THE SECRET OF SELF CONTROL- INCREASE YOUR SELF-CONTROL

ARVIND UPADHYAY

ISBN 979-888521635-7

Self-control is the ability to regulate and alter your responses in order to avoid undesirable behaviors, increase desirable ones, and achieve long-term goals. Research has shown that possessing self-control can be important for health and well-being.

Common goals such as exercising regularly, eating healthy, not procrastinating, giving up bad habits, and saving money are just a few worthwhile ambitions that people believe require self-control.

People use a variety of terms for self-control, including discipline, determination, grit, willpower, and fortitude.

Psychologists typically define self-control as:

The ability to control behaviors in order to avoid temptations and to achieve goals

The ability to delay gratification and resist unwanted behaviors or urges

A limited resource that can be depleted

Still, some researchers believe that self-control is partly determined by genetics, with some just born better at it than others.

How important is self-control in your day-to-day life? The 2011 Stress in America survey conducted by the American Psychological Association (APA) found that 27% of respondents identified a lack of willpower as the primary factor keeping them from reaching their goals. The majority of people surveyed (71%) believed that self-control can be both learned and strengthened.

Researchers have found that people who have better self-control tend to be healthier and happier, both in the short-term and long-term.

In one famous 2005 experiment, students who exhibited greater self-discipline had better grades, higher test scores, and were more likely to be admitted to a competitive academic program. The study also found that when it came to academic success, self-control was a more important factor than IQ scores.

The benefits of self-control are not limited to academic performance. One long-term health study found that high levels of self-control during childhood predicted greater cardiovascular, respiratory, and dental health in adulthood, as well as improved financial status

The ability to delay gratification, or to wait to get what you want, is an important part of self-control. People are often able to control their behavior by delaying the gratification of their urges. For instance, someone who wants to attend an expensive concert might avoid splurging their money on weekend shopping trips. They want to have fun, but they know that by waiting and saving their money, they can afford the exhilarating concert instead of the everyday mall trip.

Delaying gratification involves putting off short-term desires in favor of long-term rewards. Researchers have found that the ability to delay gratification is important not only for attaining goals but also for well-being and overall success in life.

The psychologist Walter Mischel conducted a series of famous experiments during the 1960s and 1970s that investigated the importance of delayed gratification. In these experiments, children were offered a choice: They could choose to eat one treat right away (usually a cookie or a marshmallow), or they could wait a brief period of time in order to get two snacks.

At this point, the researcher would leave the child alone in a room with a single treat. Not surprisingly, many of the kids chose to eat the single treat the moment the experimenters left the room. However, some of the kids were able to wait for the second treat.

Researchers found that children who were able to delay gratification in order to receive a greater reward were also more likely to have better academic performance than the kids who gave in to temptation immediately.

The "Hot-and-Cool" System

Based on his research, Mischel proposed what he referred to as a "hot-and-cool" system to explain the ability to delay gratification. The hot system refers to the part of our willpower that is emotional, impulsive, and urges us to act upon our desires. When this system takes over, we may give in to our momentary desires and act rashly without considering the potential long-term effects.

The cool system is the part of our willpower that is rational, thoughtful, and enables us to consider the consequences of our actions in order to resist our impulses. The cool system helps us look for ways to distract us from our urges and find more appropriate ways to deal with our desires.

Research has found that self-control is a limited resource. In the long-term, exercising self-control tends to strengthen it. Practicing self-control allows you to improve it over time. However, self-control in the short-term is limited. Focusing all of your self-control on one thing makes it more difficult to exercise your self-control on subsequent tasks throughout your day.

Psychologists refer to this tendency as ego depletion. This happens when people use up their reservoir of willpower on one task, making them unable to muster any self-control to complete the next task.

Self-control is also important for maintaining healthy behaviors. What you eat for breakfast, how often you work out, and whether you have a consistent sleep schedule are all decisions that can be impacted by your levels of self-control and have the potential to affect your health.

Researchers have found that self-control can have a number of potential influences on health and well-being. One longitudinal study found that adults who had greater self-control in childhood were less likely to have:

Substance dependence or addiction to tobacco, alcohol, or cannabis

Sexually transmitted infections

Elevated inflammation

Periodontal disease

Airflow obstruction

Metabolic abnormalities

While it is clear that self-control is critical for maintaining healthy behaviors, some experts believe that overemphasizing the importance of willpower can be damaging.

The belief that self-control alone can help us reach our goals can lead to people to blame themselves when their health is influenced by factors beyond their control. It may also lead to feelings of learned helplessness where people feel that they cannot do anything to change a situation.As a result, people may give up quickly or simply stop trying in the face of obstacles.

According to psychologist and researcher Roy Baumeister, lack of willpower is not the only factor that affects goal attainment. If you are working toward a goal, three critical components must be present:

There needs to be a clear goal and the motivation to change. Having an unclear or overly general goal (such as getting stronger) and insufficient motivation can lead to failure. You are more likely to achieve a clearly defined goal (like bench-pressing 150 pounds) with a specific motivation.

You need to track your actions toward the achievement of the goal. Simply setting the goal is not enough. You need to monitor your behavior each day to ensure that you are doing the things that need to be done in order to reach your goal.

You need to have willpower. Being able to control your behavior is a critical part of achieving any goal. Fortunately, research suggests that there are steps people can take in order to make the most of their available willpower.

Contents

Foreword

It's estimated that 95%of our behavior runs on autopilot. That's because neural networks underlie all of our habits, reducing our millions of sensory inputs per second into manageable shortcuts so we can function in this crazy world. These default brain signals are so efficient that they often cause us to relapse into old behaviors before we remember what we meant to do instead.

Mindfulness is the exact opposite of these default processes. It's executive control rather than autopilot, and enables intentional actions, willpower, and decisions. But that takes practice. The more we activate the intentional brain, the stronger it gets. Every time we do something deliberate and new, we stimulate neuroplasticity, activating our grey matter, which is full of newly sprouted neurons that have not yet been groomed for "autopilot" brain.

But here's the problem. While our intentional brain knows what is best for us, our autopilot brain causes us to shortcut our way through life. So how can we trigger ourselves to be mindful when we need it most? This is where the notion of "behavior design" comes in. It's a way to put your intentional brain in the driver's seat. There are two ways to do that—first, slowing down the autopilot brain by putting obstacles in its way, and second, removing obstacles in the path of the intentional brain, so it can gain control.

Shifting the balance to give your intentional brain more power takes some work, though. Here are some ways to get started.

Put meditation reminders around you. If you intend to do some yoga or to meditate, put your yoga mat or your meditation cushion in the middle of your floor so you can't miss it as you walk by.

Refresh your reminders regularly. Say you decide to use sticky notes to remind yourself of a new intention. That might work for about a week, but then your autopilot brain and old habits take over again. Try writing new notes to yourself; add variety or make them funny. That way they'll stick with you longer.

Create new patterns. You could try a series of "If this, then that" messages to create easy reminders to shift into the intentional brain. For instance, you might come up with, "If office door, then deep breath," as a way to shift into mindfulness as you are about to start your workday. Or, "If phone rings, take a breath before answering." Each intentional action to shift into mindfulness will strengthen your intentional brain.

Preface

What is it about self-control that makes it so difficult to rely on? Self-control is a skill we all possess (honest); yet we tend to give ourselves little credit for it. Most people don't realize it's a special skill but never figure in list of must have skill set.

When it comes to self-control, it is so easy to focus on our failures that our successes tend to pale in comparison. And why shouldn't they? Self-control is an effort that's intended to help achieve a goal. Failing to control yourself is just that—a failure. If you're trying to avoid digging into that bag of chips after dinner because you want to lose a few pounds and you succeed Monday and Tuesday nights only to succumb to temptation on Wednesday by eating four servings' worth of the empty calories, your failure outweighs your success. You've taken two steps forward and four steps back.

With this success/failure dichotomy in mind, I give you six strategies for self-control . Some are obvious, others counter-intuitive, but all will help you eliminate those pesky failures and ensure your efforts to boost your willpower are successful enough to keep you headed in the right direction for achieving your goals.

Prologue

Can self-control be improved through practice? Several studies have found that repeated practice of tasks involving self-control improves performance on other tasks relevant to selfcontrol. However, in many of these studies, improvements after training could be attributable to methodological factors (e.g., passive control conditions). Moreover, the extent to which the effects of training transfer to real-life settings is not yet clear. In the present research, participants (N = 174) completed a 6-week training program of either cognitive or behavioral self-control tasks. We then tested the effects of practice on a range of measures of self-control, including labbased and real-world tasks. Training was compared to both active and no-contact control conditions. Despite high levels of adherence to the training tasks, there was no effect of training on any measure of self-control. Trained participants did not, for example, show reduced ego depletion effects, become better at overcoming their habits, or report exerting more self-control in everyday life. Moderation analyses found no evidence that training was effective only among particular groups of participants. Bayesian analyses suggested that the data was more consistent with a null effect of training on self-control than with previous estimates of the effect of practice. The implication is that training self-control through repeated practice does not result in generalized improvements in self-control.

Does Self-Control Improve With Practice? Evidence from a 6-Week Training Program Self-control, or the ability to control thoughts, behaviors, and feelings, seems to be important for success in most areas of life (De Ridder, Lensvelt-Mulders, Finkenauer, Stok, & Baumeister, 2012). During the past 15 years, much of the research into self-control has been inspired by the strength model, which draws the analogy between self-control and a physical muscle (for a review, see Muraven & Baumeister, 2000). This model proposes that, just as using a muscle leads to temporary fatigue, exerting self-control leads to temporary reductions in selfcontrol performance; a phenomenon that has been termed 'ego depletion' (Baumeister, Bratslavsky, Muraven, & Tice, 1998). However, the strength model also suggests that if selfcontrol is repeatedly exerted over time (interspersed with periods of rest), then the opposite effect should occur. In other words, just as a muscle grows stronger with exercise, so self-control should improve over time with practice (Muraven, 2010a; Muraven,

Baumeister, & Tice, 1999). The ego depletion effect has been the subject of hundreds of empirical tests, extensive analysis of mediating and moderating factors, and much lively theoretical debate (e.g., Hagger, Wood, Stiff, & Chatzisarantis, 2010; Inzlicht & Schmeichel, 2012; Carter, Kofler, Forster, & McCullough, 2015). However, the strength model's predictions about the long-term effects of exerting self-control have received less attention. If practicing self-control improves subsequent self-control, as has been suggested by several studies (e.g., Muraven, 2010a; Muraven et al., 1999), then self-control training could benefit people facing everyday self-regulatory struggles such as controlling emotions, breaking bad habits, and overcoming impulses. Yet, there are many things that we do not yet know about the effects of training self-control through practice (see Berkman, in press; Inzlicht & Berkman, 2015; Inzlicht, Schmeichel, & Macrae, 2014, for discussion). For example, how reliable are training effects? Can we be sure that the observed improvements are the result of practicing self-control? Perhaps most importantly from an applied perspective, does training self-control indeed influence real-life outcomes that depend on selfcontrol? The present research sought to address these unanswered questions. What Do We Already Know About the Effectiveness of Self-Control Training? Table 1 provides an overview of prior studies of self-control training. Studies investigating the effect of self-control training typically ask one group of participants to perform a task requiring self-control over a period of weeks, while another group performs either no task, or a task that does not require self-control. The performance of the two groups is then compared on a subsequent self-control task, usually different to the one that was trained. A wide range of tasks has been used to train self-control, such as using one's non-dominant hand, developing and executing a personalized study or exercise program, completing the Stroop task, squeezing a handgrip, or performing a logical reasoning task. The effect of training has also been assessed using a wide range of tasks, such as tolerating pain, inhibiting aggressive inclinations or behavior, ignoring a distracting video while performing a visual tracking task, solving anagrams, or holding a handgrip. The common feature of all of these tasks is that they are believed to require self-control. How effective are these interventions in improving self-control performance? Hagger et al. (2010) meta-analyzed the findings of studies that measured the effects of training on ego depletion (i.e., performance on the second of two sequential tasks involving self-control). Across 9 tests, taken from 7 published papers, they observed that training significantly reduced ego depletion, with an overall effect size of d+ = 1.07. This suggests that practicing self-control is an extremely effective intervention. To put this effect size in context, it places the effect of selfcontrol training on ego depletion at roughly the 95th percentile in terms of both the average effectsize of psychological interventions (Lipsey & Wilson, 1993) and the average effect size observed in social psychology (Richard, Bond, & Stokes-Zoota, 2003). Effect sizes from individual studies ranged from medium (d = 0.48, Hui et al., 2009) to extremely large (d = 8.59, Oaten & Cheng, 2006a). However, close inspection of previous findings suggests that there is variation in the effect of training across studies. For example, some studies found effects of training on outcomes relevant to self-control only after participants had exerted self-control on an initial task (Finkel, DeWall, Slotter, Oaten, & Foshee, 2009; Gailliot, Plant, Butz, & Baumeister, 2007; Oaten & Cheng, 2007). Other studies obtained effects of training only among subgroups of participants – typically those with a predisposition to perform worse on the self-control task, such as participants with higher levels of trait aggression (Denson, Capper, Oaten, Friese, & Schofield, 2011; Gailliot et al, 2007). Finally, some studies found no improvements after training on outcomes relevant to self-control. For example, Muraven et al. (1999) found that trying to improve mood, a task that requires self-control, led to worse performance on a measure of selfcontrol when compared with control groups. Bertrams and Schmeichel (2014) found that participants who spent a week practicing logical reasoning subsequently performed worse than a control group on an initial anagram task, and performed no better than the control group on the same task when depleted.

CHAPTER ONE

Self-Control Secret #1 – Meditate

How to Meditate

When we meditate, we inject far-reaching and long-lasting benefits into our lives: We lower our stress levels, we get to know our pain, we connect better, we improve our focus, and we're kinder to ourselves. Let us walk you through the basics in our new mindful guide on how to meditate.

we're learning how to pay attention to the breath as it goes in and out, and notice when the mind wanders from this task. This practice of returning to the breath builds the muscles of attention and mindfulness.

When we pay attention to our breath, we are learning how to return to, and remain in, the present moment—to anchor ourselves in the here and now on purpose, without judgement.

The idea behind mindfulness seems simple—the practice takes patience. Indeed, renowned meditation teacher Sharon Salzberg recounts that her first experience with meditation showed her how quickly the mind gets caught up in other tasks. "I thought, okay, what will it be, like, 800 breaths before my mind starts to wander? And to my absolute amazement, it was one breath, and I'd be gone," says Salzberg.

While meditation isn't a cure-all, it can certainly provide some much-needed space in your life. Sometimes, that's all we need to make better choices for ourselves, our families, and our communities. And the most important tools you can bring with you to your meditation practice are a little patience, some kindness for yourself, and a comfortable place to sit.

When we meditate, we inject far-reaching and long-lasting benefits into our lives. And bonus: you don't need any extra gear or an expensive membership.

Here are five reasons to meditate:

Understanding your pain

Lower your stress

Connect better

Improve focus

Reduce brain chatter

Meditation is simpler (and harder) than most people think. Read these steps, make sure you're somewhere where you can relax into this process, set a timer, and give it a shot:

1) Take a seat

Find place to sit that feels calm and quiet to you.

2) Set a time limit

If you're just beginning, it can help to choose a short time, such as five or 10 minutes.

3) Notice your body

You can sit in a chair with your feet on the floor, you can sit loosely cross-legged, you can kneel—all are fine. Just make sure you are stable and in a position you can stay in for a while.

4) Feel your breath

Follow the sensation of your breath as it goes in and as it goes out.

5) Notice when your mind has wandered

Inevitably, your attention will leave the breath and wander to other places. When you get around to noticing that your mind has wandered—in a few seconds, a minute, five minutes—simply return your attention to the breath.

6) Be kind to your wandering mind

Don't judge yourself or obsess over the content of the thoughts you find yourself lost in. Just come back.

7) Close with kindness

When you're ready, gently lift your gaze (if your eyes are closed, open them). Take a moment and notice any sounds in the environment. Notice how your body feels right now. Notice your thoughts and emotions.

Meditation is no more complicated than what we've described above. It is that simple ... and that challenging. It's also powerful and worth it. The key is to commit to sit every day, even if it's for five minutes. Meditation teacher Sharon Salzberg says: "One of my meditation teachers said that the most important moment in your meditation practice is the moment you sit down to do it. Because right then you're saying to yourself that you believe in change, you believe in caring for yourself, and you're making it real. You're not just holding some value like mindfulness or compassion in the abstract, but really making it real."

We've gone over the basic breath meditation so far, but there are other mindfulness techniques that use different focal points than the breath to anchor our attention—external objects like a sound in the room, or something broader, such as noticing spontaneous things that come into your awareness during an aimless wandering practice. But all of these practices have one thing in common: We notice that our minds ARE running the show a lot of the time. It's true. We think thoughts, typically, and then we act. But here are some helpful strategies to change that up

The divine will be born in you according to the intensity with which you seek it. That does not mean that some supreme soul or energy from outside will enter your being. The seed is already present within you, and it will start growing. But it will grow only if you are able to give some warmth to your thirst, some heat and some fire to your thirst. The more you long for the divine, the more is the possibility that the seed which is hidden within your heart will grow, that it will sprout and become the divine; that it will break open, that it will blossom. If you have ever thought of experiencing the divine, if you have ever experienced a desire for silence, for truth, then know that the seed within you is longing to sprout. It means that some hidden thirst within you wants to be fulfilled. Try to understand that a very significant struggle is taking place within you; you will have to help this struggle and support it. You will have to support it because it is not enough that the seed has sprouted: a more nourishing environment is also needed. And even if the seed has sprouted, it does not mean that it will also bloom. For that, much more is needed. Out of the many seeds scattered on the ground, only a few will grow into trees. There is this possibility in all of them: they could all sprout and grow into trees and each could in turn produce many more seeds. One small seed has the power, the potential to produce a whole forest; it contains the potential to cover the whole earth with trees. But it is also possible that the seed with this immense power and potential will be destroyed and that nothing will come out of it. 3 T H E PAT H O F MEDITATIO N And this is only the capacity of a seed - man is capable of much more than this. One seed can create something so vast.... If a small stone can be used to create an atomic explosion.. .immense energy can be produced out of it. Whe n someone experiences this fusion within his being, within his consciousness, this blossoming, this explosion, the energy and light are the experience of the divine. We don't experience the divine from the outside. The energy that we produce through this explosion of consciousness, the growth, the flowering of our being, that energy itself is the divine. And you have a thirst for this energy: this is why I welcome you. But it does not necessarily follow that just because you have come here that you have this thirst. It is possible that you are here merely as a spectator. It is possible that you are here out of some vague curiosity - but no doors can be opened through superficial curiosity, and no secrets will be revealed to mere spectators. In life, one has to pay for everything one receives, and much has to be sacrificed. Curiosity is of no value; this is why curiosity will not get you anywhere. Curiosity will not help you to enter into meditation. Wha t is needed is an essential thirst for freedom, not curiosity. Last evening I was saying to someone that if you are near an oasis and you are dying of thirst, if your thirst is intense and you reach a state where you feel that soon you will die if you don't get water, and if at that point someone offers you water but with the condition that after drinking the water you will die - that the price of the water will be your life - you will even be willing to accept this condition. Whe n death is certain, then why not die with your thirst quenched? If you carry this intense longing and hope within you, 4 T H E FOUNDATIO N O F MEDITATIO N then under this tremendous pressure the seed within you will break open and start growing. The seed will not sprout on its own, it needs certain conditions. It needs much pressure, much warmth for its hard outer skin to crack and the tender sprout inside to grow. Each of us has this hard covering, and if we want to come out of it, just curiosity will not do. So remember this: if you are here simply out of curiosity you will leave with that curiosity, and nothing can be done to help you. And if you are here as a spectator you will leave as one, and nothing can be done for you. So it is necessary that each one of you look within himself to see whether or not he has an authentic longing for the divine. Each of you should ask himself this question: "Do I want to know truth?" Be very clear if your thirst for the divine is authentic, whether you have a yearning for truth, for silence, for bliss. If not, then understand that whatsoever you do here will have no meaning; it will be meaningless, without any purpose. If your meaningless efforts don't bear any fruits, meditation will not be responsible - you will be responsible for it. So to begin, it is necessary that you look for an authentic seeker within you. And be clear about it: do you really seek something? And if you do, then there is a way to find it. Buddha was once visiting a village. A man asked him, Every day you say that everyone can become enlightened. Then why doesn't everyone become enlightened?" "My friend," Buddha replied, "do one thing: in the evening make a list of all the people in the village and write down their desires next to their names." 5 T H E PAT H O F MEDITATIO N The man went into the village and he asked everyone; it was a small village with only a few people, and they gave him their answers. He returned in the evening and gave the list to Buddha. Buddha asked, "How many of these people seek enlightenment?" The man was surprised because not a single person had written that he wanted enlightenment. And Buddha said, "I say that every man is capable of enlightenment, I do not say that every man wants enlightenment." That every man is capable of enlightenment is very different from every man wanting to be enlightened. If you want it, then consider it to be possible. If your quest is for truth, there is no power on earth that can stop you. But if you don't long for truth, then too there is no power which can give it to you. So first you need to ask if your thirst is a real one. If so, then rest assured that a path is available. If not, then there is no path - your thirst will be your path to truth. The second thing I would like to say by way of an introduction is that you often have a thirst for something, but you are not hopeful of ever getting what you desire. You have a desire, but you are not optimistic about it. There is the desire, but with a sense of hopelessness. Now if the first step is taken optimistically, then the last step will also end optimistically. This too should be understood: if the first step is taken without any optimism, then the last step will end in despair. If you want the last step to be a satisfying and successful one, the first step should be taken with optimism. I am saying that during these three days - and I will be 6 T H E FOUNDATIO N O F MEDITATIO N saying this as long as I live - you should have a very optimistic attitude. Do you realize that as far as your state of consciousness is concerned, much depends on whether your acts are rooted in positivity or negativity? If you are a pessimist to begin with, then it is as if you are sitting on the branch of a tree, and cutting the branch at the same time. So I say to you that to be open is very important in this search. To be optimistic means you feel that if there has been a single person on this earth who has understood truth, if there has been a single person in the history of mankind who has experienced divine bliss and peace, then there is no reason why you also cannot experience it. Don't look at the millions of people whose lives are filled with darkness, whose hopes have never seen the light of day: look at the people in history who have experienced truth. Don't look at the seeds which never grew into trees, which rotted and were wasted: look at those few who were successful and who experienced the divine. And remember, what was possible for those seeds is possible for every seed. What one man can experience, every other man can also experience. Your capacity as a seed is the same as that of Buddha, of Mahavira, of Krishna or Christ. Where enlightenment is concerned nature has shown no favoritism; every man has an equal possibility. But it does not appear to be so because there are many among us who have never even tried to turn this possibility into a reality. So to be optimistic is a basic necessity. Carry this assurance with you that if anyone has ever experienced peace, if anyone has ever experienced bliss, it is also possible for you. Don't humiliate yourself by being pessimistic. To feel pessimistic is insulting to yourself. It means that you don't see yourself as 7 T H E PAT H O F MEDITATIO N worthy of experiencing truth. And I say to you, you are worthy and you will certainly achieve it. Try it and see! You have lived your whole life with a sense of hopelessness; now for these three days of the meditation camp nourish a feeling of optimism. Be as optimistic as possible that the ultimate will happen, that it will definitely happen. Why? In the outer world it is possible to approach something with optimism and not be successful. But in the inner world optimism is a very useful device. Whe n you are full of optimism, every cell of your body is filled with optimism, every pore of your skin is filled with optimism, every breath is filled with optimism, every thought is highlighted with optimism, your lifeforce throbs with optimism and your heartbeat is suffused with optimism. Whe n your whole being is filled with optimism, then this will create a climate in you in which the ultimate can happen. Pessimism also creates a personality, a character where every cell is crying, is sad, is weary, is in despair, lifeless, as if one is living only in name but is dead in spirit. If this person sets out on a journey to seek something.... And the journey on the spiritual path is the greatest journey - no man has climbed a mountain peak higher than this, no man has ever dived into a deeper ocean. The depth of the self is the deepest, and the height is the highest. Someone who wants to walk this path has to be very optimistic. So I say to you, for these three days maintain a very optimistic state of mind. Tonight, when you go to bed, fall asleep filled with optimism. And sleep with the assurance that tomorrow morning when you get up something will happen, something can happen, something can be done. Have an optimistic attitude, and along with it I would also 8 T H E FOUNDATIO N O F MEDITATIO N like to say this: after many years of experience I have come to the conclusion that man's negativity can be so strong that even if he begins to achieve something, he may not be able to see it because of his negativity. Some time ago a man used to come to me, and he would bring his wife. The first time we met he told me that his wife could not sleep. He described her condition to me: "She cannot get any sleep without medicines, and even with medicine she can only sleep for three or four hours. And my wife is afraid; strange fears seem to trouble her. She is afraid to step out of the house, and if she is in the house she is afraid that the house will collapse. If there is no one around she is afraid that if she is alone she will die, so she constantly needs someone around. At night she keeps all her medicines close to her just in case there is an emergency." I suggested that she start doing a small meditation that would be helpful. She began to do the experiment. After seven days I met him and I asked him, "What happened? How is your wife?" He said, "There has not been much progress - she just sleeps better." After a week I met him again and asked him, "Any change?" And he said, "Her condition has not changed very much, but she is a bit less afraid." I met him again after another seven days and asked him, "Has anything happened?" "Nothing significant," he said. "She manages to get some sleep now, is less fearful and doesn't keep the medicines close to her anymore - nothing much." I call this a negative outlook. Even if this man were to 9 T H E PAT H O F MEDITATIO N experience something he would not be able to see it, to recognize it. And this outlook is built into this person. It means that a negative person will not experience anything, and even if he does experience something he will not be able to recognize it - and much that might otherwise be possible will be obstructed. In addition to having a positive approach, I also suggest that during these three days you think only about what is happening to you - don't try to think about what is not happening. In these three days whatsoever happens, watch. And forget about what does not happen, what could not happen. Just remember what you did experience. If you have even a little taste of peace, of silence, nourish that. It will give you hope and it also will push you forward. Because if you nourish something that didn't happen your momentum will be lost, and what actually did happen will also be destroyed. So in these three days, in your experiments with meditation, pay attention to every little thing you experience and make that the basis for your progress. Don't give any energy to what doesn't happen. Man has always been unhappy because he forgets what he has and tries to get what he cannot get. To have this kind of basis for life is absolutely wrong. Be someone who understands what he has and live on the basis of that. I read somewhere that one man was complaining to another, "I am a very poor man, I don't have anything." So the second man said, "If you are that poor you can do one thing: I want your right eye. I will give you five thousand 10 T H E FOUNDATIO N O F MEDITATIO N rupees for it. Take these five thousand rupees and give me your right eye." And the first man said, "That is very difficult. I cannot give my right eye." So then the other man offered, "I will give you ten thousand rupees for both of your eyes." Again the first man replied, "Ten thousand rupees! But still, I cannot give my eyes." At which point the other man offered, "I will give you fifty thousand rupees if you will give me your life." At this the first man said, "But that is impossible! I cannot give my life." The first man said, "This shows you have many valuable things. You have two eyes which you will not sell for ten thousand rupees, and you have your life - and you were saying that you don't have anything!" I am talking about this kind of person and this kind of thinking. Value what you have, and also what you experience through meditation, even the small things. Think about it, talk about it, because whether or not you will experience more depends on this way of thinking - and your optimism will create more. And what you don't get.... A woman used to come to me - she was well educated, a professor in a college, a Sanskrit scholar. She was attending a seven-day meditation camp, and on the first day of the camp after the meditation she came out and said to me, "Forgive m e , but I did not have any communion with the divine." It was just the first day of the experiment and she said she did not meet with the divine! 1 I T H E PAT H O F MEDITATIO N So I said, "If you had met the divine it would have been dangerous, because if you could meet the divine so easily you would not value it." And I also said, "A person would have to be really stupid to think that by sitting silently with his eyes closed for ten minutes, he will then be ready to know the divine." So if you experience even the smallest ray of silence, consider that you have seen the whole sun because even the smallest experience of light will help you to reach to the sun. If I am sitting in a dark room and I see a thin ray of light, there are two ways I can relate to it. One way would be to say, "What is this small ray of light compared to the deep darkness surrounding me? Wha t can one small ray of light do? - there is so much darkness all around me." The other way would be to think, "In spite of all this darkness, there is at least one ray of light available to me, and if I go towards that ray of light I may reach the source where the sun is." This is why I am telling you not to think about all the darkness; if there is even the faintest, the tiniest ray of light, concentrate on that. It will give rise to a positive vision in you. Usually, your life is just the opposite. If I show you a rosebush you might say, "What is there to see?

Existence is so unfair, there are only three or four roses and thousands of thorns." This is one approach: to see a rosebush and say, "Existence is so unfair! There are thousands of thorns and only a few roses." This is one way of perceiving, one approach. Another way would be to say, "Existence is so mysterious: amidst those thousands of thorns it creates a rose." You could also see it like this and say, "A rose among all those thorns.... Isn't this a mysterious world! It really seems like a miracle, the possibility of a rose blooming amongst all those thorns." 12 T H E FOUNDATIO N O F MEDITATIO N So I would like to ask you to take the second approach. In these three days make your foundation from the slightest ray of hope that you see in your meditation, and let it become stronger. The third thing is that during these three days of meditation you will not be living in the same way that you have been living up until this evening. Man is a robot, full of habits, and if one remains within the confines of one's habits, the new path to meditation will be very difficult. Hence, I suggest that you make a few changes. One change will be that during these three days you are to talk as little as possible. Talking is the greatest affliction of this century! And you are not even aware of just how much you talk. From morning to night, until you go to sleep, you go on talking. Either you are talking to somebody else, or if there is nobody to talk to, you talk to yourself. During these three days be conscious about stopping your habit of continuously talking. And it is just a habit. For a meditator, this is vital. During these three days I would like you to talk as little as possible, and when you do talk, it should be pure, not the ordinary chitchat that you do every day. What in fact do you talk about every day? Does it have any value? Would it be harmful to you if you didn't talk? You are simply chattering; it is not worth much. And if you didn't talk would it be harmful to others? Would others feel something is missing by not hearing what you have to say? During these three days remember that you are not to talk much with anyone. This will be tremendously helpful. And if you do talk, it would be better if it were connected with meditation and nothing else. But it would be so much better if you did not talk at all: be in silence as much as possible. 13 T H E PAT H O F MEDITATIO N I don't mean it to be so strict that you force yourself to be in silence, that you write what you want to say. You are free to speak, but not to chitchat. Talk consciously, and only when necessary. This will help you in two ways. One benefit will be that you will save all the energy that is wasted by talking. Then that energy can be used for meditation. And the second benefit will be that it will disconnect you from the others and you will be in your aloneness during this time. We have come to this mountain place, and it would be a waste if all two hundred people that are gathered here were to just talk with each other, chat with each other. Then you would still be in a crowd, as you were before, and you will not be able to experience silence. To experience silence just to be in the mountains is not enough. It is also necessary to separate yourself from others and be alone. You should make contact only if it is absolutely necessary. Imagine that you are the only person on this mountain and there is no one else around. You have to live as if you have come here alone, you are staying alone and moving around alone. Sit under a tree, alone. Don't go about in groups of people. Live separately and alone for these three days. The truth of life has never been known through living in a crowd, and it cannot be experienced like that. No experience of any significance has ever happened in a crowd. Whosoever has had a taste of silence has tasted it in absolute solitude, in aloneness. Whe n you stop talking to others and when all your chattering inside and outside stops, nature starts communicating with you in a mysterious way. Nature is continuously communicating with you, but you are so engrossed in your chatter 14 T H E FOUNDATIO N O F MEDITATIO N that you don't hear her soft voice. You will have to quieten yourself so that you can hear the voice speaking within you. So in these three days, talking has to be consciously reduced. If you forget and start talking out of habit and then remember again, stop right then and apologize. Be alone. You will be experimenting with this here, but you will also have to try it on your own. Go anywhere you like, sit under a tree; you have completely forgotten that you are part of nature. You also don't know that being close to nature makes it easier to experience the ultimate; nowhere else is it easier. So make full use of these three incredible days. Be in isolation, solitude, and don't talk unless necessary. And even if everyone is quiet, continue to be alone. A meditator has to be alone. There are very many people here, so when we all sit for meditation it may look as if there is a gathering of people meditating. But all meditation is individual, a group cannot meditate. Sitting here you are in a large group, but when you go inside yourself you will all feel alone. Whe n you close your eyes you will feel alone, and when you are silent there will no longer be any group. There will be two hundred people here, but each one will be only with himself and not with the other one hundred and ninety-nine meditators. Meditation cannot be done collectively. All prayer, all meditation is individual, is private. Be alone here, and also when you leave here. And spend most of your time in silence. Don't talk. But it will not be enough to simply stop talking, you will also need to make a conscious effort to stop the constant chattering that goes on inside you. You talk to yourself, you answer yourself - quieten yourself and drop that too. If it is difficult to stop 15 T H E PAT H O F MEDITATIO N this inner chatter, then firmly tell yourself to stop this noise, tell yourself that you don't like the noise. Talk to your inner self. As a meditator, it is important to give suggestions to yourself. Try this sometime. Sit alone somewhere, tell your mind to stop its chatter, tell your mind that you don't like it, and you will be surprised to see that for a moment your inner chattering will stop. For three days give yourself the suggestion that you will not talk. In three days you will notice the difference.. .that step by step, slowly, slowly the chatter is lessening. The fourth point: you may have some complaints, some problems - you are not to pay any attention to them. If you experience a small problem or difficulty, don't give it any attention. We are not here for entertainment. Recently, I read the story of a Chinese nun. She was visiting a village where there were only a few houses, and as it was getting dark and she was all alone she went to the area in front of all the houses and asked the villagers, "Please let me stay in one of your houses." She was a stranger to them, and besides that she was of a different religion, so the villagers closed their doors to her. The next village was very far away, and it was dark and she was alone. So she had to spend the night in a field and she slept under a cherry tree. In the middle of the night she woke up - it was cold, and because of this she could not sleep. She looked up and saw that the flowers had all blossomed; the tree was covered with flowers. And the moon had risen, and the moonlight was very beautiful. She experienced a moment of immense joy. 16 T H E FOUNDATIO N O F MEDITATIO N In the morning she went back to the village and thanked all the people who had refused to give her shelter for the night. Whe n they asked her, "For what?" she said, "For your love, for your compassion and kindness in closing your doors to me last night. Because of this I was able to experience a moment of unbelievable joy. I saw the cherry flowers in bloom and the moon in its glory, and I saw something that I had never seen before. If you had given me shelter I would not have seen it. That's when I realized your kindness, your reason for closing all your doors to me." This is one way to look at things. It is possible that you also might have been sent away from each door that night, and that you might have felt angry all night. You might have felt so much hatred, so much anger towards those people that perhaps you might not have noticed the flowers blossoming in the cherry tree and you would not have seen the moon rising, let alone experienced a feeling of gratitude. You would not have experienced any of these things. There is another way to relate to life - and that is when you are filled with gratitude for everything in life. And you must remember that during these three days, feel gratitude for everything. Feel gratitude for what you receive and don't be bothered about what you don't receive. This is the basis of gratitude. It is on this base that carefreeness and simplicity are born inside you. To summarize, I would like to say that in these three days you will relentlessly try to go inside, to meditate and to enter mto silence. On this journey, a very firm resolve is needed. The conscious mind where all the thought processes take 17 T H E PAT H O F MEDITATIO N place is only a small part; the rest of the mind is still deeper. If we were to divide the mind into ten parts, the conscious mind would be only one part, the other nine parts are the unconscious mind. Our thinking and reasoning take place in only one part, but the rest of the brain is not aware of this. The rest of the brain has no sense of it. Whe n we make a conscious resolution to meditate, to enter into samadhi, ultimate bliss, the major part of our brain remains ignorant of this resolution. This unconscious part will not support us in this resolution. But if we don't get support from it we cannot succeed. To get the support, a determined, conscious effort is needed. I will now explain how to make this conscious effort. Whe n you wake up, let it be with determination, and at night when you go to bed, when you lie down on your bed, think over your resolution for five minutes and repeat it to yourself as you go to sleep. I would like to explain this exercise for becoming determined, and you will be practicing it here as well as in your normal life. As I explained, with this resolution your whole mind, conscious and unconscious both, is to decide that, "I will be silent, I am determined to experience meditation." The night Gautam Buddha attained enlightenment, he was sitting under his bodhi tree and he said, "I will not get up from this place until I am enlightened." You might think, "But what is the connection? How will not getting up help him to get enlightened?" But the resolution, "I will not..." spreads all through the body - and he did not get up until he became enlightened! Amazingly, he became enlightened the same night. And he had been trying for six years, but never before did he have such intensity. I will give you a small exercise to intensify your resolve. 18 T H E FOUNDATIO N O F MEDITATIO N We will do this exercise here and also at night before sleeping. If you exhale completely and then stop yourself from inhaling, what will happen? If I exhale completely and then pinch my nose shut and don't inhale, what will happen? In a little while my total being will struggle to inhale. Won't every pore of my body and those millions of cells scream for air? The longer I try to hold my breath, the deeper the longing for breath is going to spread into my unconscious mind. The longer I hold my breath, the more the innermost part of my being is going to ask for air. And if I hold it to the last moment, my whole being will demand air. Now it is not a simple desire anymore; the top layer is not the only one affected. Now it has become a question of life and death; now the deeper layers, the layers underneath, are also going to demand more air. In that moment, when you reach the state where your whole being is starving for air, you should repeat to yourself, "I am going to experience meditation." In that moment, when your life is demanding air, you should repeat the thought, "I will enter into a state of silence. This is my resolution: I will experience meditation." In this state, your mind should repeat this thought; your body will ask for air and your mind will repeat this thought. The stronger the demand for air, the deeper your resolution will enter inside. And if your whole being is struggling and you are repeating this sentence, then the strength of your resolution will increase many times over. In this way it will reach to your unconscious mind. You will be making this resolution every day before the daily meditation, and at night you will do it before going to sleep. Repeat the sentence, and then go to sleep. Whe n you are falling asleep, at that moment also let it be constantly 19 T H E PAT H O F MEDITATIO N ringing in your mind: "I will experience meditation. This is my resolution. I will enter into silence." This resolution should go on ringing in your mind so that you don't even realize when you are falling asleep. In sleep your conscious mind is inactive and the doors are open for the unconscious mind. If your mind repeats this idea again and again while the conscious mind is inactive, it can then enter the subconscious mind. And in time you will observe a significant change - you will see it even in these three days. So now try to understand the method by which you can strengthen the resolution. This is the way to do it: first take slow, deep breaths, filling yourself up, filling your lungs up as deeply as you can. When you have inhaled as much as you can, continue to hold the thought, "I will experience meditation," and keep repeating this sentence. Then exhale, and at one point you will feel that there is no more air to exhale. But there is - so throw that out too and repeat the sentence. Now you will feel that there is absolutely no more air left - but still there is, so throw that out. Don't be afraid: you will never exhale completely That's why, when you feel that there is no more breath left in you, there always is - so try also to exhale that. Exhale as totally as you can, and keep repeating, "I will experience meditation." It is a strange phenomenon: through it a thought process is triggered in your unconscious mind. An intense resolve will arise and you will already see its effects tomorrow, so you have to make your resolution very strong. We will start the experiment before we leave this place this evening. You are to do it five times, that is, you should inhale and exhale five times and repeat the thought inside five times. If anyone has a heart problem, or any other problem, don't do it strenuously, 20 T H E FOUNDATIO N O F MEDITATIO N do it softly. Do it as gently as possible, don't make yourself uncomfortable. I have talked about the will to experience. You must practice it every night during these three days, before sleeping. Lying on your bed, repeat the sentence as you gradually fall asleep. If you follow this process diligently and your voice reaches the unconscious, the result is easy to induce and is unmistakable. I wanted to talk about these few things today, and I hope you have already understood the points that are relatively important. As I have said, there should be no talking. Naturally, you will not read the newspaper or listen to the radio, because that would also be a kind of talking. Or when I said you will be silent and alone...this means that you avoid the company of people as much as you can. Except for the time when we gather here, or when we eat... but then too you will be quiet and in silence. There should be total silence, as if you are not there at all. Whe n you come here to meditate, then too you will come in silence. You will see the results of three days in silence. Whe n you walk on the street be quiet; when sitting, standing, moving around, be quiet. And most of the time try to be alone. Select a beautiful place and sit there quietly. And if there is someone with you, they too should sit quietly; don't talk, otherwise the mountains are wasted, the beauty is wasted. You will not see that which is right in front of you. You will destroy everything with your talking. Be alone. I wanted to mention these few things which are important for everyone. If there is no thirst within you, and there seems to be no way to awaken this thirst, then tell me about this tomorrow. Let me know if you are not very hopeful about yourself and you don't feel there can be any hope, or if you find it difficult to strengthen your resolve and feel it is not possible for you to meditate. So tomorrow you can ask me about the difficulties that you think you will face in the next three days, so that no time is wasted later on. If you have any personal problem, any pain or sorrow which you want to be relieved of which is preventing you from meditating, or if you are coming across any difficulty while meditating, remember this: you can ask your question separately. It will not be for everyone; it will be for you individually, that you follow a separate procedure. And whatever problem you may have, be clear about it tomorrow morning so that we will be prepared for the next three days. I wanted to say these few things. You have to maintain a single-pointed vision. And then from tomorrow we will start with what is to be done, we will begin the real work tomorrow. Now we will sit a little apart from each other - the hall is big enough so that everyone can spread out - and we will make our resolutions before we leave here. .. .Not so jerkily, very slowly, slowly filling the lungs completely. Whe n you fill your lungs, repeat to yourself, "I will experience meditation." Repeat this sentence. Then, when the lungs are filled to the maximum, hold your breath for a while, repeating the sentence. You may get nervous, you will feel like exhaling, but continue to hold your breath and repeat the sentence. Then slowly start exhaling, again repeating the sentence. Keep exhaling until you feel you are empty, and then go on exhaling and repeating the sentence. When you feel absolutely empty, hold this emptiness. Don't inhale yet, and go on repeating the sentence as long as you can. And then, slowly begin to inhale. An inhalation plus an exhalation is one round. Everyone should follow this procedure slowly, step by step. After doing it five times straighten your back, breathe slowly, sit quietly and relax for five minutes. We will do this exercise for ten minutes and then everyone will leave this place silently. Remember, you are not to talk, and this is from now on. In that sense the meditation camp begins right now. When you go to bed repeat this exercise from five to seven times, as long as you feel comfortable, then switch off the light and fall asleep. Fall asleep thinking, "I will be in silence, this is my aim." And when sleep envelops you this thought will be with you. When you have finished doing the exercise five times, rest quietly for a while and breathe softly. Now keep your back straight. Let your body be loose. Your back is straight and your body relaxed. Close your eyes. Quietly take a deep breath and do as I have just said five times: "I will experience silence. I will experience meditation. I am determined that I will experience meditation." Let your whole being make this oath that you will enter into meditation. Let your whole being resonate with it. This should reach to the deepest layer of your consciousness. After doing this five times, very softly, very relaxedly, sit U P , straighten your back and slow down your breathing. Exhale slowly and keep on watching your breathing. Rest for five minutes. During this rest period the resolution that you have made will sink deeper inside you. Make the resolution five times, then, sitting quietly, watch your breath for five Minutes and take slow breaths. begin with the body . My Beloved Ones, AST NIGHT I spoke about how to create a foundation for meditation within yourself. My approach to meditation is not based on any scriptures, any holy books or any specific school of thought. I am only talking about the paths which I have walked on and which I have known by going within myself. This is why what I am saying is not just a theory. And when I invite you to try it, I have no doubt that you will also be successful in finding what you are longing for. Rest assured that I will only talk about that which I have experienced. I have had to go through a period of intense anguish and suffering. I had to go through a period of trial and error, and during that period I struggled to go inside myself. I made a constant effort to try all the roads, all the paths in this direction. Those days were very painful, full of anguish and suffering. But there was constant effort, and because of this effort - just as when a great waterfall is falling from a great height and the constant flow wears away even the rocks - so just like a waterfall, with continuous effort, somewhere I found an opening. And I will only talk about the methods through which I found this opening. So I can say to you with absolute confidence and assurance that if you try this method the result is absolutely guaranteed. At the time, there was pain and sorrow, but now there is no pain or sorrow within me. Yesterday somebody asked me, "People ask you about so many of their problems. Aren't you troubled by them?" I said to him, "If the problem is not yours, then you cannot be troubled by it. If the problem belongs to someone else then there is no trouble in it. The trouble starts if you take the problem as your own." In this sense I don't have any problems. But I experience a different type of sadness, and that is that I see many people around me who appear to be in so much pain, who have so many problems, and I feel that their pain and trouble can so easily be removed because there are such simple solutions to them. I feel that if they were to knock on the door, the door would open so easily. And yet they are standing right in front of it, crying. That's when I experience a very different kind of anguish and suffering. There is a short Parsi story: A blind man and his friend were crossing a desert. They were going on different journeys but they must have met on the way and the other man must have asked the blind man to join him. They were together for some days and their friendship deepened over that time. One morning the blind m a n got up earlier than his friend and felt around for his stick. It was a desert night and it was very cold, it was winter time. He did not find the stick, but there was a snake which had stiffened because of the cold so the blind man picked it U P and thanked God saying, "I had lost my stick but now you have given me a better, a smoother stick." He thanked 27 God and said, "You are very compassionate." Then he poked his friend with this stick to wake him, saying, "Get up, it's morning." Whe n the friend got up and saw the snake, he became afraid and said, "What is that you are holding in your hand? Drop it immediately! It is a snake, it is dangerous!" The blind man replied, "Friend, in a fit of jealousy you are calling my beautiful stick a snake. You want me to throw it away so that you can take it - I may be blind, but I'm not stupid." His friend replied, "Are you mad? Have you gone mad? Throw it away immediately! It is a snake and it is dangerous!" But the blind man said, "You have stayed with me for so many days and you still haven't understood how smart I am. I had lost my stick and now the Almighty has given me a more beautiful stick, and you are just trying to fool me by calling it a snake." The blind man, in his anger, thought that his friend was jealous and envious, and so he started off on his own. After a little while the sun came up and the snake warmed up and came back to life. It was no longer cold and it bit the blind man. The pain I'm talking about is the same pain that the blind man's friend must have felt for his friend. Just like him, I also feel pain for the people all around. They are carrying a snake in their hands, not a stick, but if I tell them they wonder what jealousy is provoking me to say this. And I am not talking about someone else, I am talking about you. Don't think I'm talking about the person sitting next to you, I am talking absolutely to you. And I can see snakes in all your hands; yet anything that only looks like a stick is of no help, it is not a stick. But I don't want you to leave the path. And I don't want you to think that in a jealous state I am trying to snatch away your beautiful stick, so I don't directly call it a snake. Slowly, slowly I am trying to make you understand that what you are holding on to is wrong. And in fact I am not even saying that what you are holding on to is wrong. All I am saying is that there is something higher to hold on to. There is greater jo y to be experienced, there are greater truths in life to be understood. Wha t you are now holding on to can only lead to your destruction. Wha t we spend our lives doing eventually destroys us, destroys our entire lives. And when our whole lives have been destroyed, when our whole life is finished, there is only one pain and one sorrow that man suffers at the moment of death - and that is his regret at losing a very precious life. So today, the first thing I would like to say is that the thirst of which I spoke last night will arise only when you see, when you realize that the life you are leading right now is wrong. That thirst will arise only when you realize that the way you are living your life right now is absolutely wrong, meaningless. Is this such a difficult thing to understand? And do you know with any certainty that what you have collected so far has any value? Do you know for sure whether you will be able to know immortality with what you have accumulated? With all the efforts you are making in all directions, do you really know that you are not just building sandcastles, or is there some solid foundation to it? Think this over, contemplate on it. Whe n you start to reflect and question life, a thirst begins to arise in you. A thirst for truth arises out of contemplation. There are very few who think about life, very few. Most people live life like driftwood floating down a river: it just keeps on floating and goes wherever the river takes it. If the river takes it towards the bank, it floats towards the bank; if it takes it midstream, it floats towards the middle of the river as if it had no life, a destination of its own. Most of us live the life of a piece of wood floating in the river - we go wherever time and circumstances take us. Thinking about life and its purpose will help you to find a direction: whether you should live the life of a piece of wood floating in the river, whether you should live like a dried leaf which blows wherever the wind takes it, or whether you should be an individual, a person, a thinking person, one who has a direction in life, one who has decided what he wants to become and what he should be, one who has taken his life and its unfoldment into his own hands. Man's greatest creation is himself; his greatest creation will be his own self-realization. Anything else that he creates will not be of much value. It will be like drawing a line on water. But that which he creates inside himself, that which he makes of himself, will be like a carving in stone: it can never be erased, it will be with him forever. So think about your life - are you a piece of wood floating in the river? Are you a dead leaf which is picked up and blown around by the wind? If you think about this, you will see that you are just floating like a piece of wood, and you will see that you are being blown around like one of the dead leaves on the ground, carried by the wind to wherever it is blowing. Right now the streets are covered with these leaves. Have you made any conscious progress in your life, or have you just been pushed around by the wind? And if you have been pushed around by the wind, have you reached anywhere? Has anyone ever reached anywhere like this? If there is no consciously chosen goal in life, one reaches nowhere. The thirst for a conscious goal will arise in you only if you think about it, reflect on it, meditate on it. You must have heard this story about Buddha. This story is about how Buddha renounced his life, about how he became an ascetic and how the desire for truth arose in him. It is a very famous story, and very meaningful. Whe n Buddha was a child his parents were told that their son would one day become either a great king, an emperor, or a great monk. So his father arranged everything so that Buddha would never experience any sorrow and should never feel like renouncing his life. He built a palace for him using all the artistry and craftsmanship of those times and with all kinds of luxuries, gardens.... And there were different palaces, one for every season, and he gave orders to all the servants that Buddha should never see even a wilted flower; so that he would not come to know that flowers can die and the question, "Maybe I too will die?" would never arise in him. So during the night all the dead flowers would be removed from the garden. Any weak tree would be uprooted and removed. Only young people were allowed to be around him; old people were not allowed to enter because Buddha might think, "Man becomes old.. .one day maybe I too will become old." Until he grew up to be a young man, he did not know anything about death. He had never heard about death. He was kept totally ignorant of the people that were dying in his village so that he would not think, "If people die, then maybe I too will die one day." I'm trying to explain the meaning of contemplation. Contemplation means to reflect on whatever is happening around you. If death is happening right in front of you, then contemplate on whether it will happen to you too. If you see someone who is old, then contemplate on whether this will also happen to you. Buddha's father tried in every way to prevent this kind of contemplation from happening in him - I want you to do everything so that this contemplation will arise in you. The father did everything he could to prevent Buddha from thinking, but still it happened. One day Buddha went out and saw an old man walking on the street. He asked his attendant, "What has happened to this man? Do other people look like this too?" The attendant said, "I cannot lie to you - everyone has to become old like him one day." Buddha immediately asked, "Me too?" The attendant said, "My lord, I cannot lie to you, no one is excluded." Buddha said, "Take me back to the palace! I now understand that I too can become old. If this is going to happen tomorrow, then there is nothing left." This is what I call contemplation. But the attendant said, "We are going to a youth festival, the whole village will be waiting for us. Let's go on." Buddha said, "I have no wish to go. The youth festival has no meaning because everybody will get old one day." They went a little further on and saw a funeral procession.

Buddha asked, "What is this? What are these people doing? What are they carrying on their shoulders?" The attendant was hesitant to answer. He said, "I should not tell you, but I cannot lie to you. This man has died, he has died and these people are taking him away." Buddha asked, "What is it to die?" For the first time he came to know that people die. Buddha said, "Now I have no wish to go, take me back immediately! It is not this man who has died - rather, I have died." This is what I call contemplation. A man has succeeded in contemplation if he understands that what has happened to someone else can also happen to him one day. People who don't understand what is happening all around them are blind, and in a way we are all blind. This is why I have told you the story of the blind man who was carrying a snake in his hand. So the first thing for you to do - and it is very important - is to observe all that is happening around you, and through this an understanding will arise in you. Therefore the first, the most important thing for you to do, will be to observe everything around you. Through this observation a quest will arise in you, a question will arise, and this will in turn give rise to a thirst for a higher truth. I have suffered much pain. Whe n that pain subsided, in its place I began to see the steps on the path. Now I want to talk about the first step on this path. I have come to understand that two things are necessary if you want to attain to the ultimate consciousness, to the divine, to your inner being. One is the circumference, the circumference of meditation. The other important thing is the center of meditation - the circumference of meditation and the center of meditation; or you can call it the body of meditation and the soul of meditation. Today I will talk about the circumference of meditation, tomorrow I will talk about the soul or the center, and the day after tomorrow about the fruits of meditation. Just these three things: the circumference of meditation, the center and the fruits of meditation. In other words, the foundation of meditation, meditation itself and the fulfillment of it. The foundation of meditation involves only your periphery, and the periphery of your personality is the body. Hence the periphery of meditation involves only the body. So the first step towards meditation begins with your body. So remember, whatever negative feelings you may have about your body which other people may have imprinted on you, drop them. The body is just an instrument in the material as well as in the spiritual world. The body is neither an enemy nor a friend, it is just an instrument you can use to do wrong or you can use to do good. Through it you can either get involved in the material life or you can get involved in the ultimate. The body is just an instrument. Don't hold any misconceptions about it. People usually believe that the body is antagonistic towards us, that it is sinful, that it is our enemy and that it needs to be suppressed. I tell you that this is wrong - the body is neither an enemy nor a friend; it is what you make it. That is why the body is so mysterious, so extraordinary. In the world, whenever something wrong has happened it has happened through the body, and whenever something right has happened it has happened through the body. The body is only the means, the instrument So for meditation it is necessary to start with attention to the body, because you cannot proceed without first putting this instrument in order. If the body is not in the right condition you cannot proceed. So the first step is to purify the body; the purer the body, the easier it will be to go deeper inside. What does purifying the body mean? The first meaning is that there should be no disturbance, no blocks, no complexes in the body, in the system of the body - then the body is pure. Try to understand how these complexes and blockages enter the body. If the body is without any blocks, if it doesn't have any disturbances and if there are no problems, no interferences, then the body is pure and helps you to go inside. But if you are very angry, if you get angry and you are not expressing it, the heat that this creates will accumulate in some part of your body and it will become a blockage. You must have seen how anger can lead to hysteria, how it can lead to illness. Recent experiments being done on the human body show that out of a hundred diseases, fifty of these are not of the body but of the mind. But the mental illnesses become disturbances in the body, and if there is a disturbance in the body, if the body is not healthy, then the body's whole system becomes rigid and impure. All the different schools of spiritual discipline and the different religions have tried many incredible and revolutionary experiments to purify the body, and it will be good to understand these experiments. If you try these experiments, in a few days you will discover just how mysterious your body is. Your body will not appear to be an enemy it will be a temple where the divine resides. Then it will not be an enemy but a friend, and you will feel grateful to it. The body is not you. It is made of matter. You and your body are different from each other. Yet you can make tremendous use of it, and then you will feel gratitude towards it, you will feel indebted to it because it is so supportive. Keeping the body free of blockages is the first step towards purifying the body. And there are many blockages in our bodies. For instance, a few days ago a man came and said to me, "For some days now I have been doing some meditations of a particular religion, and the mind has become very quiet."

I said to him, "I don't think your mind is quiet." He said, "How can you say that?" I replied, "Since you arrived you have been jiggling both your legs about." He was sitting and jiggling his legs. I said, "It is not possible for the mind to be silent when the legs are jiggling about so much." The agitation of the body comes from the agitation of the mind. Whe n the movement of the mind slows down, the body too slows down. The bodies of Buddha and Mahavira would have appeared to be like the stone that their statues are made of; they would have appeared stone-like. It is not coincidental that their statues are made of stone. The reason for it is that they had started looking like stone, all movement inside them had stopped. That is, they moved only when necessary; otherwise they remained absolutely still. Whe n your legs jiggle, it is the energy created by your dissatisfaction which is not finding any outlet and you dissipate it by jiggling your legs. Whe n a man is angry he gnashes his teeth and he clenches his fists - why? His eyes turn red - why? Wh y the fists? Even when you are alone and angry at someone you will clench your fist. There is no one to hit, but the energy that is created by your anger has to be released somehow. The muscles in your hands become tense and so the energy is released. These difficulties have been created by social conditioning. A man without conditioning has a purer body than yours. A wild man's body is purer than your body; it does not have any blockages because where you suppress your emotions, he expresses his emotions very easily and spontaneously. Imagine you are at work and your boss says something to you and you become angry, but you cannot tighten your fists. Now what will happen to all this energy which has just been created in you? And remember this: the energy does not simply evaporate. Energy is never destroyed, energy never comes to an end. If you say something to me which makes me angry, I will not be able to express my anger in front of all these people. I cannot gnash my teeth or clench my fist; I cannot call you names or jump around in anger or pick up a stone. Wha t happens to the energy that has been generated inside me? - this energy will cripple a part of my body. It will be used to create a blockage in some part of my body; a disharmony will form. By that I mean that most of our disharmonies emerge in the body. You may be surprised, and you might say that you don't see any such blockages. But I ask you to try an experiment; you will then discover how many blockages there are in your body. Have you ever noticed that if you are in a room alone you may clench your teeth, or when you look in the mirror you may stick out your tongue or widen your eyes in anger? You may even laugh at yourself for doing this. Sometimes it may happen that while you are taking a shower you will suddenly jump, and you will wonder, "Why did I jump? Wh y did I clench my teeth at my reflection in the mirror? Wh y do I feel like humming a song?" My suggestion to you is that once a week, for half an hour, you lock yourself in a room and let your body do whatsoever it feels like doing. You will be surprised! Your body may start dancing - let it do whatsoever it pleases, don't stop it. It may dance, it may jump or even scream. Or it may jump at an imaginary enemy, it is possible. Then you will wonder, "What is happening?" All these are the disharmonies of the body that are repressed but are still very much present and want to be expressed, but your social conditioning does not allow it. You also don't allow them to be expressed, so in this way many disharmonies have found a home in your body. And if the body is full of blockages it is not healthy and you cannot go inside. So the first step in meditation will be to purify the body, and the first step in purifying the body will be to put an end to all the disorders in the body. So you will have to stop accumulating new disorders and also find a way to release the old ones. A solution is that once or twice a month you lock yourself in a room and let your body do whatever it feels like doing. If you feel like removing all your clothes and dancing naked, then do it, then throw off your clothes. You will be surprised that after half an hour of all that jump - ing you will feel so relaxed, so quiet and fresh. It will seem strange but you will feel very silent, and you will wonder where this silence has come from. Whe n you exercise or take a walk you feel a lightness - why is that? It is because many of the blocks in the body are released. Do you know why sometimes you are just looking for someone to get into a fight with? Wh y you are so ready to fight that you jump on the first person who comes along? It is because you have collected so many energy blocks and they are all wanting to be released. Whenever there is a war - there have been two world wars - during these world wars people were really hooked on reading their daily newspaper first thing in the morning. And many curious things happen in wartime. You may not know that during these wars two very strange things happened: one was that there was a drop in the number of suicides all over the world. During the First and Second World Wars, psychologists were surprised at this phenomenon. During the whole time of the wars there were very few suicides; all over the world there was a drop in the number of suicides, and psychologists were puzzled. During that period there were also fewer murders. And another strange thing, there was also a decline in mental illness during the time of the war. Later they realized that all the news about the war and the intensity of the news had helped to release certain blocks in people. Somehow, when you hear any news about war you get involved with it. For instance, your anger.... Now imagine you are angry with Hitler, so you build an effigy of Hitler and burn it, shout slogans and scream at him. You can sit in your living room and abuse him. Hitler is not there in front of you, he is an illusionary enemy. But in this way many of your blockages are released and it will result in better psychological health. You will be surprised: consciously you don't want there to be war, but deep inside you do want it to happen. During wartime people seem to be very cheerful. Although danger may be very close by, still people seem to be cheerful. . Some time ago India was attacked by China: there was a sudden burst of energy in all of you at the time. Do you know why? The reason was that a lot of the blocks in your bodies were released through your anger and that made you feel very light. Wars will always be fought; there will be wars as long as there are people with unhealthy bodies. Wars will not end until everyone's body becomes so pure that there are no blockages in them that need wars to dissolve them. What I am telling you right now will sound very strange, but there will be war in the world as long as people's bodies are unhealthy. No matter how much effort is made to stop war, you will still derive a certain pleasure from it. And you also experience pleasure from fighting. Think about it: don't you get some kind of pleasure out of fighting? The fight can be at any level - it can be between one religion and another, between a Hindu and a Mohammedan - and you will be surprised that it has no basis. Just look, whenever a religion is born it is divided into twenty other sub-sects, and then each of these is divided into sub-branches. Why? - because man's body is so unhealthy it is so filled with disharmony that he is just looking for any excuse. People grab at even the smallest excuse to fight, because fighting gives them some release and makes them feel more relaxed. The first step of moving towards meditation is the purification of the body. I would also like to add two more things. In order to release all the old disorders, one method is to let yourself go totally wild in a closed room, dropping all the ideas that you have forced on yourself. Drop them! Then let it all happen and observe your body and see what it does. It dances, it jumps, it falls to the floor and lies there. It hits an imaginary enemy. It pretends to stab someone, to shoot someone. Observe everything it does and let it happen. A month or two of this experiment and you will be surprised at the results. You will find that your body has become very easy, healthy and pure. It has found a release; the old blocks will have found an outlet. In days gone by, seekers used to go into the forests. They liked to be in solitude and did not want to be in a crowd. One of the main reasons for this was for purification. You have no idea what Buddha or Mohammed did when they went into solitude; there is not one book that tells you what they did when they were in the forests. So what do you suppose they were doing? I tell you without a doubt that they must have been purifying their bodies. The word 'mahavira' means someone whose blocks have been destroyed - and the first step towards destroying these blocks is in the body. So first those blocks that you have accumulated have to be released. In the beginning you will find it strange, and if you feel like laughing at yourself for behaving like a madman, jumping around, then allow the laughter to happen. If you feel like crying then let it happen. If I tell you right now to let go, then some of you will start laughing. There is pain within you which could not be expressed, which was suppressed, and it will come out. Or there is laughter waiting to come out that was stopped; it is lodged in your body in the form of a blockage. Now it will come out. You will feel that what is happening is absurd, but let it happen. Try this method of body purification on your own, and the upper layer of your blockages will be removed and you will feel lighter. The second thing: you have to see to it that new blocks don't develop. I have spoken about how to release the old blocks, but you go on accumulating new blocks every day. I may say something that makes you very angry, but you will not show it because of your social conditioning and social etiquette. A fireball of energy will move into your body. Where will it go? It may create stress on some nerves, disrupt them, lodge itself there. This is why there is a difference between the eyes and face of someone who is angry and of someone who is peaceful: the fever of anger has not distorted anything in a peaceful man's face. The body blooms into its true beauty only when there is no disharmony in it. In that sense, a beautiful body is simply an indication that there is no disharmony. That's when the eyes become beautiful, and even the ugliest body seems to be beautiful. Gandhi's body was very ugly when he was young, but as he grew older he started looking more beautiful. It was very strange. The beauty was not of the body, it was the result of the dissolving of all the blocks in the body. Very few people understood when they saw this. There's no doubt that Gandhi was ugly; if we measure by any criterion of beauty, he could not have been considered beautiful. If you see photographs of him as a child and as a young man you will see that he was ugly, but as he grew older he started looking more and more beautiful. If you have led your life beautifully, then your youth is not as beautiful as your old age. Because in youth there are many forces working in you, in old age all the feverishness disappears. If you have lived, your life beautifully then old age is the most beautiful part of life, because then all the feverishness is gone. All the disorders will have disappeared if you have developed rightly and lived your life totally. BEGI N WIT H TH E BOD Y Have you ever wondered how all these blockages accumulate in your body? If I insult you and you get angry, this creates a surge of energy in you. And energy cannot be destroyed, energy is never destroyed. Energy has to be used, and if it is not used it will become perverted and selfdestructive. You have to use it - but how to use this energy? Imagine you are at work and you are angry - there is a strong feeling of anger in you and you cannot express it. I suggest you try this: transform that energy creatively. Contract the muscles of your legs - nobody can see your legs - as much as you can. Make them stiff, pull them as tight as you can. When n you feel that you can't go any further, suddenly relax them. You will be surprised to see that the anger has gone, and you will also be exercising your muscles and toning them up. And that angry impulse which could have become destructive has been released, and in the bargain your legs have been toned up. You can tone up and improve whichever part of your body has become blocked by anger, and the energy which has been created will be used in a creative way. If your hands are blocked, tighten the muscles of both your hands and all the energy of anger will be used. If your stomach is blocked, pull all the muscles of your stomach in and imagine that all the energy of your anger is being used to contract these muscles. You will see that in a minute or two the anger will have disappeared and the energy will have been used creatively. Energy is always neutral. The energy which is created by anger is not destructive in itself; it is destructive only be - cause it is being used in the form of anger. Make better use of it. And if it is not used in a better way it will continue to exist in a destructive form. It cannot disappear unless you do something. If you can learn to make use of it, it can bring a revolution into your life. So to purify the body old blocks have to be released and new blocks have to be transformed creatively. These are the two preliminary steps and they are very important. Most of the postures in yoga, the asanas, are meant for using the body creatively. Physical exercise makes creative use of the body. If you don't use your body creatively, then all this energy which could have been a blessing will become a curse. You are all suffering from your own energy; in other words, just having energy has become a problem, a burden. There was an incident in Jesus' life. He was leaving a village when he saw a man on a rooftop screaming and shouting obscenities. Jesus climbed a ladder and asked him, "My friend, what are you doing? Wh y are you wasting your life in this ugly way? You seem to be drunk." The man opened his eyes and recognized Jesus. He got up and bowed to Jesus and said, "My lord, I was very ill, I was near death. You blessed me and made me well. Have you forgotten? Now I am perfectly well, but what do I do with all this good health? This is why I drink." Jesus was surprised. The man said, "Now I am healthy, what am I supposed to do with this good health? So I drink and somehow I manage." Hearing this, Jesus felt great sadness and he climbed down from the ladder. Then he went into the village where he saw a man chasing after a prostitute. He stopped the man and asked him, "Friend, why are you misusing your eyes in this way?"BEGI N WIT H TH E BOD Y The man recognized Jesus and said, "Have you forgotten me? I was blind and you touched me, then I was able to see again. Now what am I to do with my eyes?" Jesus was very sad as he left the village. Outside the village a man was beating his chest and crying. Jesus touched him on the head and asked, "Why are you crying? There is so much beauty in the world. Life is not for crying." The man recognized Jesus and said, "You have forgotten! I died and people were about to bury me, and then with your miracle you brought me back to life. Now what should I do with my life?" This story seems to be completely fictitious, untrue - but what are you doing? Wha t are you doing with your life? Whatever energy you have collected in your life, you are only using it to destroy yourself. Life has only two paths: if the energy that we have available to us in our mind and body is used destructively, then this is the path to hell; if the same energy can be used creatively, this is the path to heaven. Creativity is heaven and destructiveness is hell. If you make creative use of your energy you will start moving closer to heaven, and if you use your energies destructively you will be going towards hell - there is no other meaning of heaven and hell. Consider what you are doing. Do you know how much energy is triggered within someone when he gets angry? Do you know that in a rage even a weak man can lift a rock that he would not even dream of lifting when he is calm? An angry man can overpower a strong but calm man in a moment. Once it happened in Japan.... There was a group of people called samurai, the warriors of that country who made their living by the sword. Life and death was a game to them. One of the samurai was a great warrior and he was chief of the army. Then his wife fell in love with one of the servants in their house. It was a custom that if your wife fell in love with some other man he would be challenged to a duel. That meant that one of them would be killed, and whoever won the duel would also get the wife. So the servant was in love with the wife of this great samurai warrior, and the warrior said to him, "You fool, now there is no other way but to fight a duel to the death. Now we have to fight. Tomorrow morning, come with a sword." The servant was very scared. His master was a very strong man and he was just a servant, sweeping and dusting; how could he fight with a sword? He had never even touched a sword. He said, "How can I lift a sword?" The samurai replied, "Now there is no way out. Tomorrow you will have to fight with a sword." He went home and he was thinking about it all night long. There was no escape. He picked up a sword next morning - he had never touched a sword - and left the house. People were shocked to see him, because when he arrived at the place for the duel he looked like a flaming fire. The samurai became nervous when he saw him, and he asked the servant, "Do you even know how to lift a sword?" - he didn't even hold the sword in the right way The servant said, "There is no question now, my death is certain. And since it is certain that I am going to be killed, then I will try to win. Death is certain, so I will try to kill you."

CHAPTER TWO

Self-Control Secret #2 – Eat

File this one in the counter-intuitive category, especially if you're having trouble controlling your eating. Your brain burns heavily into your stores of glucose when attempting to exert self-control. If your blood sugar is low, you are far more likely to succumb to destructive impulses. Sugary foods spike your sugar levels quickly and leave you drained and vulnerable shortly thereafter. Eating something that provides a slow burn for your body, such as whole grain rice or meat, will give you a longer window of self-control. So, if you're having trouble keeping yourself out of the company candy bin when you're hungry, make sure you eat something else if you want to have a fighting chance.

Healthy eating basics

Eating a healthy, balanced diet is one of the most important things you can do to protect your health. In fact, up to 80% of premature heart disease and stroke can be prevented through your life choices and habits, such as eating a healthy diet and being physically active.

A healthy diet can help lower your risk of heart disease and stroke by:
improving your cholesterol levels
reducing your blood pressure
helping you manage your body weight
controlling your blood sugar.
What does a healthy, balanced diet look like?
Canada's Food Guide recommends eating a variety of healthy foods each day. This includes eating plant-based foods more often and choosing highly-processed or ultra-processed foods less often.
This image is a copy of the version available at https://food-guide.canada.ca

A healthy diet includes:

1. Eating lots of vegetables and fruit

This is one of the most important diet habits. Vegetables and fruit are packed with nutrients (antioxidants, vitamins, minerals and fibre) and help you maintain a healthy weight by keeping you full longer.

Fill half your plate with vegetables and fruit at every meal and snack.

2. Choosing whole grain foods

Whole grain foods include whole grain bread and crackers, brown or wild rice, quinoa, oatmeal and hulled barley. They are prepared using the entire grain. Whole grain foods have fibre, protein and B vitamins to help you stay healthy and full longer.

Choose whole grain options instead of processed or refined grains like white bread and pasta.

Fill a quarter of your plate with whole grain foods.

3. Eating protein foods

Protein foods include legumes, nuts, seeds, tofu, fortified soy beverage, fish, shellfish, eggs, poultry, lean red meats including wild game, lower fat milk, lower fat yogurts, lower fat kefir and cheeses lower in fat and sodium.

Protein helps build and maintain bones, muscles and skin.

Eat protein every day.

Try to eat at least two servings of fish each week, and choose plant-based foods more often.

Dairy products are a great source of protein. Choose lower fat, unflavoured options.

Fill a quarter of your plate with protein foods.

4. Limiting highly and ultra-processed foods

Highly processed foods — often called ultra-processed — are foods that are changed from their original food source and have many added ingredients. During processing, often important nutrients such as vitamins, minerals and fiber are removed while salt and sugar are added. Examples of processed food include: fast foods, hot dogs, chips, cookies, frozen pizzas, deli meats, white rice and white bread.

Some minimally processed foods are okay. These are foods that are slightly changed in some way but contain few industrially made additives. Minimally processed foods keep almost all of their essential nutrients. Some examples are: bagged salad, frozen vegetables and fruit, eggs, milk, cheese, flour, brown rice, oil and dried herbs. We are not referring to these minimally processed foods when we are advising you not to eat processed foods.

Heart & Stroke funded research found that ultra-processed foods make up almost half of Canadians' diets. Read more about it here.

5. Making water your drink of choice

Water supports health and promotes hydration without adding calories to the diet.

Sugary drinks including energy drinks, fruit drinks, 100% fruit juice, soft drinks and flavored coffees have lots of sugar and little to no nutritional value. It is easy to drink empty calories without realizing, and this leads to weight gain.

Avoid fruit juice, even when it is 100% fruit juice. Although fruit juice has some of the benefits of the fruit (vitamins, minerals), it has more sugar than the fruit and less fiber. Fruit juice should not be consumed as alternative to fruits. Canadians should eat their fruits, not drink them.

When safe drinking water is not available, quench your thirst with coffee, tea, unsweetened lower-fat milk, and previously boiled water.

Top 5 tips from the experts

Prepare most of your meals at home using whole or minimally processed foods. Choose from a variety of different proteins to keep things interesting. Using catchy names for each day can help you plan. Try "Meatless Monday" with this meatless recipe.

Make an eating plan each week – this is the key to fast, easy meal preparation. Check out our shopping tips here.

Choose recipes with plenty of vegetables and fruit. Your goal is to fill half your plate with vegetables and fruit at every meal. Choose brightly coloured fruits and vegetables each day, especially orange and dark green vegetables (click here for more information). Frozen or canned unsweetened fruits and vegetables are a perfect alternative to fresh produce. Try this recipe.

Avoid sugary drinks and instead drink water. Lower-fat, unsweetened milk is also a good way to stay hydrated. Keep a reusable water bottle in your purse or car so you can fill up wherever you are going.

Eat smaller meals more often. Eat at least three meals a day with snacks in between. When you wait too long to eat you are more likely to make unhealthy food choices. Keep easy-to-eat snacks (like this) in your purse or bag for emergencies.

Aim for Fitness

Maintain or work toward a healthy weight.

Be physically active every day—return fun and play to your life. Get moderate to vigorous physical activity for at least 30 minutes a day 5 days a week.

Healthy eating provides the sustained energy you need to be physically active.

Learn to manage your stress with exercise, healthy eating, relaxation, and good coping skills.

Eat a variety of vegetables, especially dark green, red, and orange vegetables (3 or more servings a day).

Eat a variety of fruits (2 or more servings a day).

Eat whole-grain, high-fiber breads and cereals (3 to 6 servings a day). Reduce or eliminate refined or processed carbohydrates; most of the grains in your diet should be whole grains.

Drink fat-free or low-fat milk and eat low-fat dairy products.

Choose from a variety of low-fat sources of protein — including eggs, beans, poultry without skin, seafood, lean meats, unsalted nuts, seeds, and soy products. If you eat meat, eat white meat at least four times more often than red meat.

Reduce intake of saturated fats and trans-fats (such as partially hydrogenated oil) as much as possible.

Use vegetable oils (like olive or canola oil) instead of solid fats.

Reduce daily intake of salt or sodium. Reduce to less than 1,500 mg. per day if you are older than 50, or have hypertension, diabetes or chronic kidney disease.

Restrict or eliminate "junk food" — foods that contain refined white flour, solid fats or trans fats, added sugars, and are high in sodium.

Restrict or eliminate sodas and other sugar-added drinks that are high in calories and contain few or no nutrients.

If you drink alcoholic beverages, do so in moderation. Drink only when it doesn't put you or anyone else at risk.

To Lose Weight

Reduce the number of calories you eat daily. Eat smaller portions—don't "upsize" your meals at fast food restaurants.

Follow the dietary guidelines above.

Eliminate all sugar-added drinks from your diet. You can drink 100% fruit juice, unsweetened, but limit servings to one or two a day. Drink more water.

Decrease the amount of time spent in sedentary activities, especially watching television. Use your screen-free time working on hobbies, house cleaning, yard work, or engaging in fun activities.

Get moderate physical activity (such as walking, bicycling, swimming, or using aerobic exercise machines) for 30 to 60 minutes a day, at least five days a week.

Do muscle strengthening and toning exercises at least 2 or 3 days a week.

Eating is something that we do every day, three times a day, sometimes more, so it is important that we have correct posture while we eat. What does correct posture while we eat mean and where do we begin? Why is it important that we have good posture while we eat? We are upright creatures and that has an effect on all of our organs. When we slump, it impacts not only our spine, joints and muscles, but our organs as well— slowing down our digestion. Sitting upright when we eat can help to prevent bloating and heaviness. This means digesting and eliminating toxins with more ease. How to Start: Correct seating and positioning of the body while consuming meals is important because it improves both the enjoyment and safety of the meal. This facilitates better digestion and eating awareness. To enable the upper body or trunk to be stable, the feet must have a firm footing so they can bear weight as you eat ? Sit close to a table to prevent you from having to stretch forward to reach your meal. This prevents hunching forward and pressure on the abdomen. ? Align your ear, shoulders and hips while eating and bring your food up to your mouth. This will encourage better control of head, neck and muscles in the tongue, jaw and mouth. ? If you do have to eat in a chair or sofa, use a tray and sit up so your feet are firmly on the ground taking the weight of your trunk. ? Put cushions behind your back for support if needed. Keep your knees level with your hips and sit as far back as possible. Sitting up straight allows your food to digest uninterrupted. ? Try to stay seated upright for 10 to 20 minutes after the meal to help prevent symptoms of heartburn, indigestion or cramps. ? Avoid tight clothing around your stomach. ? Eat in good lighting. People tend to eat more if the lighting is low. (Think restaurants.) ? Avoid talking while chewing. Really think about your eating posture at each meal. Sometimes your posture is a reflection of how you feel about yourself at the time of the meal. How to Improve Your Pos ture While Eating JUL. joy "Unless some misfortune has made it impossible, everyone can have good posture. – We all know breakfast is the most important meal, but don't forget about lunch! We encourage our residents to eat at every meal to keep those metabolisms at work, to maintain a healthy weight and appetite. This summer, Chef Ricardo will start implementing new menus with more side dishes at lunch and fewer side dishes at dinner. The reason is two-fold. First, for the residents that sleep in and skip breakfast, it will be their first meal of the day! A salad alone will not cut it for the afternoon when activity is at its highest. Another reason would be to help avoid overeating at dinner, after which activities tend to wind down. Though it sounds like the best idea to sit down and tune into our evening programs with a full stomach, it can lead to indigestion and discomfort at bedtime. Chef Ricardo believes that dinner should be lighter when compared to lunch. As for all the night owls that stay up until midnight or beyond, we recommend eating something light a few hours after dinner. Snack on some fresh fruit, some crackers with peanut butter or some pudding at least two hours before sleeping! Moderate Lunch, Lighter Dinner Always Avail.

If you've made a resolution to eat healthy and exercise more, you're not alone. Losing weight and exercising are two of the most common New Year's resolutions. But as time passes, it's easy to forget your resolutions and your new nutrition plan, and let your bad habits creep back in. Here are nine ways to stay motivated to eat healthy and reach your goals for the next 12 months and beyond.

1. Have a Weigh-in

Weigh yourself every day or every other day at about the same time. Most people weigh less in the mornings before they eat, so that may be the best time of day to do it. "The reason I recommend weighing yourself daily is that you see trends, such as weight gain, sooner rather than later," says Marjorie Nolan, MS, RD, a nutritionist with a private practice in New York and a spokeswoman for the Academy of Nutrition and Dietetics. "And if you have gained weight, you can nip it before 2 or 3 pounds turns into 5 or 6 and become that much harder to lose."

2. Put Money Down

Hire a personal trainer or nutritionist to help you reach your fitness and nutrition goals. Or pay for extra fitness classes at the gym. You need to truly invest in your success, Nolan says. "When you pay for something, you're more willing to commit to it," she explains. Consider it your holiday present to yourself.

3. Start Fresh

It's a new year — not only for the calendar but also for your refrigerator and pantry. Purge the junk food from your cupboards and start with a clean slate as you move to healthier eating habits. "Don't keep three dozen Christmas cookies in your freezer if you don't have to," Nolan says. Discard the unhealthy choices you made and restock with healthier versions.

4. Plan Ahead

Plan time to exercise and to cook and eat healthy meals. If you schedule time for exercise just as you do for doctors' appointments, you'll find it's easier to stick with it. The same goes for eating healthy. Plan a healthy menu and write a shopping list to take to the store. It's easier to stick to your nutrition goals when you have a list while shopping. You'll also be better equipped to make healthy meals and snacks at home when the foods you need are handy.

5. Set Realistic Goals

You're more likely to stay motivated when you have a realistic plan rather than vague wishes or overly optimistic ideals. First be specific. Instead of saying, "I'm going to lose weight," set a goal to lose 3 to 5 pounds in one month. Then, be realistic. For example, instead of giving up sweets entirely, say "I'm going to only eat dessert three times a week instead of seven." If your nutrition plan includes realistic goals, you'll be more likely to achieve them, says Nolan.

6. Reward Your Success

Your goal could be to lose 2 pounds or to not eat seconds at any meal for a week. Whatever it is, when you reach it, reward yourself with something small — just be sure it's not a food-related treat. Go to the movies with a friend. Get your nails done. Buy that new sweater. Go for a walk in the woods with your dog. These types of rewards help provide the incentive you need to continue working toward bigger goals.

7. Write It Down

Putting your actions down on paper helps you focus what you're doing to help (or hurt) your goals. If you keep a food journal, you can look back at what you've eaten, which could be more or less than you realize. Joining an online support group where you can share your food journal with others can help, says Nolan. "When you know other people are seeing it, you'll be more motivated to stick to your healthy eating habits," she adds.

8. Try New Recipes and New Gadgets

Look for healthy recipes online and in newspapers and magazines. Try the ones that appeal to you most. Breaking up your routine with new recipes keeps your healthy eating plan interesting. And if you're not bored, it's easier to stick to your goals. Buying new cooking items is another way to stay excited about healthy cooking, says Nolan. "Whenever I get a new kitchen appliance — pots, pans, food processor, or even a knife — I want to play with it, which can help me expand what I'm eating in a healthy way."

9. Be Forgiving

What if you can't resist and you eat that piece of pecan pie from Christmas or dig into a bag of chips? Don't be too hard on yourself. You can't change what you've eaten, but you can make better choices at your very next meal, Nolan says. If you wait until tomorrow or Monday to get back to eating healthy, it will be that much harder.

Adopting a nutrition plan at the start of the year and sticking to it as the months pass can be much easier than you think, especially if you employ these tricks to help you along the way.

CHAPTER THREE

Self-Control Secret #3 – Exercise

For most of us, temptations are everywhere, from the dessert buffet to the online shoe boutique. But a new study suggests that exercise might be a simple if unexpected way to increase our willpower and perhaps help us to avoid making impulsive choices that we will later regret.

Self-control is one of those concepts that we all recognize and applaud but do not necessarily practice. It requires forgoing things that entice us, which, let's face it, is not fun. On the other hand, lack of self-control can be consequential for health and well-being, often contributing to problems like weight gain, depression or money woes.

Given these impacts, scientists and therapists have been interested in finding ways to increase people's self-restraint. Various types of behavioral therapies and counseling have shown promise. But such techniques typically require professional assistance and have for the most part been used to treat people with abnormally high levels of impulsiveness.

There have been few scientifically validated options available to help those of us who might want to be just a little better at resisting our more devilish urges.

For most of us, temptations are everywhere, from the dessert buffet to the online shoe boutique. But a new study suggests that exercise might be a simple if unexpected way to increase our willpower and perhaps help us to avoid making impulsive choices that we will later regret.

Self-control is one of those concepts that we all recognize and applaud but do not necessarily practice. It requires forgoing things that entice us, which, let's face it, is not fun. On the other hand, lack of self-control can be consequential for health and well-being, often contributing to problems like weight gain, depression or money woes.

Given these impacts, scientists and therapists have been interested in finding ways to increase people's self-restraint. Various types of behavioral therapies and counseling have shown promise. But such techniques typically require professional assistance and have for the most part been used to treat people with abnormally high levels of impulsiveness.

There have been few scientifically validated options available to help those of us who might want to be just a little better at resisting our more devilish urges.

For most of us, temptations are everywhere, from the dessert buffet to the online shoe boutique. But a new study suggests that exercise might be a simple if unexpected way to increase our willpower and perhaps help us to avoid making impulsive choices that we will later regret.

Self-control is one of those concepts that we all recognize and applaud but do not necessarily practice. It requires forgoing things that entice us, which, let's face it, is not fun. On the other hand, lack of self-control can be consequential for health and well-being, often contributing to problems like weight gain, depression or money woes.

Given these impacts, scientists and therapists have been interested in finding ways to increase people's self-restraint. Various types of behavioral therapies and counseling have shown promise. But such techniques typically require professional assistance and have for the most part been used to treat people with abnormally high levels of impulsiveness.

There have been few scientifically validated options available to help those of us who might want to be just a little better at resisting our more devilish urges.

For most of us, temptations are everywhere, from the dessert buffet to the online shoe boutique. But a new study suggests that exercise might be a simple if unexpected way to increase our willpower and perhaps help us to avoid making impulsive choices that we will later regret.

Self-control is one of those concepts that we all recognize and applaud but do not necessarily practice. It requires forgoing things that entice us, which, let's face it, is not fun. On the other hand, lack of self-control can be consequential for health and well-being, often contributing to problems like weight gain, depression or money woes.

Given these impacts, scientists and therapists have been interested in finding ways to increase people's self-restraint. Various types of behavioral therapies and counseling have shown promise. But such techniques typically require professional assistance and have for the most part been used to treat people with abnormally high levels of impulsiveness.

There have been few scientifically validated options available to help those of us who might want to be just a little better at resisting our more devilish urges.

For most of us, temptations are everywhere, from the dessert buffet to the online shoe boutique. But a new study suggests that exercise might be a simple if unexpected way to increase our willpower and perhaps help us to avoid making impulsive choices that we will later regret.

Self-control is one of those concepts that we all recognize and applaud but do not necessarily practice. It requires forgoing things that entice us, which, let's face it, is not fun. On the other hand, lack of self-control can be consequential for health and well-being, often contributing to problems like weight gain, depression or money woes.

Given these impacts, scientists and therapists have been interested in finding ways to increase people's self-restraint. Various types of behavioral therapies and counseling have shown promise. But such techniques typically require professional assistance and have for the most part been used to treat people with abnormally high levels of impulsiveness.

There have been few scientifically validated options available to help those of us who might want to be just a little better at resisting our more devilish urges.

For most of us, temptations are everywhere, from the dessert buffet to the online shoe boutique. But a new study suggests that exercise might be a simple if unexpected way to increase our willpower and perhaps help us to avoid making impulsive choices that we will later regret.

Self-control is one of those concepts that we all recognize and applaud but do not necessarily practice. It requires forgoing things that entice us, which, let's face it, is not fun. On the other hand, lack of self-control can be consequential for health and well-being, often contributing to problems like weight gain, depression or money woes.

Given these impacts, scientists and therapists have been interested in finding ways to increase people's self-restraint. Various types of behavioral therapies and counseling have shown promise. But such techniques typically require professional assistance and have for the most part been used to treat people with abnormally high levels of impulsiveness.

There have been few scientifically validated options available to help those of us who might want to be just a little better at resisting our more devilish urges.

For most of us, temptations are everywhere, from the dessert buffet to the online shoe boutique. But a new study suggests that exercise might be a simple if unexpected way to increase our willpower and perhaps help us to avoid making impulsive choices that we will later regret.

Self-control is one of those concepts that we all recognize and applaud but do not necessarily practice. It requires forgoing things that entice us, which, let's face it, is not fun. On the other hand, lack of self-control can be consequential for health and well-being, often contributing to problems like weight gain, depression or money woes.

Given these impacts, scientists and therapists have been interested in finding ways to increase people's self-restraint. Various types of behavioral therapies and counseling have shown promise. But such techniques typically require professional assistance and have for the most part been used to treat people with abnormally high levels of impulsiveness.

There have been few scientifically validated options available to help those of us who might want to be just a little better at resisting our more devilish urges.

For most of us, temptations are everywhere, from the dessert buffet to the online shoe boutique. But a new study suggests that exercise might be a simple if unexpected way to increase our willpower and perhaps help us to avoid making impulsive choices that we will later regret.

Self-control is one of those concepts that we all recognize and applaud but do not necessarily practice. It requires forgoing things that entice us, which, let's face it, is not fun. On the other hand, lack of self-control can be consequential for health and well-being, often contributing to problems like weight gain, depression or money woes.

Given these impacts, scientists and therapists have been interested in finding ways to increase people's self-restraint. Various types of behavioral therapies and counseling have shown promise. But such techniques typically require professional assistance and have for the most part been used to treat people with abnormally high levels of impulsiveness.

There have been few scientifically validated options available to help those of us who might want to be just a little better at resisting our more devilish urges.

So for the new study, which was published recently in Behavior Modification, a group of researchers at the University of Kansas in Lawrence began wondering about exercise.

Exercise is known to have considerable psychological effects. It can raise moods, for example, and expand people's sense of what they are capable of doing. So perhaps, the researchers speculated, exercise might alter how well people can control their impulses.

To find out, the scientists decided first to mount a tiny pilot study, involving only four men and women.

These volunteers, who had been sedentary and overweight, were told they would be taking part in an exercise program to get them ready to complete a 5K race, and that the study would examine some of the effects of the training, including psychological impacts.

The volunteers began by completing a number of questionnaires, including one that quantified their "delay discounting," a measure that psychologists use to assess someone's ability to put off pleasures now for greater enjoyments in the future. It tests, for instance, whether a person would choose to accept $5 today or $15 a week from now.

So for the new study, which was published recently in Behavior Modification, a group of researchers at the University of Kansas in Lawrence began wondering about exercise.

Exercise is known to have considerable psychological effects. It can raise moods, for example, and expand people's sense of what they are capable of doing. So perhaps, the researchers speculated, exercise might alter how well people can control their impulses.

To find out, the scientists decided first to mount a tiny pilot study, involving only four men and women.

These volunteers, who had been sedentary and overweight, were told they would be taking part in an exercise program to get them ready to complete a 5K race, and that the study would examine some of the effects of the training, including psychological impacts.

The volunteers began by completing a number of questionnaires, including one that quantified their "delay discounting," a measure that psychologists use to assess someone's ability to put off pleasures now for greater enjoyments in the future. It tests, for instance, whether a person would choose to accept $5 today or $15 a week from now.

So for the new study, which was published recently in Behavior Modification, a group of researchers at the University of Kansas in Lawrence began wondering about exercise.

Exercise is known to have considerable psychological effects. It can raise moods, for example, and expand people's sense of what they are capable of doing. So perhaps, the researchers speculated, exercise might alter how well people can control their impulses.

To find out, the scientists decided first to mount a tiny pilot study, involving only four men and women.

These volunteers, who had been sedentary and overweight, were told they would be taking part in an exercise program to get them ready to complete a 5K race, and that the study would examine some of the effects of the training, including psychological impacts.

The volunteers began by completing a number of questionnaires, including one that quantified their "delay discounting," a measure that psychologists use to assess someone's ability to put off pleasures now for greater enjoyments in the future. It tests, for instance, whether a person would choose to accept $5 today or $15 a week from now.

So for the new study, which was published recently in Behavior Modification, a group of researchers at the University of Kansas in Lawrence began wondering about exercise.

Exercise is known to have considerable psychological effects. It can raise moods, for example, and expand people's sense of what they are capable of doing. So perhaps, the researchers speculated, exercise might alter how well people can control their impulses.

To find out, the scientists decided first to mount a tiny pilot study, involving only four men and women.

These volunteers, who had been sedentary and overweight, were told they would be taking part in an exercise program to get them ready to complete a 5K race, and that the study would examine some of the effects of the training, including psychological impacts.

The volunteers began by completing a number of questionnaires, including one that quantified their "delay discounting," a measure that psychologists use to assess someone's ability to put off pleasures now for greater enjoyments in the future. It tests, for instance, whether a person would choose to accept $5 today or $15 a week from now.

So for the new study, which was published recently in Behavior Modification, a group of researchers at the University of Kansas in Lawrence began wondering about exercise.

Exercise is known to have considerable psychological effects. It can raise moods, for example, and expand people's sense of what they are capable of doing. So perhaps, the researchers speculated, exercise might alter how well people can control their impulses.

To find out, the scientists decided first to mount a tiny pilot study, involving only four men and women.

These volunteers, who had been sedentary and overweight, were told they would be taking part in an exercise program to get them ready to complete a 5K race, and that the study would examine some of the effects of the training, including psychological impacts.

The volunteers began by completing a number of questionnaires, including one that quantified their "delay discounting," a measure that psychologists use to assess someone's ability to put off pleasures now for greater enjoyments in the future. It tests, for instance, whether a person would choose to accept $5 today or $15 a week from now.

So for the new study, which was published recently in Behavior Modification, a group of researchers at the University of Kansas in Lawrence began wondering about exercise.

Exercise is known to have considerable psychological effects. It can raise moods, for example, and expand people's sense of what they are capable of doing. So perhaps, the researchers speculated, exercise might alter how well people can control their impulses.

To find out, the scientists decided first to mount a tiny pilot study, involving only four men and women.

These volunteers, who had been sedentary and overweight, were told they would be taking part in an exercise program to get them ready to complete a 5K race, and that the study would examine some of the effects of the training, including psychological impacts.

The volunteers began by completing a number of questionnaires, including one that quantified their "delay discounting," a measure that psychologists use to assess someone's ability to put off pleasures now for greater enjoyments in the future. It tests, for instance, whether a person would choose to accept $5 today or $15 a week from now.

So for the new study, which was published recently in Behavior Modification, a group of researchers at the University of Kansas in Lawrence began wondering about exercise.

Exercise is known to have considerable psychological effects. It can raise moods, for example, and expand people's sense of what they are capable of doing. So perhaps, the researchers speculated, exercise might alter how well people can control their impulses.

To find out, the scientists decided first to mount a tiny pilot study, involving only four men and women.

These volunteers, who had been sedentary and overweight, were told they would be taking part in an exercise program to get them ready to complete a 5K race, and that the study would examine some of the effects of the training, including psychological impacts.

The volunteers began by completing a number of questionnaires, including one that quantified their "delay discounting," a measure that psychologists use to assess someone's ability to put off pleasures now for greater enjoyments in the future. It tests, for instance, whether a person would choose to accept $5 today or $15 a week from now.

So for the new study, which was published recently in Behavior Modification, a group of researchers at the University of Kansas in Lawrence began wondering about exercise.

Exercise is known to have considerable psychological effects. It can raise moods, for example, and expand people's sense of what they are capable of doing. So perhaps, the researchers speculated, exercise might alter how well people can control their impulses.

To find out, the scientists decided first to mount a tiny pilot study, involving only four men and women.

These volunteers, who had been sedentary and overweight, were told they would be taking part in an exercise program to get them ready to complete a 5K race, and that the study would examine some of the effects of the training, including psychological impacts.

The volunteers began by completing a number of questionnaires, including one that quantified their "delay discounting," a measure that psychologists use to assess someone's ability to put off pleasures now for greater enjoyments in the future. It tests, for instance, whether a person would choose to accept $5 today or $15 a week from now.

The delay-discounting questionnaire is generally accepted in research circles as a valid measure of someone's self-control.The delay-discounting questionnaire is generally accepted in research circles as a valid measure of someone's self-control.The delay-discounting questionnaire is generally accepted in research circles as a valid measure of someone's self-control.The delay-discounting questionnaire is generally accepted in research circles as a valid measure of someone's self-control.The delay-discounting questionnaire is generally accepted in research circles as a valid measure of someone's self-control.The delay-discounting questionnaire is generally accepted in research circles as a valid measure of someone's self-control.The delay-discounting questionnaire is generally accepted in research circles as a valid measure of someone's self-control.The delay-discounting questionnaire is generally accepted in research circles as a valid measure of someone's self-control.

The volunteers then undertook a two-month walking and jogging regimen, meeting three times a week for 45 minutes with the researchers, who coached them through the sessions, urging them to maintain a pace that felt difficult but sustainable. Each week the men and women also repeated the questionnaires.

Finally, a month after the formal training had ended, the volunteers returned to the university for one more round of testing. (Later, two of them also ran 5K races.)

The results were intriguing, the researchers felt. Three of the four participants had developed significantly greater self-control, according to their delay-discounting answers, and maintained those gains a month after the formal training had ended. But one volunteer, who had missed multiple sessions, showed no changes in impulsivity.

A four-person study is too small to be meaningful, though, so the researchers next repeated the experiment with 12 women of varying ages, weights and fitness levels.

The results were almost identical to those in the pilot study. Most of the women gained a notable degree of self-control, based on their questionnaires, after completing the walking and jogging program. (In this experiment, they were told they were training for better fitness.)

But the increases were proportional; the more sessions a woman attended or the more her average jogging pace increased, the greater the improvement in her delay-discounting score.

The volunteers then undertook a two-month walking and jogging regimen, meeting three times a week for 45 minutes with the researchers, who coached them through the sessions, urging them to maintain a pace that felt difficult but sustainable. Each week the men and women also repeated the questionnaires.

Finally, a month after the formal training had ended, the volunteers returned to the university for one more round of testing. (Later, two of them also ran 5K races.)

The results were intriguing, the researchers felt. Three of the four participants had developed significantly greater self-control, according to their delay-discounting answers, and maintained those gains a month after the formal training had ended. But one volunteer, who had missed multiple sessions, showed no changes in impulsivity.

A four-person study is too small to be meaningful, though, so the researchers next repeated the experiment with 12 women of varying ages, weights and fitness levels.

The results were almost identical to those in the pilot study. Most of the women gained a notable degree of self-control, based on their questionnaires, after completing the walking and jogging program. (In this experiment, they were told they were training for better fitness.)

But the increases were proportional; the more sessions a woman attended or the more her average jogging pace increased, the greater the improvement in her delay-discounting score.

The volunteers then undertook a two-month walking and jogging regimen, meeting three times a week for 45 minutes with the researchers, who coached them through the sessions, urging them to maintain a pace that felt difficult but sustainable. Each week the men and women also repeated the questionnaires.

Finally, a month after the formal training had ended, the volunteers returned to the university for one more round of testing. (Later, two of them also ran 5K races.)

The results were intriguing, the researchers felt. Three of the four participants had developed significantly greater self-control, according to their delay-discounting answers, and maintained those gains a month after the formal training had ended. But one volunteer, who had missed multiple sessions, showed no changes in impulsivity.

A four-person study is too small to be meaningful, though, so the researchers next repeated the experiment with 12 women of varying ages, weights and fitness levels.

The results were almost identical to those in the pilot study. Most of the women gained a notable degree of self-control, based on their questionnaires, after completing the walking and jogging program. (In this experiment, they were told they were training for better fitness.)

But the increases were proportional; the more sessions a woman attended or the more her average jogging pace increased, the greater the improvement in her delay-discounting score.

The volunteers then undertook a two-month walking and jogging regimen, meeting three times a week for 45 minutes with the researchers, who coached them through the sessions, urging them to maintain a pace that felt difficult but sustainable. Each week the men and women also repeated the questionnaires.

Finally, a month after the formal training had ended, the volunteers returned to the university for one more round of testing. (Later, two of them also ran 5K races.)

The results were intriguing, the researchers felt. Three of the four participants had developed significantly greater self-control, according to their delay-discounting answers, and maintained those gains a month after the formal training had ended. But one volunteer, who had missed multiple sessions, showed no changes in impulsivity.

A four-person study is too small to be meaningful, though, so the researchers next repeated the experiment with 12 women of varying ages, weights and fitness levels.

The results were almost identical to those in the pilot study. Most of the women gained a notable degree of self-control, based on their questionnaires, after completing the walking and jogging program. (In this experiment, they were told they were training for better fitness.)

But the increases were proportional; the more sessions a woman attended or the more her average jogging pace increased, the greater the improvement in her delay-discounting score.

The volunteers then undertook a two-month walking and jogging regimen, meeting three times a week for 45 minutes with the researchers, who coached them through the sessions, urging them to maintain a pace that felt difficult but sustainable. Each week the men and women also repeated the questionnaires.

Finally, a month after the formal training had ended, the volunteers returned to the university for one more round of testing. (Later, two of them also ran 5K races.)

The results were intriguing, the researchers felt. Three of the four participants had developed significantly greater self-control, according to their delay-discounting answers, and maintained those gains a month after the formal training had ended. But one volunteer, who had missed multiple sessions, showed no changes in impulsivity.

A four-person study is too small to be meaningful, though, so the researchers next repeated the experiment with 12 women of varying ages, weights and fitness levels.

The results were almost identical to those in the pilot study. Most of the women gained a notable degree of self-control, based on their questionnaires, after completing the walking and jogging program. (In this experiment, they were told they were training for better fitness.)

But the increases were proportional; the more sessions a woman attended or the more her average jogging pace increased, the greater the improvement in her delay-discounting score.

The volunteers then undertook a two-month walking and jogging regimen, meeting three times a week for 45 minutes with the researchers, who coached them through the sessions, urging them to maintain a pace that felt difficult but sustainable. Each week the men and women also repeated the questionnaires.

Finally, a month after the formal training had ended, the volunteers returned to the university for one more round of testing. (Later, two of them also ran 5K races.)

The results were intriguing, the researchers felt. Three of the four participants had developed significantly greater self-control, according to their delay-discounting answers, and maintained those gains a month after the formal training had ended. But one volunteer, who had missed multiple sessions, showed no changes in impulsivity.

A four-person study is too small to be meaningful, though, so the researchers next repeated the experiment with 12 women of varying ages, weights and fitness levels.

The results were almost identical to those in the pilot study. Most of the women gained a notable degree of self-control, based on their questionnaires, after completing the walking and jogging program. (In this experiment, they were told they were training for better fitness.)

But the increases were proportional; the more sessions a woman attended or the more her average jogging pace increased, the greater the improvement in her delay-discounting score.

The volunteers then undertook a two-month walking and jogging regimen, meeting three times a week for 45 minutes with the researchers, who coached them through the sessions, urging them to maintain a pace that felt difficult but sustainable. Each week the men and women also repeated the questionnaires.

Finally, a month after the formal training had ended, the volunteers returned to the university for one more round of testing. (Later, two of them also ran 5K races.)

The results were intriguing, the researchers felt. Three of the four participants had developed significantly greater self-control, according to their delay-discounting answers, and maintained those gains a month after the formal training had ended. But one volunteer, who had missed multiple sessions, showed no changes in impulsivity.

A four-person study is too small to be meaningful, though, so the researchers next repeated the experiment with 12 women of varying ages, weights and fitness levels.

The results were almost identical to those in the pilot study. Most of the women gained a notable degree of self-control, based on their questionnaires, after completing the walking and jogging program. (In this experiment, they were told they were training for better fitness.)

But the increases were proportional; the more sessions a woman attended or the more her average jogging pace increased, the greater the improvement in her delay-discounting score.

The volunteers then undertook a two-month walking and jogging regimen, meeting three times a week for 45 minutes with the researchers, who coached them through the sessions, urging them to maintain a pace that felt difficult but sustainable. Each week the men and women also repeated the questionnaires.

Finally, a month after the formal training had ended, the volunteers returned to the university for one more round of testing. (Later, two of them also ran 5K races.)

The results were intriguing, the researchers felt. Three of the four participants had developed significantly greater self-control, according to their delay-discounting answers, and maintained those gains a month after the formal training had ended. But one volunteer, who had missed multiple sessions, showed no changes in impulsivity.

A four-person study is too small to be meaningful, though, so the researchers next repeated the experiment with 12 women of varying ages, weights and fitness levels.

The results were almost identical to those in the pilot study. Most of the women gained a notable degree of self-control, based on their questionnaires, after completing the walking and jogging program. (In this experiment, they were told they were training for better fitness.)

But the increases were proportional; the more sessions a woman attended or the more her average jogging pace increased, the greater the improvement in her delay-discounting score.

These gains lingered a month after the training had ended, although most of the women had tapered off their exercise routines by then.

The upshot of these results would seem to be that exercise could be a simple way to help people shore up their self-restraint, says Michael Sofis, a doctoral candidate in applied behavioral science at the University of Kansas who led the study.

These two experiments cannot tell us, though, how exercise helps us to ignore a cupcake's allure. But Mr. Sofis says that many past studies have concluded that regular exercise alters the workings of portions of the brain involved in higher-level thinking and decision-making, which, in turn, play important roles in impulse control.

Exercise also may have more abstract psychological impacts on our sense of self-control, he says. It is, for many of us, a concentrated form of delayed gratification. Exerting ourselves during a workout is not always immediately pleasurable. But it can feel marvelous afterward to know that we managed to keep going, a sensation that could spill over into later decision-making.

Of course, with a total of only 16 participants, these experiments remained small-scale and limited, relying on a fundamentally artificial, mathematical measure of self-control. The scientists did not, for example, track whether the volunteers became less impulsive in their actual daily lives. Mr. Sofis and his colleagues hope to conduct follow-up studies that will look at the real-world impacts of exercise on self-control.

But for now, he says, these results suggest that normal people "can change and improve their self-control with regular physical activity."

These gains lingered a month after the training had ended, although most of the women had tapered off their exercise routines by then.

The upshot of these results would seem to be that exercise could be a simple way to help people shore up their self-restraint, says Michael Sofis, a doctoral candidate in applied behavioral science at the University of Kansas who led the study.

These two experiments cannot tell us, though, how exercise helps us to ignore a cupcake's allure. But Mr. Sofis says that many past studies have concluded that regular exercise alters the workings of portions of the brain involved in higher-level thinking and decision-making, which, in turn, play important roles in impulse control.

Exercise also may have more abstract psychological impacts on our sense of self-control, he says. It is, for many of us, a concentrated form of delayed gratification. Exerting ourselves during a workout is not always immediately pleasurable. But it can feel marvelous afterward to know that we managed to keep going, a sensation that could spill over into later decision-making.

Of course, with a total of only 16 participants, these experiments remained small-scale and limited, relying on a fundamentally artificial, mathematical measure of self-control. The scientists did not, for example, track whether the volunteers became less impulsive in their actual daily lives. Mr. Sofis and his colleagues hope to conduct follow-up studies that will look at the real-world impacts of exercise on self-control.

But for now, he says, these results suggest that normal people "can change and improve their self-control with regular physical activity."

These gains lingered a month after the training had ended, although most of the women had tapered off their exercise routines by then.

The upshot of these results would seem to be that exercise could be a simple way to help people shore up their self-restraint, says Michael Sofis, a doctoral candidate in applied behavioral science at the University of Kansas who led the study.

These two experiments cannot tell us, though, how exercise helps us to ignore a cupcake's allure. But Mr. Sofis says that many past studies have concluded that regular exercise alters the workings of portions of the brain involved in higher-level thinking and decision-making, which, in turn, play important roles in impulse control.

Exercise also may have more abstract psychological impacts on our sense of self-control, he says. It is, for many of us, a concentrated form of delayed gratification. Exerting ourselves during a workout is not always immediately pleasurable. But it can feel marvelous afterward to know that we managed to keep going, a sensation that could spill over into later decision-making.

Of course, with a total of only 16 participants, these experiments remained small-scale and limited, relying on a fundamentally artificial, mathematical measure of self-control. The scientists did not, for example, track whether the volunteers became less impulsive in their actual daily lives. Mr. Sofis and his colleagues hope to conduct follow-up studies that will look at the real-world impacts of exercise on self-control.

But for now, he says, these results suggest that normal people "can change and improve their self-control with regular physical activity."

These gains lingered a month after the training had ended, although most of the women had tapered off their exercise routines by then.

The upshot of these results would seem to be that exercise could be a simple way to help people shore up their self-restraint, says Michael Sofis, a doctoral candidate in applied behavioral science at the University of Kansas who led the study.

These two experiments cannot tell us, though, how exercise helps us to ignore a cupcake's allure. But Mr. Sofis says that many past studies have concluded that regular exercise alters the workings of portions of the brain involved in higher-level thinking and decision-making, which, in turn, play important roles in impulse control.

Exercise also may have more abstract psychological impacts on our sense of self-control, he says. It is, for many of us, a concentrated form of delayed gratification. Exerting ourselves during a workout is not always immediately pleasurable. But it can feel marvelous afterward to know that we managed to keep going, a sensation that could spill over into later decision-making.

Of course, with a total of only 16 participants, these experiments remained small-scale and limited, relying on a fundamentally artificial, mathematical measure of self-control. The scientists did not, for example, track whether the volunteers became less impulsive in their actual daily lives. Mr. Sofis and his colleagues hope to conduct follow-up studies that will look at the real-world impacts of exercise on self-control.

But for now, he says, these results suggest that normal people "can change and improve their self-control with regular physical activity."

These gains lingered a month after the training had ended, although most of the women had tapered off their exercise routines by then.

The upshot of these results would seem to be that exercise could be a simple way to help people shore up their self-restraint, says Michael Sofis, a doctoral candidate in applied behavioral science at the University of Kansas who led the study.

These two experiments cannot tell us, though, how exercise helps us to ignore a cupcake's allure. But Mr. Sofis says that many past studies have concluded that regular exercise alters the workings of portions of the brain involved in higher-level thinking and decision-making, which, in turn, play important roles in impulse control.

Exercise also may have more abstract psychological impacts on our sense of self-control, he says. It is, for many of us, a concentrated form of delayed gratification. Exerting ourselves during a workout is not always immediately pleasurable. But it can feel marvelous afterward to know that we managed to keep going, a sensation that could spill over into later decision-making.

Of course, with a total of only 16 participants, these experiments remained small-scale and limited, relying on a fundamentally artificial, mathematical measure of self-control. The scientists did not, for example, track whether the volunteers became less impulsive in their actual daily lives. Mr. Sofis and his colleagues hope to conduct follow-up studies that will look at the real-world impacts of exercise on self-control.

But for now, he says, these results suggest that normal people "can change and improve their self-control with regular physical activity."

These gains lingered a month after the training had ended, although most of the women had tapered off their exercise routines by then.

The upshot of these results would seem to be that exercise could be a simple way to help people shore up their self-restraint, says Michael Sofis, a doctoral candidate in applied behavioral science at the University of Kansas who led the study.

These two experiments cannot tell us, though, how exercise helps us to ignore a cupcake's allure. But Mr. Sofis says that many past studies have concluded that regular exercise alters the workings of portions of the brain involved in higher-level thinking and decision-making, which, in turn, play important roles in impulse control.

Exercise also may have more abstract psychological impacts on our sense of self-control, he says. It is, for many of us, a concentrated form of delayed gratification. Exerting ourselves during a workout is not always immediately pleasurable. But it can feel marvelous afterward to know that we managed to keep going, a sensation that could spill over into later decision-making.

Of course, with a total of only 16 participants, these experiments remained small-scale and limited, relying on a fundamentally artificial, mathematical measure of self-control. The scientists did not, for example, track whether the volunteers became less impulsive in their actual daily lives. Mr. Sofis and his colleagues hope to conduct follow-up studies that will look at the real-world impacts of exercise on self-control.

But for now, he says, these results suggest that normal people "can change and improve their self-control with regular physical activity."

These gains lingered a month after the training had ended, although most of the women had tapered off their exercise routines by then.

The upshot of these results would seem to be that exercise could be a simple way to help people shore up their self-restraint, says Michael Sofis, a doctoral candidate in applied behavioral science at the University of Kansas who led the study.

These two experiments cannot tell us, though, how exercise helps us to ignore a cupcake's allure. But Mr. Sofis says that many past studies have concluded that regular exercise alters the workings of portions of the brain involved in higher-level thinking and decision-making, which, in turn, play important roles in impulse control.

Exercise also may have more abstract psychological impacts on our sense of self-control, he says. It is, for many of us, a concentrated form of delayed gratification. Exerting ourselves during a workout is not always immediately pleasurable. But it can feel marvelous afterward to know that we managed to keep going, a sensation that could spill over into later decision-making.

Of course, with a total of only 16 participants, these experiments remained small-scale and limited, relying on a fundamentally artificial, mathematical measure of self-control. The scientists did not, for example, track whether the volunteers became less impulsive in their actual daily lives. Mr. Sofis and his colleagues hope to conduct follow-up studies that will look at the real-world impacts of exercise on self-control.

But for now, he says, these results suggest that normal people "can change and improve their self-control with regular physical activity."

These gains lingered a month after the training had ended, although most of the women had tapered off their exercise routines by then.

The upshot of these results would seem to be that exercise could be a simple way to help people shore up their self-restraint, says Michael Sofis, a doctoral candidate in applied behavioral science at the University of Kansas who led the study.

These two experiments cannot tell us, though, how exercise helps us to ignore a cupcake's allure. But Mr. Sofis says that many past studies have concluded that regular exercise alters the workings of portions of the brain involved in higher-level thinking and decision-making, which, in turn, play important roles in impulse control.

Exercise also may have more abstract psychological impacts on our sense of self-control, he says. It is, for many of us, a concentrated form of delayed gratification. Exerting ourselves during a workout is not always immediately pleasurable. But it can feel marvelous afterward to know that we managed to keep going, a sensation that could spill over into later decision-making.

Of course, with a total of only 16 participants, these experiments remained small-scale and limited, relying on a fundamentally artificial, mathematical measure of self-control. The scientists did not, for example, track whether the volunteers became less impulsive in their actual daily lives. Mr. Sofis and his colleagues hope to conduct follow-up studies that will look at the real-world impacts of exercise on self-control.

But for now, he says, these results suggest that normal people "can change and improve their self-control with regular physical activity."

CHAPTER FOUR

Self-Control Secret #4 – Sleep

study examined the mediating roles of both positive and negative affects in the relationship between sleep quality and self-control. A sample of 1,507 Chinese adults (37% men; mean age = 32.5 years) completed self-report questionnaires measuring sleep quality, positive and negative emotions, and self-control. Poor sleep quality was positively correlated with negative affect and negatively correlated with positive affect and self-control. Positive affect was positively correlated with self-control, while negative affect was negatively correlated with self-control. Both positive and negative affects significantly mediated the relationship between sleep quality and self-control. Improving individuals' sleep qualities may lead to more positive emotions and less negative emotion, and these mood changes may increase resources for self-control. Regulating positive and negative affects may reduce the negative effects of poor sleep quality on self-control.

Self-control is an important component of successful psychological functioning, and it alters one's response when presented with conflicting desires (Pilcher et al., 2015). High trait self-control predicts low resting heart rate, high heart rate variability, a steep cortisol slope, stable emotional patterns, and well-being (Daly et al., 2012), which are beneficial for physical and psychological health. Self-control is also predictive of success in achievement-related domains (Choi et al., 2018). Self-control enables people to delay instant gratification and work toward long-term goals.

Neuroimaging indicates sleep deprivation affects activation and deactivation of the prefrontal cortex (PFC) (Chee and Choo, 2004), resulting in less-effective executive control function of the PFC (Nilsson et al., 2005). Poor sleep quality deleteriously impacts self-control capacity (Altena et al., 2008), such as emotion regulation (Palmer and Alfano, 2017) and cognitive inhibition (García et al., 2012). A diary study covering 10 working days reveals that a good night's sleep allows employees to regain self-control the next day (Gombert et al., 2018). The underlying mechanism by which sleep quality impacts self-control, however, remains unclear.

Bouwmans et al. (2017) suggest that sleep quality can predict positive and negative affects. Negative affect was positively correlated with the Pittsburgh Sleep Quality Index (PSQI) score, and positive affect was negatively correlated with the PSQI score (Latif et al., 2019). Positive affect is related to better sleep quality (Bower et al., 2010). Disturbed sleep engenders lower positive affect and reduced psychological well-being (Steptoe et al., 2008). Subjective sleep quality is a predictor of next-day positive affect (de Wild-Hartmann et al., 2013), which is consistent with an electronic diary study (Bouwmans et al., 2017). Poorer sleep is predictive of elevated levels of negative affect (Sin et al., 2017; Shen et al., 2018), and better sleep is predictive of increased positive affect (Hamilton et al., 2008; Kalmbach et al., 2014).

Sleep duration is not exactly the same as sleep quality, but it is usually one of the components included in measures of sleep quality, such as the PSQI. Some relevant studies have shown that individuals' sleep durations are also correlated with positive and negative affects. Franzen et al. (2008) found that experimental sleep deprivation results in reduced positive mood and increased negative mood. Sleep loss is associated with increased negative affective responses to stressors, and sleep deprivation reduces individuals' psychological thresholds for the perception of stress from cognitive demands. One study using cross-sectional data shows that insomnia was associated with negative affect, which in turn was associated with marijuana-related problems (Yurasek et al., 2020). The protective function of good sleep quality was verified by Sonnentag and Binnewies (2013) – sleep quality buffers the positive effects of negative affect during the evening on negative affect the next morning. Lack of sleep also hinders emotion regulation (Baumeister and Heatherton, 1996), whereas adequate sleep promotes self-control and emotion regulation (Zohar et al., 2005; Hamilton et al., 2008).

Negative affect may induce self-control failure (Heatherton and Wagner, 2011). Binge eating, for example, is associated with loss of self-control and is adopted to avoid negative affect (Mason et al., 2018). Anger is a common negative affect, which exerts a prominent effect on aggressive behaviors and hinders individuals' self-control (Ellwanger and Pratt, 2014). Negative affect is also associated with risky decision-making, irrational consumption (Bruyneel et al., 2009), and addictive behaviors (Wilson et al., 2014). Individuals with poor sleep quality may act more impulsively to cope with the associated negative mood, presenting as the decrease of individual self-control ability (Zhu et al., 2019).

Self-control was regarded as a limited resource in the self-control strength model (Tice et al., 2007), and positive affect compensates the depletion of self-control and facilitates self-control behaviors (Shmueli and Prochaska, 2012). Individuals with high (vs. low) positive affect are likely to consider situational details, act accordingly, and stay on uninteresting tasks longer (Isen and Reeve, 2005).

Although some have examined the mediating role of positive affect in the association between sleep quality and drug craving (Freeman and Gottfredson, 2018), few studies simultaneously investigated the mediating roles of positive and negative affects in the relationship between sleep quality and self-control. Therefore, we tested a two-mediator model assuming that sleep quality predicts self-control and that positive and negative affects mediate this association.

A total of 1,507 participants (37% men; age range = 18–59 years; mean age = 32.5 years) received a small reward (10¥≈1.49$) as compensation for participation in the study. Participants who were working in various industries and companies (e.g., governmental agencies and institutions, nationalized business, foreign companies, and private companies) in Beijing participated. To ensure heterogeneity, we collected data from participants of different ages, education levels, marital statuses, income levels, and parental situations from different urban areas in Beijing.

Sleep Quality

The Chinese version of the PSQI was applied to measure participants' sleep quality (Liu et al., 1996). The scale was designed (Buysse et al., 1989) to measure seven components of sleep quality: subjective sleep quality, sleep latency, sleep duration, habitual sleep efficiency, sleep disturbances, use of sleeping medication, and daytime dysfunction over the last month. The scale comprises 19 items (e.g., "During the past month, when have you usually gone to bed?") and each component has a score ranging from 0 to 3, with higher total scores indicating poorer sleep quality. Cronbach's α for the Chinese version of components of the PSQI in this study was 0.76.

Positive and negative affects were measured by the Chinese version (Huang et al., 2003) of the Positive and Negative Affect Schedule, which was designed by Watson et al. (1988) to evaluate the tendency to experience positive (10 items; e.g., "enthusiastic") and negative (10 items; e.g., "nervous") affect. The scale comprises 20 items, and each item was rated on a Likert scale ranging from 1 (not at all) to 5 (extremely). Cronbach's αs for positive and negative affects were 0.86 and 0.87, respectively, in this study.

The Chinese version of the Self-Control Scale (Tan and Guo, 2008) was adopted to measure participants' self-control, which was designed by Tangney et al. (2004). In this study, the scale comprised 19 items to evaluate five components of self-control: resisting temptation, impulse control, healthy habits, task performance, and entertainment temperance (e.g., "I am good at resisting temptation"). Answers were provided on a Likert scale ranging from 1 (not at all) to 5 (very much), with higher total score signifying better self-control. Cronbach's α for the Chinese version of self-control in this study was 0.88.

The questionnaires were uploaded onto Wen Juan Xing, an online platform used to collect survey data. After the questionnaire link was generated on this platform, we spread the questionnaire link through WeChat (an instant messaging software) Moments. Participants were recruited through WeChat Moments, and standardized instructions were employed to direct participants on how to complete the questionnaires. Participants completed a survey designed that comprised demographic variables, sleep quality, positive and negative affects, and self-control. Sixty participants were excluded due to incomplete answers. The time window of data collection was from August 2018 to October 2018. Informed consent was obtained from all participants, and this study was approved by the scientific ethical committee of the authors' university.

Analyses were conducted in IBM SPSS Statistics 24. Data were screened for missing values, normality, and selection bias prior to analysis. Means, standard deviations, and zero-order correlations for all study variables are shown in Table 1. The PSQI score was positively associated with negative affect ($r = 0.26$, $p < 0.01$), and negatively associated with positive affect ($r = -0.21$, $p < 0.01$) and self-control ($r = -0.25$, $p < 0.01$), indicating that people with better sleep quality tend to experience more positive affect and self-control and less negative affect. Self-control was negatively correlated with negative affect ($r = -0.49$, $p < 0.01$) but positively correlated with positive affect ($r = 0.24$, $p < 0.01$), elucidating that both sleep quality and positive affect are protective factors for self-control

CHAPTER FIVE

Self-Control Secret #5 – Ride the Wave

Desire has a strong tendency to ebb and flow like the tide. When the impulse you need to control is strong, waiting out this wave of desire is usually enough to keep yourself in control. The rule of thumb here is to wait at least 10 minutes before succumbing to temptation.

What keeps us from doing this are the Thieves of Time. "Four key drivers propel companies, teams, and human beings at work: Drive, Excellence, Information, and Activity. Despite being positive and helpful to us in their basic nature, these forces are also the biggest reason white space withers." When taken to extremes, they reduce our effectiveness. They look like this:

We mindlessly accept a meeting invite because we are driven. (Associated with burnout and overdrive)

We overtweak a presentation because we want to be excellent. (Associated with perfectionism)

We go too deep into dashboards and data because we want to be informed. (Associated with overload)

We impulsively grab the next to-do on our list because we feel we should always be active. (associated with frenzy)

You deal with these excess use of these strengths by asking the following Simplification Questions:

Drive – when it turns into overdrive – needs to hear: Is there anything I can let go of?

Excellence – when it turns into perfectionism – needs to hear: Where is "good enough," good enough?

Information – when it turns into overload – needs to hear: What do I truly need to know?

Activity – when it turns into frenzy – needs to quiet its flailing long enough to hear: What deserves my attention?

CHAPTER SIX

Self-Control Secret #6 – Forgive Yourself

Making peace and moving forward is often easier said than done. Being able to forgive yourself requires empathy, compassion, kindness, and understanding. It also requires you to accept that forgiveness is a choice.

Whether you're trying to work through a minor mistake or one that impacts all areas of your life, the steps you need to take in order to forgive yourself will look and feel the same.

All of us make mistakes at times. As humans, we're imperfect. The trick, says Arlene B. Englander, LCSW, MBA, PA is to learn and move on from our mistakes. As painful and uncomfortable as it may feel, there are things in life that are worth enduring the pain for in order to move forward, and forgiving yourself is one of them.

Focus on your emotions

One of the first steps in learning how to forgive yourself is to focus on your emotions. Before you can move forward, you need to acknowledge and process your emotionsTrusted Source. Give yourself permission to recognize and accept the feelings that have been triggered in you and welcome them.

Acknowledge the mistake out loud

If you make a mistake and continue to struggle with letting it go, acknowledge out loud what you learned from the mistake, says Jordan Pickell, MCP, RCC.

When you give a voice to the thoughts in your head and the emotions in your heart, you may free yourself from some of the burdens. You also imprint in your mind what you learned from your actions and consequences.

Think of each mistake as a learning experience

Englander says to think of each "mistake" as a learning experience that holds the key to moving forward faster and more consistently in the future.

Reminding ourselves that we did the best we could with the tools and knowledge we had at the time, will help us forgive ourselves and move forward.

Give yourself permission to put this process on hold

If you make a mistake but have a hard time putting it out of your mind, Pickell says to visualize your thoughts and feelings about the mistake going into a container, such as a mason jar or box.

Then, tell yourself you are putting this aside for now and will return to it if and when it will benefit you.

Give yourself permission to put this process on hold

If you make a mistake but have a hard time putting it out of your mind, Pickell says to visualize your thoughts and feelings about the mistake going into a container, such as a mason jar or box.

Then, tell yourself you are putting this aside for now and will return to it if and when it will benefit you.

Have a conversation with your inner critic

Journaling can help you understand your inner critic and develop self-compassion. Pickell says one thing you can do is write out a "conversation" between you and your inner critic. This can help you identify thought patterns that are sabotaging your ability to forgive yourself.

You can also use journaling time to make a list of the qualities you like about yourself, including your strengths and skills. This can help boost your self-confidence when you're feeling down about a mistake you made.

Notice when you are being self-critical

We are our own worst critics, right? That's why Pickell says one important action tip is to notice when that harsh voice comes in and then write it down. You might be surprised by what your inner critic actually says to you.

Quiet the negative messages of your inner critic

Sometimes it can be difficult to recognize the thoughts that are getting in the way of forgiveness. If you're struggling to sort out your inner critic, Pickell suggests this exercise:

On one side of a piece of paper, write down what your inner critic says (which tends to be critical and irrational).

On the other side of the paper, write a self-compassionate and rational response for each thing you wrote on the

other
side of the paper.

Get clear about what you want

If the mistake you made hurt another person, you need to determine the best course of action. Do you want to talk to this person and apologize? Is it important to reconcile with them and make amends?

If you're on the fence about what to do, you might want to consider making amends. This goes beyond saying sorry to a person you've hurt. Instead, try to fix the mistake you've made. One study found that forgiving ourselves for hurting another is easier if we first make amends.

Take your own advice

Oftentimes, it's easier to tell someone else what to do than to take our own advice. Licensed marriage and family therapist, Heidi McBain, LMFT, LPT, RPT says to ask yourself what you would tell your best friend if they were sharing this mistake they made with you, and then take your own advice.

If you're having a difficult time working through this in your head, it can help to role-play with your friend. Ask them to take on your mistake. They will tell you what happened and how they are struggling to forgive themselves.

You get to be the advice giver and practice telling your friend how to move on.

Quit playing the tape

It's human nature to spend time and energy replaying our mistakes. While some processing is important, going over what happened again and again won't allow you to take the proper steps to forgive yourself.

When you catch yourself playing the "I'm a horrible person" tape, stop yourself and focus on one positive action step. For example, instead of replaying the tape, take three deep breaths or go for a walk.

Interrupting the thought pattern can help you move away from the negative experience and reduce stress and anxiety

Show kindness and compassion

If your first response to a negative situation is to criticize yourself, it's time to show yourself some kindness and compassion. The only way to begin the journey to forgiveness is to be kind and compassionate with yourself.

This takes time, patience, and a reminder to yourself that you're worthy of forgiveness.

12 Seek professional help

If you're struggling to forgive yourself, you may benefit from talking to a professional. McBain recommends talking to a counselor who can help you learn how to break these unhealthy patterns in your life and learn new and healthier ways of coping with mistakes.

CHAPTER SEVEN

Measure Your Progress

It's not always easy to maintain consistency as we work toward our goals. And yet, consistency is often the one thing that matters most in pursuit of these goals.

Consider what Confucius wrote centuries ago:

"The man who moves a mountain begins by carrying away small stones... It does not matter how slowly you go so long as you do not stop."

The challenge with consistency is that it's quite difficult to sustain. One strategy I've found incredibly useful is Seinfeld's "Don't Break The Chain," whereby on the very days you show up to work toward your goal, you mark an X on your calendar. Your objective then becomes very simple:

Don't break that chain of X's.

The idea here is three-fold. It draws you back to the present moment, pushes you to focus on what you can control, and reminds you that growth and expansion happen in the process, not the result.

You don't become a comedian the day you walk up on stage, you grow into one day after day as you stretch yourself in the process of writing jokes. Likewise, you don't become a writer the day you finish your book, you grow into one day after day as you honour the process of sitting down to write.

But how do you sustain that consistency in your creative practice?

How do you keep your gaze fixated on the process and not the result?

The secret lies in measuring your progress.

Measure The Gain, Not The Gap

Too often, we define success by sizing up where we are today against the ideal we had set out for ourselves a year ago. We compare what we've already achieved with what we want to achieve as an end.

This happens in everyday life. When you trek up a mountain, you're curious as to how many more kilometres you still have until you summit. When you're off on a road trip, the only nagging question that buzzes through your head is "how much longer do we still need?"

But once we notice how much further we have to go, a hybrid wave formed from hopelessness and demotivation rises within us. "All this effort I've put in and I'm still so far away from where I want to be;" that's what you begin to think:

Three months of daily workouts and I'm still 20kg off my weight target.

Four months of writing daily and I still don't have a decent chapter.

One year into this newsletter project and I still haven't reached 1,000 subscribers.

It's funny how our mind plays tricks on us.

But as we both know, the way we think defines how we experience the world around us. And so, as we learn how to create a distance between our mind and our thoughts, we learn how to think about our thinking. We engage in what is known in psychology as metacognition—being aware of one's own thoughts.

We learn to observe our thoughts, rather than merely engage with them all. And so we learn how to observe progress from different angles.

Dan Sullivan, founder of Strategic Coach, an organization that thrives on mindset and entrepreneurial coaching labels the earlier examples as a way of measuring progress by focusing on "The Gap."

The gap is the distance between where you stand today and where your ideal stands way ahead. And as you continue to focus on that gap, you'll continue to see how far away you still are, and thus you'll continue to feel dissatisfied with your effort.

But Dan offers a solution to this. He reminds us that we can change the way we think by first changing the way we look at things. Instead of casting our gaze forward, we flip the coin and cast it backwards. As he explains:

"The way to measure your progress is backward against where you started, not against your ideal."

The proper way of measuring progress? Look backwards, not forward. Gaze right from where you are today, back to where you were when you first started. Do you see all the progress you've made? Do you see all the obstacles you've mounted and the raging rivers you've crossed? The many doubts you've tamed.

Do you see how far you've come?

That backward distance is defined as "The Gain," and it's much more inspiring, motivational, and rewarding, than what lies ahead in "The Gap."

Focus on Your Progress, Not Your Ideal

Another drawback from being totally fixated on "The Gap" is that the gap will constantly grow bigger, and so naturally, you'll become the rabbit chasing that elusive carrot.

How?

Well consider this: You're a constant work-in-progress. You're always changing, evolving, and growing. Who you were ten years ago is different to who you are today, and likewise, the person you will be in five years from now will be different to the person you are today.

As you constantly move and change so will your ideals move and change. As you outgrow your own clothes, so will you outgrow your own ideals. As you continue to flow forward, so will your goals and ideals.

The goal of publishing a single book suddenly becomes two. The goal of launching a small side project now becomes "let's make this a 7-figure business."

The salient point here is that what you choose to pursue will constantly elude you because your ideal is a natural moving target.

So if you fall for the trap of measuring your current self against your future self (the person who will have attained her ideal), you'll never be satisfied with where you are today because there will always be a gap to fill. You'll never feel worthy of yourself either. And that's precisely why it's best to focus on your progress and not your ideal. The progress that you've already compounded should be your primary benchmark for achievement.

So turn around and measure your progress against your starting point.

Be in The Gain, not The Gap, and you'll experience a sense of having achieved something beautiful. And that's the feeling that'll crush your inner critic's voice and motivate you to keep going.

Turn around and measure your current self against your previous self.

Compare who you are today and where you are today with who you were yesterday. Pause, look back and reflect. Realize how far you've come and how much you've grown. That's all it really takes—a single moment to alter the way you think, a multitude of moments to alter the next path you take.

So cast your gaze back upon the first day you started:

Who were you then? Who are you now?

Where were you then? Where are you now?

What are all the wonderful things you've done?

Whatever highs or lows you uncover, I promise you this:

You will feel more fulfilled. You will feel more powerful. More beautiful. More grateful. Much more confident and empowered. You will feel lighter.

You will feel happier. Simply because you gifted yourself a moment to pause, to breathe and draw your attention back to what matters most—your effort in the present—and recognized just how far you've voyaged to become the person that you are today.

But Why is it Important to Measure Progress and What Difference Does it Actually Make?

Published research in the Psychological Bulletin reveals the importance of measuring progress in order to achieve your goals. Through a meta-analysis of 138 studies comprising 19,951 participants, professor Benjamin Harkin of the University of Sheffield discovered the following:

If you're trying to achieve your goal, the more often you monitor your progress and physically record it, the greater the likelihood that you'll succeed.

Why? Because, in the worlds of Dan Sullivan, "the feeling that we're making progress is powerful and positive, but it only comes from knowing you've moved forward, and the only way to know that is through specific measurements."

You see, as humans, we're naturally forgetful.

Our brains process so much information on any given day. We're bombarded with over 5,000 ads per day. An average smartphone user receives 50 app notifications per day. Factor in the e-mails, the text messages, the social posts and all other micro-moments that distract your thinking and you begin to realize just how much information your mind juggles at any given moment.

In The Shallows, a brilliant book that explores what the internet is doing to our brains, Nicholas Carr writes:

"The influx of competing messages that we receive whenever we go online not only overloads our working memory; it makes it much harder for our frontal lobes to concentrate our attention on any one thing. The process of memory consolidation can't even get started.

Memory consolidation is simply the process by which a temporary memory is transformed into a more stable, long-term form. But since our minds are constantly consumed with stimuli and content, so much of what you think about just washes over like a breaking wave at the shore.

This means that what you don't track and make note of, you simply forget.

If you don't believe me, then let me ask you this:

How many articles have you read in the past two months?

How many times have you run to the bathroom in the past week?

How many apples have you had since the start of the year?

Now of course no one expects you to measure your progress on such mundane daily events, but consider the point I'm trying to make: You don't track these things because they don't matter to you. But you know what does?

Your goals!

So why aren't you tracking your progress on them?!

Didn't see that one coming, did you?

Look, it's imperative that you physically measure your progress, especially toward the one or two goals that matter most to you.

When I began my writing journey at the turn of 2020, I knew that it would be a long voyage forward, but I also knew that I needed a way to measure my own growth so I can keep myself accountable and motivated to keep going, especially when my energy runs low.

So I created an excel sheet and called it "The Growth Tracker."

My growth tracker that measures "The Gain." It tracks the articles I publish on this blog and on Medium every single month, along with my Medium follower growth and my newsletter subscriber growth.

In some months I didn't publish as much as I did in others, but do you notice the consistent growth month over month?

Whenever I would experience a slump in energy, I would open the sheet and look back at all the effort I've put in and all the progress that I've already made, and those two things alone would motivate me to get back on my chair and write.

As you create a visual representation of your progress and focus on "The Gain," you do three things:

You keep yourself motivated.

You lift yourself up when you're feeling low on energy to carry on.

You highlight the growth (in numbers) that you've already experienced, and that achievement alone gives you a reason to keep going.

As Dan Sullivan writes, "the only progress you can achieve is the progress you measure." Linking all this back to Seinfeld's strategy, it's no wonder how effective it has been for my writing: Seeing that chain grow longer every day is a way of seeing my progression grow deeper by day.

Remember: There's Nowhere For You to Arrive at, You're Already There

Measuring your progress is crucial for both, your motivation and growth; but your attitude in life matters more.

You see, we've been wired to believe that success is a measure of speed. That success is somewhere we must arrive at. That achievement is found in the hustle and grind. That there's always more action to take, more targets to hit. And all this kind of thinking has left us running around feeling empty, chasing new goals, and constantly raising the bar of what it means to 'make it.'

As a result, we never truly cultivate a sense of being that is rooted in self-worth and contentment with where we are, right here, right now.

And as long as we continue to chase that big elusive dream of an imaginary future, we'll never be able to truly find happiness and self-worth at the present moment that is happening today.

So here's what I want you to remember as you work toward your goals and measure your progress:

Your happiness and wellbeing have nothing to do with how well you think you're doing, how far into the journey you've crossed, or what's coming next. Your happiness and wellbeing have everything to do with how present, accepting, and content you are with all that is.

That's one of the five powerful teachings of the Wabi-Sabi philosophy.

As you write, you are becoming a writer. As you build your company, you are becoming an entrepreneur. As you sow, you are also weaving the very fabric through which you shall reap. It's in the process where we grow and expand and mould our identity, one day at a time.

Measurement! I just love measurement. That's because it tells you how you're doing and how much progress you've made. Progress checks can motivate you, help you catch yourself when you're slacking, and tell you when to change course.

Without giving thought to how you define progress, however, you can measure the wrong thing, or measure the wrong way. You might end up demoralized for no reason, or falling behind unknowingly on a project, or missing opportunities. So if you're going to measure progress, do it right! Turn off auto-pilot "gut checks" and measure progress thoughtfully.

Measure process goals

If you're Type A like me, you probably overwork yourself, under the assumption that more work gives more progress. But does it? Have you ever measured? Just being busy and stressed doesn't mean we're getting anything done. We need to track how far we are from our goal, and whether we're closing that gap.

First determine the kind of goals you're chasing. Episode 462, "Grow a Pair for Your Career," outlines the difference between outcome goals and process goals. Outcome goals—like getting a promotion—are something you strive for, not something you just do. Process goals, on the other hand, are measurable actions that help you get closer to your outcome goal, like making ten more sales calls each day.

If you're going to measure progress, do it right! Turn off auto-pilot "gut checks" and measure progress thoughtfully.

On a daily basis, measure progress through movement toward your process goals. It doesn't matter how much you work, only whether that work takes you closer to finishing that day's process goals. Then check that your process goals are doing what they should, by tracking overall movement toward an outcome goal.

For example, if you work in sales, your process goal might be to make fifty cold calls a day. If that's your goal, sending two hundred emails should not count as progress. What's more, if your outcome goal is to close sales, and you haven't closed one in months, you may need to rethink if you have the right process goals. Maybe "number of calls" doesn't lead to sales. Maybe you need to make progress on the quality of your calls, instead. So make your new process goal tweaking your sales pitch, and direct some work toward that.

Measure how far you've come

Another way to track progress is to look at how far you are from your starting point.

Sam is a twenty-something who's just started up a fairly successful online delivery company. The vision of being the next Amazon.com seems impossible! Or at least, light years away. And it is. But knowing that it's not Amazon yet isn't a useful measure for evaluating progress. Furthermore, it's so far away that it isn't even clear which paths lead to that result.

Sam can instead concentrate on what's been accomplished so far. They started sitting around a dining room table. Now they have office space, customers, a business model that works, money in the bank, and profit. By measuring progress based on how far they've come, not on how far they have left to go, Sam can realize they've made tons of progress, and can make sure it continues to unfold, as more and more milestones get added to the list.

Measure distance to your goals

At some point your goal is within reach. Then, you can start measuring how far you are from your goal, and concentrate on closing the gap.

Don't do this too soon! You can hurt morale. At my last Harvard Business School reunion, for example, doing an "Am I there yet?" progress check gave me a soul-crushing burst of inadequacy as I was moderating a panel of my classmates, whose combined net worth was enough to purchase a third world country and pave it over. In gold.

When you're out on a long run, you get a surge of fresh energy when you see you're only ten feet from the finish line, and there's an entire 55-gallon drum of gummy bears waiting at the end. And an Oreo ice cream cake. The next thing you know, you're barreling over the finish line.

When you've passed the halfway point, start measuring your progress by how quickly you're closing on your goal. Keep that Oreo ice cream cake in mind, and set new goals to push you those last few feet.

Even if you get some steps wrong, just making the plan will energize you and be motivating.

A good way to do this is to make a checklist of things you'll need to do to reach the end point. These can be high-level things like, "Run A/B testing with focus groups," or low-level things like, "Write an email to call for A/B testing participants." Once your plan is on paper, finishing your project will seem much more doable, since all the steps left to take are right there in front of you. And as I talked about in episode 466, "Make a Plan for Motivation," even if you get some steps wrong, just making the plan will energize you and be motivating.

Re-measure often

Once you figure out the best way to track your progress, and the types of progress you need to track, choose how often you'll track. Sometimes, tracking progress once a week is plenty. But from my experience, it's best to track progress every two to three days.

That way, if you suddenly notice you're not where you should be, you only have to make up two or three days' worth of work. If you were only checking once a week, you could get an entire week behind before you'd notice it.

From my experience, it's best to track progress every two to three days.

What gets measured gets managed. And we love to manage progress. On a daily basis, concentrate your measurements on your progress goals, rather than your outcome goals. Then choose a less-frequent measurement that is based on where you are in your project: distance to your goal, or distance from your starting point. With a little experimentation, you can find the magic balance that keeps you on top of your game.

CHAPTER EIGHT

Learn How To Manage Stress

Have you been feeling stressed out lately? As if you can't handle work, home, family, or life in general. The stress is piling up and you are not sure what to do. Well here are some quick tips to managing stress so you don't feel so chaotic in your life:

1.Take a 10 minute walk. According to a few experts if you take a walk it will help reduce endorphins in the system that cause stress.

2. Practice mindfulness. Learning to focus on your breathing can help you reduce stress. If you are able to take a few minutes out of day and breath in silence this can greatly help you reduce your stress.

3. Create an exercise regiment. If you can spend some time of your day getting in a workout that you enjoy for about 45 this can also help reduce the amount of stress that you recieve and help you manage it.

4. Write a reflection journal. Create a journal where you can write down your thoughts and process events that have happened to you. This can help you get a fresh prospective about the situations you are in.

5. Organize yourself. Set aside a few minutes a day to create a planner in order to get your thoughts straight and take in a chill pill to avoid the chaos that might be taking place around you currently.

These are just a few points and tips to help get the stress you may have under control. One of the best ways you can help control your stress is by coming up with ideas on your own that have worked on reducing those stressful moments. The best stress manager is yourself.

ways to reduce stress and keep blood pressure down

When it comes to preventing and treating high blood pressure, one often-overlooked strategy is managing stress. If you often find yourself tense and on-edge, try these seven ways to reduce stress.

Get enough sleep. Inadequate or poor-quality sleep can negatively affect your mood, mental alertness, energy level, and physical health.

Learn relaxation techniques. Meditation, progressive muscle relaxation, guided imagery, deep breathing exercises, and yoga are powerful relaxation techniques and stress-busters.

Strengthen your social network. Connect with others by taking a class, joining an organization, or participating in a support group.

Hone your time-management skills. The more efficiently you can juggle work and family demands, the lower your stress level.

Try to resolve stressful situations if you can. Don't let stressful situations fester. Hold family problem-solving sessions and use negotiation skills at home and at work.

Nurture yourself. Treat yourself to a massage. Truly savor an experience: for example, eat slowly and really focus on the taste and sensations of each bite. Take a walk or a nap, or listen to your favorite music.

Ask for help. Don't be afraid to ask for help from your spouse, friends, and neighbors. If stress and anxiety persist, talk to your doctor.

Along with these ways to reduce stress, add in a healthy lifestyle — maintaining a healthy weight, not smoking, regular exercise, and a diet that includes fruits, vegetables, whole grains, lean protein, and healthful fats — and high blood pressure could be a thing of the past.

CHAPTER NINE

THE LINK BETWEEN SELF-CONTROL AND EMPATHY

I recently read an article by Ed Yong that suggests your ability to have empathy for someone else is produced in the same area of the brain as your ability to have self-control. As empathy allows a person to put their opinions and perspective aside and step into the shoes of another, Yong describes this as true for self-control. Think about cheating on a diet. You are eating mostly fruits, vegetables and proteins but you get the sudden urge for chocolate cake. When you have the self-control to resist the urge to order a slice of cake, you are taking a hit now so Future You can feel healthier. This is you having empathy for your Future Self.

Here are more examples that you may have experienced:

Present you not going out with friends for a night as a way to help your future bank account/savings. If you are trying to save up for a trip, to pay your rent, or to save up for your kid's education, sometimes it becomes a challenge to take time for yourself. At that moment, saying "no" to a friends' night out is a form of having empathy for your future self and your future financial goals.

Present you ordering a salad for dinner rather than ordering a pizza. This self-control could demonstrate an example of you looking out for your future self's health goals. Maybe you are trying to lose weight, feel more comfortable in that bridesmaids dress or are trying to get your 5 vegetables a day. Although choosing pizza might be more pleasurable at the moment, this self-control is empathic towards your future health outcomes.

Present you taking the bus on a rainy day rather than calling an Uber/Lyft. This self-control to take the cheaper, and less convenient means of transportation shows empathy towards your future bank account and financial goals. Those 3x surge charge rates are not worth it- especially if that means you have limited money to buy groceries later in the week.

This article helped me reframe these situations that happen on a regular basis. Self-control around food is the most challenging for me but using this article as a frame of reference has allowed me to have more empathy and understanding for my decision making. I have found that this self-control is dependent on the significance I place on the desired outcome. If I am saving up for something, it is easier for me to resist the urge to grab a cab when it is raining, or cook at home rather than going out, because I know exactly what the money is going towards. The same might go for those who have goals around exercise and food. Identifying that you want to fit back into those pair of jeans, or the goal to look a certain way for spring break, might trigger more self-control, as the future goal is more desired. This self-control, even though it may not be as desirable in the present moment, allows you to be empathic towards your future perspective, and weigh your decision with your future goals in mind.

Self-Control Is Just Empathy With Your Future Self

The same part of the brain that allows us to step into the shoes of others also helps us restrain ourselves.

a stream of kids, confronted with a single, alluring marshmallow. If they can resist eating it for 15 minutes, they'll get two. Some do. Others cave almost immediately.

This "Marshmallow Test," first conducted in the 1960s, perfectly illustrates the ongoing war between impulsivity and self-control. The kids have to tamp down their immediate desires and focus on long-term goals—an ability that correlates with their later health, wealth, and academic success, and that is supposedly controlled by the front part of the brain. But a new study by Alexander Soutschek at the University of Zurich suggests that self-control is also influenced by another brain region—and one that casts this ability in a different light.

Press your right index finger to the top of your right ear, where it meets your head. Now move up an inch and back an inch. You're now pointing at your right temporoparietal junction (rTPJ). This area has long been linked to empathy and selflessness. But Soutschek, by using magnetic fields to briefly shut down the rTPJ, has shown that it's also involved in self-control.

Which makes perfect sense. Empathy depends on your ability to overcome your own perspective, appreciate someone else's, and step into their shoes. Self-control is essentially the same skill, except that those other shoes belong to your future self—a removed and hypothetical entity who might as well be a different person. So think of self-control as a kind of temporal selflessness. It's Present You taking a hit to help out Future You.

"For a long time, people have speculated that we use the same mechanisms to reason about other people as about our hypothetical selves," says Rebecca Saxe from MIT. "So this new study fits really well."

Saxe should know. She was one of the first scientists to link the rTPJ to theory of mind—the ability to understand the mental states of other people. In 2005, she and Nancy Kanwisher scanned people's brains while they listened to stories in which protagonists made poor choices based on false beliefs. This experiment showed that the TPJ is active specifically when people are "reasoning about the contents of another person's minds"—the essence of theory of mind. This region, the duo wrote, helps people to think about thinking people.

At the same time, many other neuroscientists were doing similar experiments and getting the same answers. The consensus was striking, Saxe later wrote. "Because there was almost no pre-existing neuroscience of theory of mind, researchers came to the topic with unusually few preconceptions about where to look in the brain. In those circumstances, neuroimaging is notoriously fickle, producing many false positives and false negatives. Yet every group that sought to identify brain regions implicated in ToM got essentially the same answer; and in study after study, we still do."

Many other studies have since expanded on those early results. If the rTPJ is bigger, people are more likely to behave altruistically. If the neurons within it are better-connected (and well-linked to other parts of the brain), people show less bias towards their own in-groups. If the area is stimulated by electric currents, people become better at taking someone else's perspective.

And if the region is disrupted, it changes our ability to reason about morality. Consider a woman who poisons her friend's coffee—if she does so deliberately, we'd judge her more harshly than if she acted accidentally. Intent matters, and we need the rTPJ to judge intent. When Liane Young, one of Saxe's former students, disrupted the rTPJ using magnetic fields, she found that people were more lenient towards the deliberate poisoner, as long as her friend survived. With their ability to gauge intent disrupted, they started looking to outcomes instead.

Not everything fits with the idea of the rTPJ as a nexus for theory of mind. For example, many studies suggest that it affects our ability to shift our attention from one part of space to another, like a technician moving a spotlight around. "Even in my own small lab, people disagree about the function of the rTPJ," says Young, now a professor at Boston College.

If you look at the debate and relax your eyes, you can probably merge the two viewpoints into one. Maybe the rTPJ is a region that redirects our attention from one thing to another—whether between objects in the world around us, or between our minds and other people's. Alternatively, it's likely that what we call the rTPJ is not actually a singular bit of the brain. "There's a lot of work suggesting that there are different sub-regions—one of which does spatial reorienting, and the other does perspective-taking," says Young.

That's where Soutschek's study comes in. He specifically focused on the back half of the rTPJ—the one that's been more heavily linked to empathy—and disrupted it in 43 volunteers. When that happened, the recruits became more likely to pocket a pile of cash for themselves rather than splitting it with a partner, and especially when the partner was a stranger. But they were also more likely to pick a small immediate lump of cash over a larger future one, especially when the delays were long.

A second experiment explained why. This time, the volunteers saw a picture of a man standing in a room with red discs on the wall. The volunteers could see all the discs, but they had to say how many the man in the room could see. They had to shift their perspective to his, and they became worse at that when their rTPJ was disrupted. What's more, Soutschek showed that the extent of their bias—their inability to leave their own heads—predicted both how impulsive and how selfish they were in the earlier experiment.

This tells us that impulsivity and selfishness are just two halves of the same coin, as are their opposites restraint and empathy. Perhaps this is why people who show dark traits like psychopathy and sadism score low on empathy but high on impulsivity. Perhaps it's why impulsivity correlates with slips among recovering addicts, while empathy correlates with longer bouts of abstinence. These qualities represent our successes and failures at escaping our own egocentric bubbles, and understanding the lives of others—even when those others wear our own older faces.

You are an achiever, working hard each day to realize your dreams. But what about those days when you hit the snooze button on your alarm or opt for watching an extra hour of TV? Later you might berate yourself for having poor self-control, but what really happens in those moments when you decide between short-term comfort and future goals? Researcher Alexandar Soutscheck at the University of Zurich has found evidence that the same part of the brain responsible for empathizing with others also plays a role in self-control. According to the results of Soutscheck's study, another way to think of self-control is "empathy with your future self"

CHAPTER TEN

Ways To Increase Your Self-Control

Of all the things that are in short supply in our lives, self-control likely tops the list for most of us. When people were asked to list their character strengths in a study conducted in 54 nations and the 50 U.S. states, self-control came last. Self-control is the ability to control our feelings, emotions and reactions. A recent public example of a lapse in self-control comes from Tim Armstrong, the chief executive officer of AOL, who had to apologize for publicly firing an employee. "It was an emotional response," Armstrong said in his apology.

More scientists are discovering the importance of self-control as a force we can tap into to have a more successful and satisfying life. But self-control is a limited resource that is depleted with use. When we exercise control in one situation, we're less likely to keep our cool the next time we're faced with a situation that requires self-control. As Kelly McGonigal notes in The Willpower Instinct: How Self-Control Works, Why It Matters, and What We Can Do to Get More of It, "Trying to control your temper, stick to a budget or refuse seconds all tap into the same source of strength. And because every act of willpower depletes willpower, using self control can lead to losing self-control ... if you do turn down that tempting tiramisu, you may find it more difficult to focus when you're back at your desk."

Luckily, there's a lot we can do to mitigate willpower depletion and enhance our ability to exercise self-control, including the following eight tips.

1. Look at the big picture.

A study shows that abstract and global or high-level thinking promotes self-control success. That is, people are more likely to exercise self-control when they see the proverbial forest beyond the trees and when they don't get bogged down by specific minutiae.

For example, when working on a long-term project, it's easy to get frustrated by the multitude of small steps required to get you there. Instead, periodically reminding yourself and others on the team of the end goal serves to promote self-control by preventing discouragement.

2. Know the perils of inadequate sleep.

A University of Washington study, reported in Harvard Business Review, indicates that sleep deprivation drains glucose in the prefrontal cortex, thereby depleting the fuel needed for self-control. Sleep restores it. This was found to make a difference at work the next day between ethical and unethical behavior, such as cheating by falsifying receipts. Those who slept six hours or less were more likely to engage in deviant work behaviors than those who slept more than six hours.

The implications for those running a business are too important to ignore. "Organizations," says the lead researcher Christopher M. Barnes, "need to give sleep more respect. Executives and managers should keep in mind that the more they push employees to work late, come to the office early, and answer emails and calls at all hours, the more they invite unethical behavior to creep in." Are you driving your people too hard? Do you encourage team members to prioritize sleep in their lives? Do you set a good example yourself? Tired workers are not good for business.

3. Relax already.

Popular views of self-control are that we should try to control impulses, fight temptations and actively exercise willpower. Nothing could be further from the truth, it seems. A new study from researchers at the University of Illinois found that people primed with words suggesting action, such as "start," or "get on with it," were more likely than others to make impulsive decisions that undermine their long-term goals. In contrast, those primed to "rest" or "stop" found it easier to avoid impulsive decisions. "Our research," says Dr. Dolores Albarracín, "suggests that the relaxed state is better at inhibiting the pull of temptations." This may very well have some impact in how we manage people. Pushing them to "move on" may result in more risky behavior or impulsive decisions.

4. Do some short bouts of exercise.

Do you find yourself with limited time to undertake a full exercise program? The good news is that, when it comes to self-control, short bouts of moderately intense exercise is all you need to boost your strength in this area. The pre-frontal cortex is responsible for self-control, and research reported in Science Daily shows that short bouts of exercise result in increased blood and oxygen flow to the pre-frontal cortex, which may explain the boost in self-control ability. No matter how busy you are, plan to include a short burst of exercise in your daily routine.

5. Get digital self-control support.

There is a plethora of apps that can help you exercise self-control, even apps that can help you exhibit control when you're online. There are many other ways to help you outsource your self control: a self-blackmailing service to help keep you from quitting—whether it's writing a blog or losing weight; Stick.com that keeps you committed to any goal; GymPact to ensure you never miss another workout, as well as other similar apps to track your workouts; and Mint.com or Expense Manager to keep track of your spending and help you make better money decisions.

6. Know yourself.

Emotional self-control, or impulse control, are cornerstones of emotional intelligence. Know yourself so you can manage your emotions and impulses. For example, are you in the habit of reacting hastily to issues? Once you get started, do you find it hard to stop talking? Are you able to stay composed and positive in stressful circumstances? Can you exercise patience in annoying situations? The ability to keep disruptive emotions and impulses in check is the mark of a seasoned leader.

Self-awareness precedes self-management. Here are two emotional intelligence assessments to help you increase your self-knowledge in this area: the Emotional Quotient Inventory and the Emotional Competence Inventory. You can also find out how you score on self-control measures by taking the free online VIA Inventory of Strengths—it's a psychological assessment of 24 character strengths, one of which is self-control.

7. Avoid decision fatigue.

Self-control has important implications in the quality of our decisions. Roy F. Baumeister, author of Willpower: Rediscovering The Greatest Human Strength, notes that after people have made a number of decisions, no matter how small, they've used up their willpower, and their self-control is compromised. Decision fatigue has a negative impact on our decisions. For example, some people react by preferring not to make a decision at all; others may make impulsive decisions or decisions that are more subject to irrational bias. Avoid making decisions about important matters at the end of the day, when you have already made a multitude of decisions as we all do during the normal course of a day. One study, for example, shows that some judges in court have been known to make poorer decisions at the end of the day.

Put some aspect of your life on default mode so you don't have to make too many unnecessary decisions. Steve Jobs, for example, always dressed in 501 jeans and black turtlenecks. President Obama wears only blue or grey suits. "I'm trying to pare down decisions," he told Vanity Fair. "I don't want to make decisions about what I'm eating or wearing. Because I have too many other decisions to make ... You need to focus your decision-making energy. You need to routinize yourself. You can't be going through the day distracted by trivia." Take an inspiration from this to see what you can do to simplify decision-making in the more mundane aspects of your life.

8. Sip some lemonade.

In an interview with the American Psychological Association, Baumeister talks about the role of glucose in self-control. Glucose is the chemical in the bloodstream that carries energy to the brain, muscles and other organs and systems. "In simple terms," Baumeister says, "glucose is fuel for the brain. Acts of self-control reduce blood glucose levels. Low levels of glucose predict poor performance on self-control tasks and tests." Willpower can be restored by raising your blood sugar. He recommends periodically replenishing glucose, even if it's just with a glass of lemonade, to strengthen your ability to maintain self-control.

For many people, self-control represents a deeply desired; yet, allusive attribute that too often slips through our fingertips.

There is a multitude of areas in everyday life where so many of us want to do better.

This is particularly evident given the millions of people (including almost half of Americans) who make New Year's resolutions each year. Such resolutions often involve goals related to diet and fitness, finances, relationships, and the reduction of unhealthy behaviors (i.e., smoking).

Unfortunately, however; an 80 percent failure rate has been estimated for such resolutions (Luciani, 2015). Moreover, general efforts to change behaviors result in relapse over half of the time (Kottler, 2012).

Why are we so consistently disappointed by our failed efforts at self-improvement? For one thing, these objectives are not easy. Fulfilling one's dreams "takes an awful lot of determination, dedication, self-discipline, and effort" (Jesse Owens, brainyquote.com).

This article will look into the research behind self-control and self-discipline (terms to be used interchangeably); including the many benefits thereof and how to attain them. Several interesting research studies will also be described.

So, let's begin our inquiry by exploring the evidence supporting the many benefits of self-control to health and socioemotional well-being.

Before you continue, we thought you might like to download our three Self-Compassion Exercises for free. These detailed, science-based exercises will not only help you increase the compassion and kindness you show yourself but will also give you the tools to help your clients, students, or employees show more compassion to themselves.

What are the Benefits of Self-Control and Self-Discipline?

1. Weight, Fitness, and Health

It has been said that "eating constitutes the greatest obstacle to self-control" (Mahavira, brainyquote.com). Of course, the endless stream of weight loss-related advertising, including gym memberships, weight loss programs, and even weight loss surgery is ample evidence for the enormous business surrounding weight loss. Not to mention the personal weight-related struggles experienced by numerous people.

Losing weight is an all too common goal that is greatly enhanced by self-control. For example, in a 12-week diet and self-discipline exercise program among overweight adults (e.g., a body mass index of at least 25 kg/m2), researchers found higher levels of trait self-control among those who were more successful in achieving program goals.

More specifically, participants with relatively higher self-control ate fewer calories (including less fat), burned more calories, and achieved greater weight loss (Crescioni, Ehrlinger, & Alquist et al., 2011).

Several additional studies investigating self-control (also referred to as 'self-regulation') and weight loss have included youth participants, often with a particular interest in how early self-control might protect against and subsequent weight gain during adolescence.

This topic was researched in a large-scale longitudinal study, including ten U.S. sites (Francis, & Susman, 2009). Participants included 1061 children from age 3 to 12 years. Self-control and body mass index (BMI) were assessed at baseline, as well as at multiple time-points covering a total of 9 years.

Interestingly, children with lower self-regulatory skills had higher BMI's and more weight gain at each time-point. In other words, self-control had a significant impact on weight gain from childhood through early adolescence.

In a similar study by Duckworth, Tsukayama, and Geier (2010); self-control was assessed among fifth graders who were followed until eighth grade. This study found that fifth graders who were higher in self-control evidenced significantly decreased BMI's over the following three years.

Finally, weight gain during the transition from childhood to adolescence was examined in another longitudinal study among 844 children (Tsukayama, Toomey, & Faith et al., 2010). This study, which included both parent and teacher ratings of self-control, indicated that those who were higher in self-control were less likely to be overweight at age 15.

The authors noted that the ability to control impulses and delay gratification represented significant factors affecting the avoidance of weight gain during adolescence. The combination of these studies provides compelling evidence for the power of self-control early in life to predict healthy weight over time— including during early and middle adolescence.

Along with weight, a more general measure of physical fitness has been examined concerning self-control. Specifically, in a cross-sectional (non-longitudinal) study including young male participants, various fitness-related outcomes were assessed including BMI, muscle fitness, aerobic fitness, and leisure time physical activity (Kinnunen, Suihko, & Hankonen et al., 2012).

Findings indicated that self-control was associated with lower BMI and higher levels of muscular and aerobic fitness. Interestingly, fitness indicators remained significantly related to self-control, even regardless of participants' BMI measures.

Medical conditions in adulthood have also been linked to measures of self-control during adolescence. For example, in a compelling study by Miller, Barnes, and Beaver (2011), 9 out of 10 physical and brain-based health issues were significantly less likely among adults who were rated as higher in self-control during adolescence.

More specifically, lower self-control was predictive of a higher odds of experiencing depression, ADHD, other mental illnesses, poor hearing, stuttering speech patterns, asthma, cancer, high cholesterol, and high blood pressure. These findings represent a powerful example of the benefits of self-control.

2. Academic and Career Success

Fred Rogers (e.g., 'Mr. Rogers') referred to discipline "as the continual everyday process of helping a child learn self-discipline" (brainyquote.com). He had a point.

Along with health-related outcomes, self-discipline also plays an important role when it comes to children's education. For example, a longitudinal study, including 164 eight graders, found that self-discipline assessed in the fall was related to a variety of important educational outcomes measured in the spring (Duckworth, & Seligman, 2005).

This study indicated that self-control had a significant positive impact on grades, attendance, and time spent doing homework. Being higher in self-control was also related to fewer hours spent watching television.

The importance of self-discipline reported in this study was maintained after statistically adjusting for IQ and achievement test scores. This research lends support to parents who have consistently—and perhaps frustratingly— tried to impress upon their adolescents the importance of being disciplined when it comes to homework, screen time, and general study habits.

With rapid increases in technology related to office automation, large numbers of people are working from home. While telecommuting has several advantages for employees, such as increased flexibility; it also has its challenges.

Primarily, when employees work in a potentially distracting environment without in-person supervision, productivity may be negatively impacted. Indeed, employees require a certain degree of self-discipline and motivation to succeed in their jobs (Olson, 1983).

To address predictors of occupational success; Converse, Pathak, and DePaul et al. (2012) took a comprehensive look at self-control. The researchers conducted two studies, with the first one examining self-control among 249 full-time employees. In this study, self-control was related to higher salary and occupational prestige.

The second study consisted of an impressive longitudinal design and 1,568 participants whose self-control was assessed during childhood. After 20 years, those who were rated higher in restraint achieved greater career and occupational success (i.e., job satisfaction, salary, and prestige).

It was also reported that self-control benefited educational achievement; which, in turn, predicted higher wages and occupational prestige (Converse et al., 2012). These findings are particularly relevant for employers, given their implications regarding which employees will be most successful. And they are undoubtedly salient to telecommuters.

3. Risky and Problem Behaviors

Behavioral theories seeking to explain deviant, unhealthy, and risky behaviors often address the role of self-control. For example, Gottfredson and Hirschi's (1990) self-control theory posits that inclinations toward criminal actions occur as a function of an individual's ability to control his/her tendency to engage in such behaviors.

Those people who are higher in self-control are predicted to be better able to postpone immediate gratification in favor of long-term rewards. More specifically, "long-term consequences influence the actions of a person with ample self-control, whereas the elements of criminal behavior reflect easy and immediate gratification of universal, fundamental, human desires.

A person with adequate self-control is less likely to attend to, or invest in, these features of a situation than is how or her less-controlled counterpart" (Gibbs, Giever, & Martin, 1998, pgs. 41-42).

This theory was tested using a large sample (N = 1000) of American college students (Ford, & Blumenstein, 2012). Researchers found a higher risk of binge drinking, cannabis use, and prescription drug misuse among participants who were lower in self-control.

A review of risky behavior would be remiss if not addressing the period of adolescence. Adolescence is marked by substantial increases in dangerous behaviors such as fast driving, substance use, and risky sexual behavior— among others.

While it is not uncommon for youth to misjudge the risks involved in their actions (i.e., adolescent drivers tend to overestimate their driving skills), there are other factors at play when it comes to significant increases in preventable forms of death that occur during this period. One such factor is self-control; as holding-off on temptations can be particularly challenging among young people.

Consequently, several studies have investigated the various constructs (i.e., self-control) that predict dangerous behavior among adolescents. For example, self-control theory has been investigated concerning youth sexual behavior because of its potential for undesirable and unhealthy outcomes (i.e., unplanned pregnancy and sexually transmitted disease).

For example, Hope and Chapple (2004) examined data from a longitudinal study consisting of 709 participants who were between 15 and 17 years of age at the final assessment. A sub-sample of this group was also created, consisting of participants who had initiated sexual behavior (n = 223).

Researchers found that lower self-control significantly predicted having initiated sex, increased numbers of sexual partners, and a more casual (versus committed) relationship with sexual partners.

Research has similarly indicated that the lack of self-control is related to more impulsive or under-controlled sexual behavior, as well as the inability to resist engaging in sexual conduct with an individual who is not the primary sexual partner (Gailliot, & Baumeister, 2007).

Similarly, Wills and Stoolmiller (2002) followed a sample of 1,526 6th graders through 9th grade. A composite substance use score incorporating cigarette, alcohol, and marijuana use were created. Researchers found that increases in substance use over time were higher for those who were lower in self-control.

Finally, in a study examining criminal behavior and substance use among adolescent males already involved in the criminal justice system, a global scale of low self-control incorporating multiple subcategories was included as the predictor. Results indicated that the self-control sub-factors of risk-seeking and volatile temper were significant predictors of drug use, and both property and violent crimes (Connor, Stein, & Longshore, 2009).

4. Various Additional Outcomes Related to Self-control

Research addressing the benefits of self-control also has taken a look at broader spectrum outcomes. For example, in a study by Tangney, Baumeister, and Boone (2004); two extensive investigations were conducted using a new measure of self-control among college students.

Findings indicated that higher self-control was related to better relationships and interpersonal skills, higher grade point average, less binge eating, more secure attachments, and better adjustment as defined by less psychopathology and higher self-esteem (Tangney et al., 2004).

An additional study suggesting that self-control is related to a range of outcomes was conducted by de Ridder, Lensvelt-Mulders, and Finkenauer (2012). In their meta-analysis of 202 self-control studies, the investigators found positive relationships between higher self-control and the following outcomes: Happiness, good grades, committed relationships, and love.

Lower self-control was related to the following non-adaptive outcomes: Binge eating, alcohol use, occasional speeding, and lifetime delinquency. The authors further noted that the effect of self-control was about the same regardless of whether it was being examined as a risk or protective factor (de Ridder et al., 2012).

These findings are consistent with other research supporting a significant association between self-control and both happiness and general well-being (Hofmann, Luhmann, & Fisher et al., 2014). Overall, these studies provide convincing evidence for the impact of self-control across a range of critical psychosocial outcomes.

Most Interesting Scientific Findings

1. Processes, Measurement, and Moderators

Hofmann et al. (2014) conducted three studies aimed at explaining relationships between self-control and life satisfaction. Using adult participants in each study, a measure of relatively stable, trait self-control was examined in relation to life satisfaction ratings.

The authors reported evidence for a significant relationship between self-control and both positive emotions and life satisfaction. Perhaps more interestingly, high self-control, and positive outcomes were moderated by the ability to manage conflict.

More specifically, those with higher self-control also were able to act in a way that reduced conflict and distress. Moreover, individuals with high self-control were also better able to avoid temptations and thereby avoid 'vice-virtue' temptations (Hofmann et al., 2014).

This research suggests that there is more involved in how self-control affects outcomes, with conflict avoidance representing a key mechanism.

In the previously noted meta-analysis by de Ridder et al. (2012), additional interesting information about factors affecting the link between self-control and desired outcomes were also presented. Namely, the authors reported a stronger association between self-control and automatic behaviors versus more consciously control behaviors.

Automatic behaviors are those that are more habitual (i.e., writing pages in a novel each day as part of a routine); as opposed more controlled behaviors that require adjustments (i.e., trying to manage multiple competing resources to make time to work on a novel).

The authors suggest that self-control is not as related to resisting temptations as is often thought, but may instead be more about forming and breaking habits. Associations between self-control and outcomes have also been found to differ when it comes to real versus imagined behaviors.

Unlike actual behaviors, imagined behaviors consist of those "that one intends to do, thinks one can do, or thinks one should do" (de Ridder et al., 2012, p. 80). Imagined behaviors are more akin to wishful thinking (i.e., "I'm going to sail the world next year!").

In a study by de Ridder and colleagues (2012), behaviors and self-control were more strongly associated with imagined versus real behaviors. The authors suggest self-control measures and constructs may be convoluted by the types of behaviors included, and how they are defined and measured.

Along with the need to unpack the nature of specific behaviors (i.e., real versus imagined; automatic versus control), the researchers also suggest that self-control is overestimated when only self-reports of behaviors are included.

In a research article by Duckworth and Gross (2014), self-control was examined in relation to grit. The authors define grit as "the tenacious pursuit of a dominant superordinate goal despite setbacks" (Duckworth, & Gross, 2014, p. 319).

Grit is thus more consistent with strength of character or perseverance in the face of adversity. The authors note that, while self-control and grit are indeed correlated; they represent distinct constructs that should not be used interchangeably. In other words, a person may have one, but not the other.

A person who is high in grit is described as someone who works persistently toward achieving a primary goal, perhaps even for years. He/she may be a highly productive person who can suppress conflicting lower order goals; as well as to deal with setbacks by creating alternative lower order goals and continuing to work tenaciously toward the primary goal (Duckworth, & Gross, 2014).

Consistent with this example, grit involves exceptional achievements that often cover a lengthy period to complete; whereas, self-control involves making decisions on more of a day-to-day basis (Duckworth, & Gross, 2014). Overall, this research and the proposed models provide important directions for future research addressing these concepts, as well as important treatment implications.

Treatment and Intervention

Intervention strategies that include self-discipline components have found some promising results, including within educational settings. For example, Cincinnati implemented a district-wide program aimed at helping instructors to teach self-discipline to K-12th-grade students (Brown, & Beckett, 2006).

Teachers were supported with tools needed to deal with disciplinary issues without removing students from the class. While there were multiple components to this large-scale intervention, promoting student self-discipline was an essential factor in achieving desired outcomes.

Impressively, the program resulted in reductions in both suspensions and expulsions within the Cincinnati school district (Brown, & Beckett, 2006).

Lastly, in a paper by Moffitt, Arseneault, and Belsky et al. (2011), the implementation of large-scale self-control programs are discussed. The authors propose that such programs could have significant societal benefits by improving health, wealth, and public safety.

Longitudinal, prospective studies that assessed self-control in children and followed them over time are presented. It is proposed that the multitude of positive outcomes predicted by increased self-control imply that large-scale self-control programs have the potential to realize important societal outcomes related to taxpayer costs and overall prosperity among citizens (Moffitt et al., 2011).

In sum, each of the studies described herein presents important evidence for the benefits of self-control; as well as the justification for continued interventions promoting it.

22 Things You Can Do to Realize These Benefits

Happiness is dependent on self-discipline. We are the biggest obstacles to our happiness. It is much easier to do battle with society and with others than to fight our own nature.

Dennis Prager

While becoming more self-disciplined isn't easy— as it often goes against our immediate desires and impulses, it is attainable.

Here are several ways to become more self-disciplined:

Be informed: Don't jump into the idea of achieving an important goal without doing your research. While you may be excited and eager to get started; by understanding what it takes to be successful and the steps needed to get there, your objective will be much more obtainable.

Avoid labeling yourself: We all have that voice in the back of our head that repeats all sorts of nonconstructive information. If your voice is telling you things like "That's just not 'you;'" or "you're just not the type to succeed at that goal" – it is essential that you learn and practice a more positive story about yourself.

Don't put your life on hold: Sure, it's better to attend that big reunion, wedding, or other meaningful events when you are looking your best. But don't make living life contingent upon fulfilling all of your goals. Keep striving toward achieving them, but enjoy your life in the meantime.

Consider the timing: Be conscious of the timing in which you want to exercise more self-control. If certain times of year are more challenging (i.e., for many, the holidays are not the best time to initiate health and fitness plans), focus on a more reasonable period.

Don't beat yourself up for perceived failures and setbacks: As you are on your journey toward better control, there will be occasional setbacks. Do not conceive of them as failures that define your entire attempts at self-improvement. All of your hard work thus far is not defined by one set-back today. Forgive yourself and get back in the program.

Identify your short- and long-term goals— and be specific: Simply stating "I'm going to be more disciplined in how I deal with my finances," or "I'm going to become more fit," won't cut it. You need to write out the specific goals along the way, and to display such goals in a place where you will see them each day— like on a big piece of paper in on your kitchen wall.

Choose goals that are right for you; don't succumb to others' expectations: How you achieve self-control benefits is dependent upon your personal goals, abilities, and motivation. Pick objectives that are meaningful to you.

Aim for realistic goals: A sure way to fail at achieving self-control objectives is by choosing unattainable goals. If you've never run before, a marathon probably is not in your near future. Realistic goals are essential to success.

Don't overdo it: As you are enthusiastically plunging forward with your new self-control program, if you notice that it's wearing you down or impeding other areas of your life, you may be overdoing it. It is important to check-in with yourself regularly to make sure all is on track.

Self-monitor your progress: Self-monitoring means keeping a consistent record of your progress. Psychologists often include self-monitoring as part of intervention programs, not only as a way to collect data; but also because it is related to improved compliance with program objectives. How you monitor your progress is up to you (i.e., could be on your phone, your computer, or a piece of paper), the important thing is that you do it.

Share your plan with a friend: By sharing your new self-control objectives with others, you will be more likely to stick with them.

Seek help as needed: If your plan is proving exceedingly tricky because something is blocking or sabotaging your progress, it may be time to ask for help from a friend or professional.

Be optimistic; picture your end goal: It seems obvious, but by always imagining yourself in a positive light and having an upbeat attitude, you will be more likely to succeed.

Take breaks: Sometimes, a new self-discipline approach can become overwhelming and will cause the person to feel deprived. By giving yourself reasonable breaks (i.e., a person trying to lose weight may allow one day a week in which the demands are less stringent), you will be less likely to give up altogether.

Practice self-care: While you may be doing great toward achieving your goals, remember to take care of yourself in other areas, so that you remain well-rounded and healthy.

Don't create new problems: Becoming more disciplined should not involve unreasonably expensive programs, foods, practitioners, classes, etc. For example, individuals attempting to achieve New Year's resolutions may eat all sorts of unhealthy foods during the holidays, only to be followed by overly expensive healthy foods after the new year (Pope, Hanks, & Just et al., 2014).

Reward yourself: Don't forget to reward yourself along the way. Small, but meaningful, rewards help maintain motivation.

Identify positive role models: As you venture toward your objective, be aware of individuals who either inspire or sabotage your efforts by their behaviors. Stick with the first group.

Avoid distractions and temptations: Along with timing, efforts at self-control are enhanced when you are not subjected to conditions that interfere with your progress (i.e., a kitchen full of junk food will not help someone working toward healthy eating).

Adjust goals, but only as necessary: If you are finding that your original goals were either too hard to be realistically met or not challenging enough, it's okay to adjust them.

Share your successes: As you find yourself doing well with your plan, share your progress with others who will be proud of you. This will enhance your self-esteem and continued motivation.

Be IN for the long-haul: Remember, becoming more self-disciplined may be a new mindset for you; and mindsets can be difficult to change. Changing our behaviors and expectations is always challenging, and rewards take time to realize. But if you stick with it, while also framing your goals as lifestyle (as opposed to temporary) changes, you will be more likely to see results.

You must adopt the sort of lifestyle changes you can maintain for as long as you live. The same is true with any change you are prepared to initiate. This isn't a sprint but a marathon.

Kottler, J. (2012, p. 15).

A Take Home Message

While becoming more self-disciplined is not easy, it is manageable. After all, "emotional self-control is the result of hard work, not an inherent skill" (Travis Bradberry). This idea leads to some important takeaways:

Research indicates that improving self-control is 100% worth it. There are a myriad of benefits of self-control that cover multiple domains of functioning (i.e., fitness, diet, risky behaviors, school and career success, happiness, etc.). Moreover, the benefits of self-control are evident among all age-groups.

You do have control over your self-control— you were not born lacking in it, and thus you can change it.

Along with intervention research indicating that self-control programs have shown effectiveness, there are many specific ways in which you can improve your efforts at achieving more self-control (i.e., realistic goals, appropriate timing, regular self-monitoring, and meaningful rewards— among many others).

From a research standpoint, self-control is not exactly straightforward. Researchers need to investigate both further how self-control is measured and researched; while also addressing important moderators that affect its relationship to outcomes. In doing so, readers will better understand what is meant by 'self-control' and what can be done to increase it and reap the benefits.

Consumers have access to a vast amount of useful information when it comes to increasing self-control and realizing aspirations. If you, like so many of us, have a specific self-improvement goal in mind or would like to be more disciplined in general, you can do it. Once you gather as much information as possible and devise your strategy; be excited and positive about the future— for you are on your way toward a more disciplined and fulfilled life.

"Self-control is often used to describe a favorable character trait in people. The word is used fairly frequently, but what exactly is self-control, and why is it important?"

Here, we'll share some secrets of self-control and ways to pass on the practice of self-control to your children.

WHAT IS SELF-CONTROL?

Self-control is the war between impulsivity and doing what's right or beneficial. It's the ability to control emotions, impulses or behaviors to achieve a greater goal.

A common example of this is people attempting to maintain their New Year's Resolution and lose a few pounds. It can be very difficult to refuse seconds of dinner or dessert afterward, but those practicing self-control know that they are working toward a long-term goal. While the immediate satisfaction would be sweet, the long-term results probably wouldn't be weight loss.

WHY IS SELF-CONTROL IMPORTANT?

This may seem self-explanatory, but it's helpful to work through this question thoughtfully.

Is self-control really that important, or is it better to enjoy the moment and not concern oneself with future outcomes?

Besides risking the ability to achieve long-term goals, there are other problematic issues with a lack of self-control.

People who lack self-control often give in to impulsive behavior and emotions as well. This means that they may make poor choices that harm themselves or others and react poorly when they don't get what they want.

Imagine a toddler who wants something but the parent says no. Often, the initial reaction is to behave impulsively. They may throw a tantrum and hit and scream. Toddlers are still learning to regulate their emotions and respond appropriately when things don't go their way.

The same is true for people of all ages. Self-control is an important skill to develop because these same emotions occur in any person who feels that their needs or desires are not being met. However, a person who lacks self-control may respond in a variety of ways including with anger, physical violence or by turning to unhealthy coping mechanisms.

Ecclesiastes 7:9 says, "Do not be quickly provoked in your spirit, for anger resides in the lap of fools."

A person who lacks self-control may be an unstable person, prone to fits of anger and unethical decisions. There's more at stake to a lack of self-control than a forgotten New Year's Resolution—it may mean the difference between a person who is successful in personal relationships and careers, and one who is not.

THE LINK BETWEEN SELF-CONTROL AND EMPATHY

Researchers have recently discovered that the same part of the brain that controls empathy also controls self-control. This section of the brain is called the right temporoparietal junction, or rTPJ.

In the study, Alexander Soutscheck temporarily altered the part of the brain long-associated with empathy using a magnetic field. He discovered that a person's self-control was inhibited when this part of the brain was shut down.

Rebecca Saxe from MIT weighed in by saying, "For a long time, people have speculated that we use the same mechanisms to reason about other people as about our hypothetical selves. So this new study fits really well."

In other words, a person's self-control to avoid dessert in the present helps a hypothetical future self lose weight. The effects are not immediate, so a person's use of self-control now benefits a future version of themselves.

In Soutscheck's study, when he disrupted the rTPJ part of the brain, his test participants were less likely to behave altruistically. They were given a scenario where they could take a sum of money for themselves or share it with a partner. When the rTPJ part of the brain was disrupted, they were less likely to share. This confirmed the link between rTPJ and empathy.

But interestingly, the same participants were also more likely to take a small sum of money in the immediate as opposed to a larger amount in the future—linking rTPJ to self-control responses as well.

WHAT ARE THE SECRETS OF SELF-CONTROL?

If self-control is important, what do you do when it doesn't come naturally? How can you develop this vital skill?

Here are three ways to begin a journey of self-control.

PRAY, MEDITATE, BE MINDFUL

Prayer and meditation are powerful ways to help you reset your thought processes.

Taking time to pray or meditate during the day is a good way of refocusing your mind and giving yourself a chance to calm down if something is irritating you. Instead of getting worked up about a problem, offer your concern to God in prayer, as Philippians 4:6 says, "Do not be anxious about anything, but in every situation, by prayer and petition, with thanksgiving, present your requests to God." Or consider using meditation by setting aside some time to close your eyes, breathe deeply and focus on what you can control and how you can move forward.

If you're trying to stop a bad habit, these can be good options to curb your impulse to do it. You can replace those old habits with prayer or meditation.

GET ENOUGH SLEEP

It's not always easy to catch the z's that you need, but a lack of sleep has been linked to self-control issues.

In a Harvard Business Review article, author Christopher Barnes discussed the link between a lack of sleep and poor choices.

Building on previous research that showed a lack of sleep may lead to lower self-control, Barnes and his colleagues conducted a study of their own. Their results showed overwhelmingly that those suffering from sleep deprivation exhibited high levels of unethical behavior.

Many adults are living on less sleep than they probably should be getting—some living on less than six hours a night. Unfortunately, sleep deprivation may lead to making poor choices. If you're suffering from a lack of sleep, try to rearrange your schedule to make sure you're getting enough snooze time.

CREATE A RITUAL

It may seem unlikely, but participating in a simple ritual may give you the ability to avoid unhealthy impulses.

Scientific American conducted a study that gave participants a simple (and random) ritual to perform to help them achieve weight loss. They chose females from a university gym who were already striving toward weight loss.

Half of the participants were told to be mindful about their food habits. The other half was told to do a three-step ritual before consuming their food which involved cutting their food into pieces before they ate it, rearranging the food so it was symmetrical on their plate and pressing their eating utensil on their food three times before eating.

The study showed that the women who performed the ritual ate fewer calories and also ate less sugar and fats.

HOW TO TEACH CHILDREN THE ART OF SELF-CONTROL

If you have or work with children, you may be wondering how to teach them self-control. Learning self-control at a young age is a great way of setting them up for success in the future.

Self-control, or self-regulation as it is sometimes referred to, is a skill that can be taught. While some people are born with more natural ability, most often it is a skill that individuals can help develop.

One way of doing this is to help children replace negative responses with positive ones. Dr. Matthew Rouse, a clinical psychologist at the Child

Mind Institute, explains that to teach children to self-regulate, you should not avoid situations that may be difficult. Instead, you should coach your children through difficult times.

When you coach kids through a frustrating moment, you're providing a framework that clinicians call "scaffolding," or showing the child the behavior that you want the child to have. Once that child understands the concepts they can begin to overcome challenges on their own.

One way to work through this process is by doing practice runs. For example, suppose a child throws tantrums when going to the store. Child Mind Institute suggests taking a short trip to the store and helping your child practice things like staying with you or keeping their hands to themselves. You could use a reward system for every time the child behaves.

Even with a short trip, the child may still act out or misbehave. This can be discouraging. However, Dr. Rouse explains that consistency is what's important. If necessary, make the trip very short and as simple as possible. As the child begins to get better at the activity, they can be given more independence.

SELF-CONTROL IN THE FUTURE

Self-control is linked to many good things including success and the ability to achieve goals. However, it's important to keep in mind that one mistake in self-control shouldn't mean that a person should give up. No one is capable of perfectly controlling their impulses or decision making at all times.

This is even more apparent in habits or responses that have become hard-wired into a person. Channeling anger into positive energy or resisting unhealthy habits is not an easy task. Consider it a victory each time you are able to use self-restraint in a situation that you would ordinarily respond in a negative way.

If you make a mistake, see it as an opportunity to learn rather than a reason to quit trying. Self-control is a lifelong journey to continue to work on.

GROW IN INFLUENCE WITH A DEGREE

Use the virtue of self-control to pursue your personal and professional goals by opening the door to new skills and opportunities with a degree from Cornerstone University's Professional & Graduate Studies division. Take that next step along your path to achieving your goals through practical application to make a change in your life now while maintaining your vision for your future.

How to Live a Strict Life

Many people are born with strict personalities, are raised in strict homes, and want to live strict for the rest of their lives

Understand what strict living is. Strict in this context means disciplined and is not about self- restricting any pleasures or good things in life. It is about getting your life on track in a healthy way.

Create order. There are several aspects of keeping your life orderly:

Aim at getting rid of the chaos, anxiety, confusion, fear etc. Aiming directs you to the positives of being otherwise. Then you have to follow strictly with determination.

Decide on your goals. Think about what you really want: it may be saving up for a holiday, or improving your health etc.

Accept that you will be fighting your demons like procrastination, ignorance, etc.

Your goals should be S.M.A.R.T. Each letter stands for a word, as below:

Sensible/Specific: Make sure the goal is precise. Don't just say, "Exercise and Do Homework." Instead, say things like "Do 30 minutes of stretching and work on your essay for english class." This will allow you to achieve more because if you are not specific, then you will only do a small amount.

Measurable: Make sure you can measure progress. For example, a goal should not be 'write the first part of a new blog post.' Instead, a goal should be something like 'write 500 words of a new blog post.'

Achievable/Attainable: Make sure you can achieve your goal. If you are going to be awake for 16 hours one day, then doing 15 hours of work and leaving the remaining hour for eating is not going to be achievable. You need to assign a realistic amount of time to do work, and leave time to do other things.

Realistic/Relevant: First, do not try to do things which have a very low likelihood of success. For example, a business owner may plan to be the leader of the market within three months. However, if they are going through a hard time and three other companies are giving strong competition, this will probably not happen. Secondly, do not do irrelevant things. If you are asked to write a report on the effects of flooding to Victorians, then you do not need to research the causes of rainfall.

Time based: Set a time limit to accomplish things. Deadlines increase productivity quickly.

Decide the best way to achieve this plan. What can you do and what will you need help from others to do? Do you need to get kits or equipment first for your project?

Set a time frame. If, for example, you need to have a project finished in time for a meeting, chart out how much time you'll need to do the job and where you can fit it in. Use a diary or calendar or even put reminders on the fridge.

Balance your judgements. Stand firm on your goal without trying to go to the extreme of being too control conscious. If you find yourself making excuses, then it's time to step back and re-evaluate if your goal is really important.

void distractions. They will make your life more difficult.

Let people involved know what you need and when. They are doing you a favor by helping you, but by the same token, you also need to be independent. If your goal is to wake up and exercise at 6 a.m., make sure they respect your decision.

Don't expect others to be extra helpful or to feel obligated to do anything extra for you.

If no one supports you, work alone.

Put your plan into action. Monitor how it goes and improve things you feel can be improved. Have fun and enjoy completing whatever project you're working on.

Be organized. Keep a notepad with pen and a calendar to write things on.

The moment you realize you are thinking too much about something or someone, turn to your goal and continue with it.

Adjust each task according to the time available and keep aiming at fulfilling them on time.

Be clean. A good life is a lot about being clean both inside and outside. For being tidy, make sure you dust and vacuum and have everything put away. Rejuvenate your body by making way for its cycle on time. Refresh your senses with breaks and fun activities that you enjoy. Don't lose anything by underestimating its value. Little things make a big difference when done well and well on time.

Eat well. To control food intake, limit your portion to a required serving and eat it slowly with a drink of water or milk. Give yourself time to eat your meal slowly so that you not only enjoy it more, but that you don't eat too much and still feel hungry. It's okay to have dessert, but choose healthy snacks between meals.

Replace junk food with a well-defined diet including proteins, calcium, vitamins etc. Include fruits, vegetables, and nuts as you can. No need to add them if you don't like them. Just use a good substitute.

Get into tidy habits,and clean as you go in the different areas of your home. Take care of the spaces around you. Your surroundings affect your sense of comfort, so do what you can to keep them clean and do not add clutter in any way.

Practice letting go. Let go of any goal or project you're not able to do, or you'll be miserable.

You are free to be liberal with your capacities. You don't have to satisfy all your mind's cravings and planning. Do what you can by listening to your body.

Multi-task. If you can multi-task right away, go for it. If you need time, learn your ways and balance it per your circumstances. For being flexible, this means to have time to be able to do things spontaneously. Do it appropriately or don't do it at all if you don't get the hang of it. Just fulfill one thing at a time.

If a friend calls you and invites you out for a meal, you don't want to say no just because it will ruin your daily routine. Check your schedule to see if you have time, and let your friend know about any dietary restrictions you have.

Clean out your home by getting rid of anything you don't wear or use. Give them to charity.

If you think you don't have to contribute to charity, think of it in terms of decluttering your space and your home. It is for your own good too because when you don't have a lot of things around, you will finally be able to see what you really want.

Work with yourself, other people, and events. By finding a balance, you can improve your life and regain some self-control. Working harmoniously with others can create a satisfying balance since we are social animals. Arguing less, staying silent when appropriate, and helping when asked can all create balance in your immediate surroundings. Doing this won't make you weaker, it will build your self-control.

Learn to say No. You can't be a people-pleaser to all and do your work well. Pleasing others is a cycle that goes on and on and takes up your time. Do what is feasible for others and fulfill your responsibilities as you must. Be polite and explain why you can't help others and get back to your work.

15 Bible Verses on Self Control

Do you struggle with willpower and self-discipline in your eating (or any area of your life)? Use these 15 Bible verses on self-control to grow in this Fruit of the Spirit.

Food cravings are no joke. They are strong and convincing and usually lead you to eat way more junk food than you need.

God created food to sustain us, fuel us, bring people together, and bring us enjoyment, but food was never meant to control us.

Just like other pleasures in life.

If you are growing in self-control for your weight loss journey or just to draw nearer to Christ, memorizing Scripture is a fantastic way to improve your self-discipline.

I like to write these verses on note cards and keep them in areas where I tend to experience temptation – on the fridge, in my car, on my nightstand, etc.

It helps me to turn to God in those moments of temptation and listen for God's voice (like in the midst of emotional eating).

Here are my favorite Scriptures to use.

Scripture on Self-Control

Galatians 5:22-23

But the fruit of the Spirit is love, joy, peace, forbearance, kindness, goodness, faithfulness, gentleness and self-control. Against such things there is no law.

Self-control is listed in the Bible as one of the Fruits of the Spirit – a sign that Christ is in us.

If we let our desires lead our decisions, our lives (and our bodies) can quickly spin out of control.

Self-control is a discipline that God grows in us when we continually choose to die to our flesh and live in Him.

Fulfilling those cravings feels so good at the time, but Christ offers us a freedom that is only found in honoring those healthy boundaries.

Romans 7:18

For I know that good itself does not dwell in me, that is, in my sinful nature. For I have the desire to do what is good, but I cannot carry it out.

It is SO frustrating to know what is right and still not be able to manage to do it.

So what is the missing piece between our knowledge and action?

Jesus.

Sin runs deeps insides of us, but as Christians, we have the One in us who can give us the strength to stand up and say no to temptation.

We don't have the strength on our own to be able to choose what is right, especially when it doesn't feel good.

Fortunately, we serve a very good, ever-faithful God who works wonders in our weakness as we seek Him.

Proverbs 25:27-28

It is not good to eat too much honey, nor is it honorable to search out matters that are too deep. Like a city whose walls are broken through is a person who lacks self-control.

Honey itself is not a bad thing. It tastes so sweet and wonderful. Food is such a blessing when you eat it for the right reasons!

But it seems as humans, when we get a taste of something good, our appetite becomes insatiable and we crave more and more and more.

Have you ever thought to yourself, "Well, I've already had 3 cookies...what's 1 more?"

That's how the enemy works.

He convinces you that just a little bit more is okay. And then a little bit more after that.

Don't be like a city whose walls are broken. Stand firm, knowing when enough is enough.

1 Corinthians 7:5

Do not deprive each other except perhaps by mutual consent and for a time, so that you may devote yourselves to prayer. Then come together again so that Satan will not tempt you because of your lack of self-control.

This verse is referring to sex, but the concept of self-control here is the same.

As I mentioned about, small lapses in our judgement, giving in to just a little bit of temptation doesn't always feel sinful.

It doesn't always feel like we need to fight it.

When we give in to temptation once, even just a little bit, it's like Satan sticking his foot in the door, giving him more power to tempt you even more.

That's the lie of temptation. It tells you that when you give in, it's going to feel so good and you'll feel so satisfied...

But that satisfaction never comes and all you're left with is that feeling that you want more.

1 Timothy 3:2-3

Now the overseer is to be above reproach, faithful to his wife, temperate, self-controlled, respectable, hospitable, able to teach, not given to drunkenness, not violent but gentle, not quarrelsome, not a lover of money.

In this verse, Timothy was explaining what they should look for in a person before appointing them as an overseer.

In their list of character traits, self-control is a biggie and applicable to just about everything else on the list.

It takes self-control to accomplish all of those things – staying faithful to your wife, keeping your cool in frustrating situations, not drinking too much, not losing your temper, not arguing (even when you think you're right), and not becoming too focused on money.

2 Timothy 3:1-5

But mark this: There will be terrible times in the last days. People will be lovers of themselves, lovers of money, boastful, proud, abusive, disobedient to their parents, ungrateful, unholy, without love, unforgiving, slanderous, without self-control, brutal, not lovers of the good, treacherous, rash, conceited, lovers of pleasure rather than lovers of God— having a form of godliness but denying its power. Have nothing to do with such people.

I included 5 verses here because they are all so powerful.

This is a strong warning to avoid people lacking self-control.

It uses strong wording, saying that people without self-control love pleasure more than God.

Yikes! I never want that to be something that defines me!

And the end of the verse instructs them to, "Have nothing to do with such people."

Don't be such people. Be an example of Christ that others can look up to.

Titus 2:11-12

For the grace of God has appeared that offers salvation to all people. It teaches us to say "No" to ungodliness and worldly passions, and to live self-controlled, upright and godly lives in this present age..."

Titus is full of encouragement to be self-controlled. It mentions that elders need to be self-controlled (Titus 1:8), older men should be taught to be self-controlled (Titus 2:2), older women need to be self-controlled (Titus 2:5), and younger men should be encouraged to be self-controlled, as well (Titus 2:6).

So, basically, the Bible says every age group of people really need to work on this character quality!

And this passage explains that it's the grace of God that teaches us to say no to sin (because, I'm certainly not strong enough to resist without His help!).

2 Peter 1:5-8

For this very reason, make every effort to add to your faith goodness; and to goodness, knowledge; and to knowledge, self-control; and to self-control, perseverance; and to perseverance, godliness; and to godliness, mutual affection; and to mutual affection, love.

For if you possess these qualities in increasing measure, they will keep you from being ineffective and unproductive in your knowledge of our Lord Jesus Christ.

There is a growth process listed in this verse to help us live powerfully and purposefully.

Becoming a Christian is not the end of the road!

After you have faith, strive to add goodness, knowledge, self-control, and so on.

I want people to know how Jesus has transformed my life and developing self-control is an important way to prevent myself from being "ineffective and unproductive."

2 Timothy 1:7

For the Spirit God gave us does not make us timid, but gives us power, love and self-discipline.

It's crazy how often we let fear guide our decisions.

With money, food, and all kinds of other pleasures in life, there is this fear that there isn't enough to go around.

Instead of gathering up as much of those things for ourselves as we possibly can, God calls us to live a different way.

He calls us to be content with what we have, knowing that He is our provider.

We don't need to live in fear or timidity because the Hold Spirit is our source of all the power, love, self-discipline we need.

1 Corinthians 10:13

No temptation has overtaken you except what is common to mankind. And God is faithful; he will not let you be tempted beyond what you can bear. But when you are tempted, he will also provide a way out so that you can endure it.

This is my go-to verse when it comes to food cravings (and other temptations!).

It is a powerful reminder of a few different things.

#1 – I am not alone. Temptation can be so isolating if we believe we are the only one struggling.

#2 – I can do this. God is faithful and knows my limits. He won't tempt me more than I can bear, which means He knows I have the strength to overcome it.

#3 – There is always another way. It makes sense in the moment to think that the only way to satisfy my (crazy) strong desire for Oreos is to give in and eat them, but there is always another way to respond to that urge.

I'm not saying it's easy, but this verse reminds me to stop, think, and look for the way out of temptation.

Romans 12:1

Therefore, I urge you, brothers and sisters, in view of God's mercy, to offer your bodies as a living sacrifice, holy and pleasing to God—this is your true and proper worship.

There is no denying that developing self-control requires sacrifice.

Often, we view sacrifice as just giving up something we really want. It's about deprivation and missing out on happiness.

My pastor explains sacrifice differently.

He says sacrifice is giving up something you love for something you love more.

That really resonated with me. It's helped me learn to offer my body as a living sacrifice in a way that honors God in my eating and worships Him in my exercise.

James 1:19-20

My dear brothers and sisters, take note of this: Everyone should be quick to listen, slow to speak and slow to become angry, because human anger does not produce the righteousness that God desires.

Self-control is a character trait that affects so many aspects of your life – your weight loss journey, the words you speak, the way you express frustration and anger.

The incredible thing about self-control is that when you improve it in one area (like making healthier food choices when you really want to eat a whole chocolate cake), it spreads to other areas.

You learn not to respond to your emotions and urges right away, so you become more patient and temperate in all things.

1 Corinthians 9:24-25

Run in such a way as to get the prize. Everyone who competes in the games goes into strict training. They do it to get a crown that will not last, but we do it to get a crown that will last forever.

We were all created for a unique purpose. It's an incredible honor that God would create you and I to do good works to serve Him and others.

But all purposes in our lives require strict training – losing weight, learning to read, running a marathon, earning your PhD, and so much more.

Doing great things requires great self-control.

1 Corinthians 6:12

"I have the right to do anything," you say—but not everything is beneficial. "I have the right to do anything"—but I will not be mastered by anything.

Human freedom tells us, "Do whatever makes you happy. You deserve it."

God knows that is not the best way to live and will never bring us true happiness anyways. He gives us healthy boundaries to enjoy the good things in life, but not to the point of excess.

You have the choice to live however you'd like. You can go eat a family size bag of Cheetos right now if you want to.

But just because you can doesn't mean you should.

Food cravings have a way of starting small ("a cookie sounds good right now") and growing into a monstrous problem that dictates our decisions ("you need to go through a drive-thru on your way home and toss the evidence before your husband can see").

Be watchful that you aren't being mastered by those things.

2 Corinthians 12:9

But he said to me, "My grace is sufficient for you, for my power is made perfect in weakness." Therefore I will boast all the more gladly about my weaknesses, so that Christ's power may rest on me.

As humans, we love to be independence. We can't wait to get our driver's licenses, move out of the house, and earn our way in the world with promotions, certifications, and achievements.

We want to prove that we can do it all – balance family, run our schedules, find success.

We desperately try to hide any sign of weakness because that would show others that we are failing.

But God isn't limited by our human standards.

If you are struggling with lapses in self-control due to temptation, cravings, and mistakes, know that God's grace is still enough.

And when we admit our struggles and seek Him to fill in our gaps, it's only then that we can be complete.

What an amazing God we serve who can work even more powerfully in our shortcomings.

Here's How to Help Kids Master the 3 Types of Self-Control

Self-control is a key component in our children's ability to effectively function in day-to-day life, and is a lot more complicated and detailed than you might suspect.

In our children's early years, self-control is expressed by their ability to trust adults, integrate the concept of rules, delay gratification, control their angry impulses, find internal methods of practicing patience despite their frustrations, empathize with the feelings of others, exhibit an understanding of fairness by waiting their turn, and find ways to make them self feel better when facing sadness.

Delaying Gratification

We want our children to be able to regulate their behavior and emotions. The goal is to "delay, defer, and accept substitutions without becoming aggressive or disorganized by frustration, and [to] cope with arousal, whether due to environmental challenge or fatigue".

Self-control develops when our child begins the process of differentiating between short-term and long-term outcomes, and the understanding that a long-term outcome is far greater than the one they might experience at the moment through instant gratification. This ability to project into the future and grasp the idea of cause and effect is what allows our children to comprehend the concept that first they must do their homework before they are allowed to play.

Establishing a working model to delayed pleasure is a necessary component for our children to eventually live responsible and balanced lives.

There Are Three Kinds of Self-Control

Impulse Control is our child's ability to stop and think before they act upon a thought.

The pros:

It allows our little ones to visualize the future consequences of their actions.

Constantly interrupt and speak when it's not their turn

Talk too much

Not practice self-regulation, and procrastinate with tasks like homework

Carelessly rush through assignments or chores

Be inconsistent with following rules from one day to the next

Emotional Control is the ability of our kids to manage their feelings by focusing on future goals.

It helps our children keep powering through, even when they are confronted by upsetting or unexpected circumstances.

Become easily frustrated and prematurely give up

Become sensitive to constructive criticism/being corrected

Have a difficult time winding down enough to focus on tasks (like homework)

Become easily agitated by others and unable to control their temper

Struggle with the concept of delayed gratification, thus can't prioritize homework or chores before playing

Movement Control is our children's ability to control their body movements.

The pros:

It allows our kids to regulate their physical actions and reactions in an appropriate way.

Be constantly fidgety, hyper, or anxious

Have difficulty sitting still through quiet or seated events

Be disruptive with their movements during games or conversations

Struggle standing patiently in line and waiting their turn

Affirming relationships are vital components in the healthy development of our children. More specifically, a strong attachment between us and our children increases their ability to control impulses, and develop a healthy level of self-control.

Teaching Kids Self-Control

In order to teach and reinforce the value of self-control, there are a few things to keep in mind:

Consistency: Self-regulation has a greater opportunity to develop in our children if they are in a coherent environment, where expectations are clear and rules are consistently enforced. We can't tell them they have to do their school work one day and forego playing, only to let them play before their work is completed the following day. In order for self-control to be meaningful, it must be consistent. It's our job as parents to instill and enforce that consistency.

Praise: Children who successfully master self-control are typically those who have supportive parents or caregivers. Our children need to know that they are special little people to us, and that we value their struggles to work toward self-control. Self-control is not an easy task for anyone. Lecturing our kids about their lack of control – when they are clearly out of control – is not the most effective method, because their brain's receptivity becomes compromised during stress. Words of admiration and praise reinforce positive behavior, so encourage them to do better and praise them when they do great.

Reward: Let's be honest – practicing self-control isn't a walk in the park. So when our children are successful in their efforts of delaying gratification, reward them!

Positive Self-Talk: Teaching our children to foster healthy self-talk is a key element in maintaining balance and self-control in their lives. Successfully talking themselves through a task that needs to be completed, doing their best to ignore distractions – that's self-control!

Modeling Self-Control: Our children have a greater chance of developing self-control when they see us focusing on problem-solving instead of punishment, retribution, and anger. When we calmly use words to express our feelings, our children have the opportunity to model after our positive behavior, and in turn, do the same. We are the greatest teacher our children will ever have.

Control Your Destiny with 4 Types of Self Control

4 Types of self-control
    Physical movement
    Emotion
    Concentration
    Impulses
    Brief body scan

Start off by taking a single, deep breath in through the nose and out through the mouth. You are welcome to gently close your eyes, or keep them open. Notice your body where it is: the positioning of your body, and also how your body is feeling. If you're feeling any tension anywhere, see if you can allow that to soften, or adjust your body as needed.

Tune in to your environment

Begin to allow your awareness to wander a little bit. Notice the sounds inside your environment or outside your environment. Be aware of how sounds have a nature of disappearing and reappearing, and also how your mind comes up with different comments or images on these sounds, or on your experience. Allow for all of this.

Notice thoughts and emotions

Now begin to gently open your eyes, noticing how there's also visuals in your environment. Notice how you feel. Take stock of how you're feeling physically, mentally, and emotionally.

According to the Merriam-Webster Dictionary, the definition for self-control is "restraint exercised over one's impulses, emotions, or desires." In other words, we can prevent ourselves from doing something we don't want to do or from feeling something we don't want to feel, especially when we're tempted.

It's an incredibly helpful skill. For example, when a doctor urges a patient to lose weight, self-control prevents them from eating too much junk food. If they need to go to the gym, it also keeps them from watching TV instead. When someone has an important assignment or a project due soon, they might procrastinate unless they have enough self-control.

Emotional self-control is important, too. It prevents us from screaming at others when we're angry or from punching someone when they wrong us. It also stops us from crying uncontrollably when we do not get our way or from becoming distracted in situations that require attention.

Although we learn to self-soothe as babies (by, for example, sucking on a pacifier), we're not born with self-control. We develop this skill throughout our childhood and arguably our entire lives. This is why it's not unusual to see an upset toddler throw a toy across the room, but the same behavior would be bizarre in an adult.

Sometimes, however, individuals reach adulthood with too little or too much self-control. Neither situation is ideal. In addition to the physical and emotional challenges this might bring, too little or too much self-control can also have social and mental effects like isolation, depression, or anxiety. You might be wondering what a healthy amount of self-control looks like, but to best understand that, it's important to know what too much or too little looks like first. We'll start there.

Signs Of Too Much Self-Control

Self-control is usually a quality that people admire. However, when someone has too much of it, they can struggle. Sometimes, people suffering from excessive self-control come off as perfectionists or seem overbearing. Experts call this behavior "overcontrol." Someone dealing with "overcontrol" might experience the following:

Difficulty relaxing

Distance toward others

Rigid personality

Overly focused on details

Lack of feelings or display of feelings

Being responsible (to a fault)

Avoidance of risk

In general, people with too much self-control don't stand out as much as those who lack self-control. Why? Because their behavior is often confused with being hard-working, introverted, or highly sensible. With that in mind, how do we know if someone has too much self-control or is simply mature? Well, it depends on the individual.

If someone's behavior works for them and causes little to no distress, it's likely that everything is fine. However, if excessive self-control makes their physical, mental, emotional, or social life a challenge, they may benefit from seeing a licensed counselor.

Signs Of Too Little Self-Control

Someone who lacks self-control is easy to spot. They generally have difficulty committing to positive habits, and they may not be able to regulate their feelings or actions as well as their peers. Signs of low self-control could be:

Little or no self-discipline

Lack of goals or inability to reach goals

Low motivation

Little to no willpower

Difficulty controlling emotions

Lack of attention

Quick to blame others

Difficulty maintaining friendships

Dangerous or overly-passive lifestyle

Having little self-control (or none at all) has a major impact on one's day-to-day life. Not only is it difficult to build self-confidence, but it's also hard to work with others and reach goals. If someone runs into the same obstacles over and over again, they may need to work on self-control. Similarly, if they seem to lack direction or appear immature, too little self-control might be the cause.

How To Have Self-Control

Everyone has a different amount of self-control, and it can vary by situation, too, but most of us could use a boost to find a better balance between too little and too much. Here are a few tips to get you started.

Relax

It can be hard to have self-control when we trick ourselves into thinking something must be done urgently or stopped immediately. We also struggle with self-control when we're driven by our gut reactions. Imagine you're driving down the road at high speed, and a slow driver cuts you off. Your gut reaction is what makes you want to honk your horn and scream at them or worse.

To give yourself the best chance at a calmer response and a better day, learn to slow your thoughts, so you can postpone your gut impulses. Relaxation can help. Meditation, deep breathing, and mindfulness are all excellent ways to practice relaxation. The more you relax, the more likely you are to calmly approach stressful events and choose thoughtful responses instead of acting on impulse alone.

Learn To Plan

Self-control is hard to achieve without direction. For example, if you want to lose 10 pounds, and therefore need to skip your nightly dessert, it helps to plan ahead. Instead of hoping you'll be strong enough when the time comes, think of ways to curb your appetite in advance, so you're more likely to succeed.

To avoid relying on willpower, make a plan for what you will do the next time you're tested. Perhaps you can plan on doing 15 minutes of yoga or reading a good book when you have a craving for sugar. Using distractions like this can help you improve your self-control in the long run. You will eventually learn that you can overcome unpleasant feelings and that you don't need to act on all of your desires.

Find Out What You Want

Sometimes we lack self-control because we're not clear on exactly what we want. For example, if it feels like you're going nowhere in your current job, make sure it's not because you don't know where you want to go next. When you have a clear goal, it's easier to exercise self-control because you can make choices that point you in the right direction. A licensed therapist can help you figure out exactly what motivates you, and can be a powerful tool in helping you reach your goals using self-control.

That said, it's important to have goals that are meaningful to you. Do not set a goal just because someone or something else pushes you toward it. Look deep within yourself, and find out why your goal matters to you. If it doesn't mean anything to you, it will be very hard to dedicate yourself to it.

Remember The Consequences

Often, an honest look at the consequences is enough to motivate someone struggling with self-control. Imagine finding an extra $100. Part of you knows you should use it to pay off your credit card, but another part of you wants to spend it on dinner and a movie instead. To make the right decision for you, consider the consequences.

If you pay off your credit card, will you be working toward financial freedom and taking steps to eliminate your debt? If you treat yourself, will you still have enough money to pay the credit card bill on time, or will you end up with another late fee or worse?

Look beyond short-term gratification, and think about the long-term value. If you set yourself up for success by taking care of yourself tomorrow, your self-control will naturally grow over time as you start to reap the benefits.

Role-Play

If practicing self-control is a challenge for you, role-play with a friend, a family member, or a therapist. This will help you confront your feelings in a controlled environment without the threat of negative consequences. To start, think about a simple situation where you typically struggle with self-control. As your self-control improves, branch out to more difficult or challenging situations.

Get Healthy

As with any proactive behavior, being in the right physical, mental, and emotional place makes a big difference. If it's been a while since your last physical exam, call your primary health care physician, and schedule an appointment. An underlying condition might be exacerbating your self-control issues. To that end, if you're experiencing symptoms of depression, anxiety, or other mental health issues, please get help immediately.

And in general, remember to take care of the basics. Eat a healthy diet, drink plenty of water, and get roughly eight hours of sleep per night. This will help you keep a clear mind on your journey to better self-control.

BetterHelp Can Help

Self-control plays a major role in our lives, and it's often a big factor in our overall levels of satisfaction. While it's possible to display too much self-control, a lack of self-control tends to get us into trouble. To master self-control, we need to find balance, and a counselor can help. Reach out to the mental health professionals at BetterHelp to see the best results. You can read reviews for some of our therapists below.

Counselor Reviews

"Erin is an amazing therapist. She listens to me and relates to me very well. I feel very supported and safe talking to her. Erin always helps me set goals for myself and pushes me to work hard on my own mental health in a comforting way. I've had a lot of therapists, and Erin is by far the best one I've ever had. She has sincerely helped me turn my life around."

"Diane gets right to understanding the problem so we can find solutions. She's not judgmental or harsh, but she says what I need to hear. I feel like she understands my issues and is attentive and puts as much effort as I am into therapy. I enjoy her approach which is gentle yet assertive and I feel confident in her suggestions. She offers a fresh perspective and I end the session feeling hopeful and motivated."

The Dark Side of Self-Control

People with great willpower are often lauded over their peers with less self-control. But having strong character may not always be a good thing.

A few years ago, 80 Parisians were given the chance to take part in the pilot of a new gameshow, called La Zone Xtrême. The producer greeted each participant at the studio and told them that they would appear in pairs – one as a "questioner", and one as the "contestant".

It was only once the participants arrived on stage, and the host explained the rules, that things got decidedly dark. The questioner was told to punish the contestant for any wrong answers with a sharp electric shock. They would have to increase the intensity each time, up to a total of 460 volts – more than twice the voltage of a European power outlet. If the pair made it through 27 rounds, they would win the show. The contestant was then taken into a chamber and strapped into a chair, while the questioner sat centre stage, and the game commenced.

Since it was simply a pilot show, the participants were told there was no monetary prize for winning the game – yet the vast majority of the questioners continued to administer the shocks, even after they could hear the screams of pain emanating from the chamber.

Thankfully, these cries for help were just an act – there was no electric shock. The questioners were unknowingly participating in elaborate experiment that allowed scientists to explore the way various personality traits could influence moral behaviour. You might expect the worst offenders to have been impulsive and antisocial – or, at the very least, with no strength of character. Yet the French scientists found the exact opposite. It was the participants who scored highest on conscientiousness – a trait normally associated with careful, disciplined and moral behaviour – who were willing to administer the greatest shocks.

"The people who are accustomed to being agreeable and organised, and whose social integration is good, find it more difficult to disobey," explains Laurent Bègue, a behavioural scientist at the University of Grenoble-Alpes who analysed the participants' behaviour. And in this case, that personality profile meant they were willing to torture another human being.

These findings join a spate of new studies showing that people with high self-control and discipline have a surprising dark side. This research can help us understand why model citizens sometimes turn toxic, with important implications for our understanding of unethical behaviour in the workplace and beyond.

Overcoming impulses

For decades, self-control had been seen as an unalloyed advantage. It can be assessed in various ways – from the questionnaires studying conscientiousness (which considers someone's preference for self-discipline and organisation) to experimental measures of willpower (such as the famous "Marshmallow Test").

The traits that lead people to act immorally may not just be mundane – but actually desirable – in other situations

In each case, people with high self-control were seen to perform better at school and work and to adopt healthier lifestyles; they are less likely to overeat or take drugs, and more likely to exercise. Their ability to overcome their baser urges meant that people with higher self-control were also less likely to act aggressively or violently, and were less likely to have a criminal record. For these reasons, self-control was believed to contribute to the strength of someone's "character"; some scientists even went as far as to argue that it comprises a kind of "moral muscle" determining our capacity to act ethically.

In the mid-2010s, however, Liad Uziel at Israel's Bar-Ilan University began to investigate whether context might play an important role in determining the consequences of our self-control. He speculated that the trait was just a useful tool that allows people to achieve any goal – both good and bad. In many situations, our social norms reward people cooperating with others, and so people with high self-control happily toe the line. And if we change those social norms, then people with high self-control might turn out to be less than scrupulous in their treatment of others.

To test the idea, Uziel turned to a standard psychological experiment called the "dictator game" in which one participant is given a sum of money, and offered the chance to share it with a partner. Thanks to our social norms to be cooperative, people are often quite generous. "Rationally, there is no reason to give the second player any sum," explains Uziel, "but people often give about a third of the endowment to others." The researchers found that the people with high self-control were generous if they feared that they would be judged for their stingy behaviour. If their actions were private, however, without the fear of judgement from others, then they were much more selfish than people with low self-control – choosing to further their own self-interests rather than help others. In these circumstances, they kept almost all the sum to themselves.

People high in self-control also appear to be more careful about when they commit an anti-social act and avoid getting caught. David Lane and colleagues at Western Illinois University in the US recently questioned people about certain dubious behaviours and whether they had suffered the consequences of their actions. Sure enough, they found that people with high self-control were more likely to avoid punishment for dangerous driving and cheating on tests, compared to people with poorer self-control. Once again, they seem to be carefully judging the social norms of what is acceptable behaviour, and adhering to them when the misdeed is more likely to affect their reputation.

Extermination machines

These are dubious moral acts, but if the social norms allow it, strong willpower can contribute to acts of cruelty. In one macabre study, psychologist Thomas Denson at the University of New South Wales in Australia invited participants into the lab with an unusual task – to feed bugs into a coffee grinder. Unbeknown to the participants, the "extermination machine" was rigged to allow the bugs to escape before they were killed – but the grinder still made an unnerving crunching sound as the insects worked their way through machine. The aim of the experiment, the participants were told, was to better understand certain "human-animal interactions" – a justification for the task that should have rendered the act more socially acceptable to the participants.

The effects of self-control, it turned out, depended on people's sense of moral responsibility. For people who were particularly concerned about the ethical consequences of their actions, increased self-control made little difference to the outcome. They killed a moderate number of bugs, but their greater self-control didn't seem to make it any easier to obey the orders. For the rest of the participants, however, greater self-control significantly increased the number of bugs they were willing to crush. They seemed keener to carry out the scientists' request, and they were better able to override any feelings of aversion to the task – turning them into more efficient killers.

People high in self-control appear to be more careful about when they commit an anti-social act and avoid getting caught

The "players" of La Zone Xtrême showed a very similar pattern of behaviours – only on a much larger scale. The experiment was inspired by Stanley Milgram's controversial experiments in the 1960s, which had tested whether participants would be willing to torture another person with electric shocks in the name of science. Milgram's experiment was taken to show people's unflinching obedience to authority – but the French researchers wanted to know which kinds of personalities were most susceptible. They found that the participants with higher self-control (as measured through a test of conscientiousness) were willing to dish out around 100 volts more to their partner in the game – to the point that their partner fell silent, feigning unconsciousness or death.

Interestingly, high agreeableness – the desire to please others – was the only other personality trait to increase this callous behaviour. "They tended to electrocute the victim more, probably to avoid an unpleasant conflict with the TV presenter," says Bègue. "They wished to be reliable people and to keep their commitment."

In their paper, Bègue's team contrast the discoveries with 20th Century philosopher Hannah Arendt's assessment of high-ranking Nazi Adolf Eichmann. Arendt famously coined the phrase "the banality of evil" to describe how mundane people, like Eichmann, can commit acts of great cruelty. According to Bègue's research, the traits that lead people to act immorally may not just be mundane – but actually desirable – in other situations. People with high conscientious and agreeableness are the people we would normally choose to be our employees or our spouses.

People with lower self-control are less likely to adopt healthy lifestyles – but one study showed that those with higher self-control were much more selfish

Toxic workplace

Bègue emphasises that this research needs to be replicated before we can draw general conclusions about human nature, but it is interesting to speculate whether traits like high self-control could predict someone's involvement in many everyday acts of immorality – large and small.

It would all depend on the strength of the social norms, says Lane. "I do think these results could generalise to other behaviours if people could convince themselves they were victimless crimes that others already do," says Lane. There is some evidence, for instance, that tax avoidance increases with conscientiousness – which would fit these findings. In the workplace, meanwhile, the model employees may also be the people who steal from the company "under the perception 'they won't even miss that money'," says Lane.

Uziel, meanwhile, suspects that someone with high self-control is more likely to act ruthlessly when group cohesion starts to fall apart, including times when their own sense of power or authority is threatened, or when they feel in competition with others. They could proverbially stab you in the back to gain a new promotion, for instance – or kowtow to a boss while disregarding how their behaviour will affect others.

If so, we might start to appreciate the people around us who are a little bit less disciplined and agreeable than the rest. They may frustrate us with their unreliability, but in La Zone Xtrême, at least, they are the ones you would want to decide your fate.

In the late 1950s, noted psychologist Walter Mischel spent several summers doing field research in a remote village on the Caribbean island of Trinidad. The villagers consisted of two ethnic groups—the Africans and the East Indians.

Each group lived in its own enclave and held negative stereotypes about the other group. According to the East Indians, all the Africans ever did was take it easy and party all day, never giving a thought for the future. And the Africans said, all the East Indians ever did was work hard and stuff their money under the mattress, never enjoying the moment.

When Mischel was working the children in a local school, he offered them a choice between a small treat right away or else a larger treat the next time he came to class. He found that the African children tended to choose the smaller treat right away, whereas the East Indian children often asked for a larger treat later. This was the birth of the so-called marshmallow test, what Mischel is most known for today.

In the classic marshmallow-test scenario, a preschooler is seated at a table with a small treat in front of them. (It could be a marshmallow, piece of chocolate, or a pretzel.) An adult tells them that they can have the treat now, but if they wait until the adult returns, they can have two treats instead. The adult then leaves the room, but a hidden camera records the child's anguished attempts to resist the temptation.

Some children waited and got their double reward, but others gave in and gobbled the single treat before the time was up. Looking at the films, it became clear that the successful children employed strategies such as closing their eyes or looking away, while those who failed the test focused their attention on the treat.

It's quite impressive to learn that at least some five-year-olds know how to divert their attention away from temptations, but even more amazing was the result of a follow-up study years later. Mischel found that the children who'd passed the marshmallow test at age five performed much better in school and scored higher on the SAT. In other words, an early ability to delay gratification has major implications for success later in life.

As Israeli psychologist Liad Uziel points out in a recent article, self-control is an even better predictor of academic success than IQ. Apparently, persistence is more important that intelligence when comes to getting good grades in school. Furthermore, adults high in self-control tend to be better adjusted psychologically and more emotionally stable. With so many benefits, many psychologists think we should be working harder to find ways to help people boost their self-control.

However, this "more is better" attitude is dangerous, Uziel argues. In particular, he points to three unresolved issues concerning self-control:

Different psychologists use the term self-control in different ways that don't seem to point to the same basic skill. So what kind of self-control should we be encouraging, anyway?

While a certain amount of self-control is good, in some situations too much can actually hinder a person, causing them to make worse decisions than if they'd just followed their feelings in the moment. So clearly more is not always better.

Encouraging people to exercise more self-control can also backfire, because doing so reminds them of something they lack. And since they believe they have little self-control, they don't exercise any.

Let's consider each of these issues in depth.

Regarding the first point, Uziel indicates that most people think of self-control as the ability to persevere in the face of hardship or temptation. This is exactly the situation that is set up in the marshmallow test. However, adults with good self-control know there are clear limits to how much they can resist giving in to instant gratification. The ice cream in the freezer or the potato chips in the cupboard go uneaten as long as you're in a good mood, but at the first sign of stress you're munching away before you even realize it.

Instead, adults with healthy levels of self-control know that the best way to resist temptations is to avoid them altogether. You don't keep ice cream or potato chips in the house if you don't want to let them be the outlet for your stress—few people binge on healthy snacks like apples and bananas. In other words, people with high self-control know their weaknesses and arrange their lives accordingly.

Regarding the second point, Uziel remarks that too much self-control is also detrimental to a person's well-being. People who exhibit over-control engage in rigid behaviors and thought patterns that keep them from adapting to current circumstances. For example, people who are very high in self-control tend to adhere strictly to social norms. Thus, someone who is fundamentally unhappy in their marriage may stick it out for fear of what others would think of them if they got a divorce.

Further, over-controllers will persist in activities intended to achieve a socially sanctioned goal even at the risk of their own health. Uziel cites a study that found binge drinkers were in fact more likely to have high versus low self-control. This is because those with low self-control stop drinking when their bodies tell them they've already had more than enough. But the high self-controllers ignore these body cues for the sake of winning the drinking game, and presumably, the respect of their peers. The same can be said for all those workaholics out there who risk their health through lack of exercise, poor diet, and inadequate sleep all so they can achieve whatever goal seemed so glorious at the outset.

Regarding the third point, Uziel comments on the elusive pursuit of self-control. When people are reminded that they need to exert more self-control, they're less successful at achieving their goals than when they're not reminded of it. This is because a self-fulfilling prophecy arises when people are reminded of the need for controlling their impulses.

This self-fulfilling prophecy goes something like this: I need more self-control. Which means I have no self-control. And since I have no self-control, I can't help but give in to temptation. Thus, self-control seems to depend on self-efficacy, which is the belief that we're capable of accomplishing the task we set before us. If you want to lose ten pounds, believing you have the ability to cope with any challenge that might arise as you pursue that goal is more important than your ability to stare down a pint of Rocky Road or bag of Lay's.

In the end, Uziel isn't saying that self-control is bad. Rather, it's the "more is better" mindset that's problematic. We need a certain amount of self-control to achieve our goals. But we also need to listen to our intuition and seriously consider what it's telling us. By persevering in this goal, am I endangering my health or my best interests? Am I so focused on myself that I'm hurting my relationships with the people who are important to me? These are questions that can only be answered through the wisdom of intuition—listening to what your body tells you about the current moment, rather than what your mind tells you about the far-off future.

Self-Control: Can You Have Too Much of a Good Thing?

Self-control – the ability to inhibit competing urges, impulses, behaviors, or desires and delay gratification in order to pursue future goals – is often equated with success and happiness. Indeed, failures in self-control characterize many of the personal and social problems afflicting modern civilization, including substance abuse, criminal activities, domestic violence, financial difficulties, teen pregnancy, smoking, and obesity (Baumeister, Heatherton, & Tice, 1994; Moffitt et al., 2011).

Due to the high value most societies place on capacities to delay gratification and inhibit overt or public displays of potentially destructive emotions and impulses—problems linked with excessive inhibitory control or 'overcontrol' have received little attention, or been misunderstood, and in these conditions it has been difficult for clinicians to recognize such problems.

However, too much self-control can be equally problematic. Excessive self-control is associated with social isolation, poor interpersonal functioning, and severe and difficult-to-treat mental health problems, such as anorexia nervosa, chronic depression, and obsessive-compulsive personality disorder (e.g., Lynch & Cheavens, 2008; Zucker et al., 2007).

Individuals with disorders of overcontrol are often quietly suffering, even though their suffering may not be apparent

Maladaptive overcontrol is characterized by four core deficits:

Low receptivity and openness: manifested by low openness to novel, unexpected, or disconfirming feedback, avoidance of uncertainty or unplanned risks, suspiciousness, hyper-vigilance for potential threat, and marked tendencies to discount or dismiss critical feedback.

Low flexible-control: manifested by compulsive needs for structure and order, hyper-perfectionism, high social obligation and dutifulness, compulsive rehearsal, premeditation, and planning, compulsive fixing and approach coping, rigid rule-governed behavior, and high moral certitude (e.g., there is only one right way of doing something).

Pervasive inhibited emotional expression and low emotional awareness: manifested by context inappropriate inhibition of emotional expression (e.g., exhibiting a flat-face when complimented) and/or insincere or incongruent expressions of emotion (e.g., smiling when distressed, showing concern when not feeling it), consistent under-reporting of distress, and low awareness of body sensations.

Low social connectedness and intimacy with others: manifested by aloof and distant relationships, feeling different from other people, frequent social comparisons, high envy and bitterness, and reduced empathy.

CHAPTER ELEVEN

Who's in charge anyway?

nfluenced by the discoveries of cognitive science, many of us will now accept that much of our mental life is unconscious. There are subliminal perceptions, implicit attitudes and beliefs, inferences that take place tacitly outside of our awareness, and much more. But we are apt to identify ourselves with our conscious minds. People who take the implicit attitudes test, for example, are often horrified to discover that they harbor racial prejudices or gender biases they were unaware of. If they accept the science, they are forced to believe that these attitudes are in some sense part of themselves. But they are an unwelcome part, an alien part, something to be got rid of if possible.

We are also apt to think that it is our conscious minds that are in control, much of the time; or at any rate, that our conscious minds are capable of taking control. When we pause to reflect, and act on our reflections, it is our conscious thoughts — our conscious beliefs, goals, and decisions — that get to control what we do. Or so we think. But this sense of self-control is an illusion. In reality our conscious minds are controlled and manipulated by unconscious processes.

'Untitled', 19th July 2015, by Rachael Carruthers. Image used with permission.

The reason is simple. Beliefs, goals, and decisions are never conscious. Rather, these states pull the strings in the background, selecting and manipulating the sensory-based contents that do figure in consciousness. Our conscious reflections are exclusively composed of sensory-like events such as visual images, episodic memories, inner speech, and so on. But because we swiftly and unconsciously interpret these events as manifestations of corresponding beliefs, goals, or decisions, we have the impression that we are consciously aware of such thoughts. You can, as it were, hear yourself as deciding to do something when the appropriate sensory-like episode — "I'll do it now", say — figures in consciousness. But your access to the underlying decision is just as indirect and interpretive as is your access to someone else's decision when they say such a thing out loud. In our own case, however, we are under the illusion that the decision is a conscious one.

What are my grounds for making these surprising claims? In short, the science of working memory. This is the sort of memory that is involved when one needs to keep in mind an image or a phone number to report or write down a while later. It is also the short-term memory system in which episodes of inner speech take place. Indeed, many in cognitive science think that working memory is the system in which all conscious episodes play out. It is sometimes described as a "global workspace" because its contents are simultaneously available to many different faculties of the mind (for forming explicit memories, for drawing inferences, for guiding reasoning and planning, and for reporting in speech). But working memory is a sensory-based system. It uses so-called "top-down attention" to activate and sustain imagistic representations in conscious form. There is no place within it for purely abstract non-sensory states such as beliefs, goals, or decisions.

Consider a particular example. You are studying for a French class, trying to learn the meanings of the designated words. But all the while images and memories are being sparked unconsciously by aspects of what you read, see, and hear. These are initially unconscious, but are evaluated by the bottom-up attentional network for relevance to current goals and values. These ideas then compete for top-down attention to enter working memory and become conscious. At a certain point you take a decision (unconsciously) to switch attention from the French words to an image of yourself on a sandy beach, with palm trees, blue sky, and green sea. Before you know it you are drifting in fantasy, while your goal of learning vocabulary struggles to regain control of attention. At a certain point it wins the competition and you snap back, tell yourself off for time-wasting, and focus your attention on the textbook again.

In this manner our conscious minds are continually under the control of our unconscious thoughts. We decide what to pay attention to, what to remember, what to think of, what to imagine, and what sentences to rehearse in inner speech. There is control, of course, and it is a form of self-control. But is not control by a conscious self. Rather, what we take to be the conscious self is a puppet manipulated by our unconscious goals, beliefs, and decisions. Who's in charge? Well, we are. But the "we" who are in charge are not the conscious selves we take ourselves to be, but rather a set of unconsciously operating mental states. Consciousness does make a difference. Indeed, it is vital to the overall functioning of the human mind. But a controlling conscious self is an illusion.

5 tips for impulse control issues

An impulse control disorder is characterized by the inability to resist impulsivity in a particular activity. A person with an impulse control disorder can't seem to stop himself from doing something that might hurt himself or people around him. When a person with an impulse control disorder begins to feel the urge or the temptation to commit this activity, he typically feels a rising anxiety, as if he'll explode if he doesn't do it. Once he performs the action, he may feel a huge sense of relief or even a rush of satisfaction and happiness, no matter how dangerous the activity was, or despite the negative or dangerous consequences of that activity.

There are officially recognized impulse control disorders, and they include kleptomania, pyromania, pathological gambling, trichotillomania and intermittent explosive disorder. More are increasing in popularity. These impulse control disorders are defined by how they limit a person's ability to control his or her actions, no matter how negative or devastating the end result.

A short breakdown of the officially recognized impulse control disorders

Kleptomania is pathological stealing – but it's not that simple. People with kleptomania typically steal items with little or no value. When a kleptomaniac steals, it's not usually a premeditated act, and the things he or she steals aren't often anything they even need in the first place. Those stolen items may be discarded, given away to friends, or sometimes even secretly returned. Like all other impulse control disorders, kleptomania takes over usually when the person is stressed, frustrated or anxious. The person with kleptomania feels as though the only way to feel better, happier or excited is to steal.

Pyromania is the act of setting fire, not out of malice, revenge or financial gain, but just to relieve the need to set fire. It is not an intent to harm anyone, but rather to witness the start of a fire or to learn about how to control or end it. The pyromaniac will feel a sense of anxiety or pressure before committing the behavior, and will often feel relieved or joyful immediately after setting and watching the fire burn.

Pathological gambling is the dangerous and often financially debilitating disorder that many times interferes with an individual's personal and professional life. People who are addicted to gambling report losing relationships, jobs, homes and savings. Most compulsive gamblers often seek ways to "fix" their financial problems their gambling caused by gambling even more, causing a cycle that leads to even deeper, and sometimes irreversible, grave financial losses.

Trichotillomania is the rare impulsive condition that causes an individual to pull out his or her hair. A trichotillomaniac will pull hair out from the scalp, eyelashes, legs, eyebrows, arms and pubic area. When trichotillomania becomes severe, the results are highly noticeable, so many with the condition take to wearing hats, wigs, or theatrical makeup that hides the hair loss. People with this condition say that they'll pull hair out due to stress or anxiety, but the after-effects of the hair pulling causes even further stress and anxiety. Many will pull hair out during regular activities like driving, watching movies or studying. Read more about this impulse control.

Intermittent explosive disorder is the condition that causes a person to lash out in anger, often in a hostile or violent manner. People with this condition have reported causing damage or destruction to property, or injury to individuals. Usually, a person with intermittent explosive disorder will feel anxious, stressed or nervous before an outburst, only to feel embarrassed, shocked or regretful after lashing out.

How to help a child control their aggression.

A sixth impulse control disorder is gaining more attention, and that's compulsive sexuality. People with this disorder report having sex with multiple partners they may not even know, have sex in dangerous situations or circumstances, or have sex in unsafe conditions. Many times, a person with compulsive sexuality spends more time thinking about sex and planning for sexual activity more than anything else. The act eventually becomes less pleasurable and exciting and just becomes an urge that can never be satisfied. Because of the stigma surrounding this disorder, it often goes unreported and undiagnosed, and is a secret kept from spouses, partners, friends or mental health professionals.

The exact causes of impulse control disorders remain unknown, but experts have linked them to other mental health disorders, biological or genetic factors, social circumstances and brain chemistry. Impulse control disorder treatment includes cognitive behavioral therapy and medication, although individuals living with any impulse control disorder can employ the following strategies for reducing impulsivity in an effort to help manage day-to-day challenges.

Five tips to controlling impulse control disorders

1. Know your triggers. Knowing what your triggers are is the first step to avoiding them and being able to better control your behavior and your day.

Jonathan, a 48-year old father of three and a person recovering from compulsive gambling, says he recognizes that his triggers are plenty.

"When people think of triggers (to gambling), they think of driving by a casino, or for people addicted to scratch tickets or whatever, walking by a convenience store," he shares. "But the truth is, it's so much more than that – it starts way before you think about the gambling."

Jonathan says that when he's stressed at work – like when his boss is micro-managing him, or his sales quota for the month seems too far from reach, he gets anxious. When his daughter starts talking to him about heartbreak, or the things all 18-year-old girls go through, he says, he gets anxious. Anything that propels him to feel stress, anxiety or frustration lead him to desire what he has grown to enjoy most, which is gambling.

"My trigger, if it had a face, would be anything that causes me severe stress," he admits. "I know now to catch that stress before it gets really big. I try to think bigger, outside of that initial reaction, and if I can catch it there, I prevent myself from fantasizing and craving the casino."

2. Plan for your triggers. Impulsive behavior treatment includes coming up with solutions to your weaknesses, and being prepared physically and mentally to deal with your triggers.

For Kyle, a 40-year-old musician and diagnosed pyromaniac, his trigger, he says, are candles.

"Just walking by candles does something to me, so I don't keep them at home," he says. For emergencies, while other people keep a small stock of candles in case of an electric blackout, he chooses to keep several battery-operated flashlights. Close friends who know of his disorder are sensitive to this, and don't put candles on birthday cakes, for example.

"I could be having the best day," he says, "but if I see a candle, I'll turn. They can't always be avoided though – I know that." It's in those situations, Kyle says, that he employs tactics he's learned in therapy – to see past the candle and understand that it's not the candle triggering him, but the memories surrounding it. He then seeks a different, healthier and more positive perspective.

"It takes a ton of work, and it's definitely easier to run," he says. "But the power you get from being able to stare down that fear in the face… it's a good high, every time."

Alyson, a young woman who has been living with and managing kleptomania, has discovered that running is a helpful practice.

"When I start to feel that angst-y, kind of panicked feeling, I run – literally," she shares. "I put on my running shoes and I just run. That rush of endorphins is amazing. I don't know how, but when I run, I just feel so relaxed and driven at the same time, like I can overcome or do anything."

3. Practice meditation. Meditation is one of the most effective ways to keep track of one's internal dialogue.

Simply put, meditation is the practice of concentration and self-regulation. Mindfulness is a type of meditation, which is the act of focusing on one's senses and being fully present in the moment. Mindfulness meditation, as it's often referred to, helps reduce impulsive behavior because if you're focused on what's happening in the here and now, you're a lot less likely to run off and do something else.

Meditation also increases your awareness of your thoughts and feelings – the good and the bad. It helps you recognize what might be an unproductive state of mind, so you can pause before you act.

Meditation doesn't have to be a formal exercise completed in a yoga studio; it can be done anytime, anywhere (just don't do it while driving!) You can be mindful when you're out walking, breathing in fresh air and appreciating nature. You can be mindful when exercising (walking, swimming, doing yoga). You can meditate by closing your eyes and focusing on each part of your body from toes up. There are many ways to meditate, and not one is better than the other – you simply have to find what's best and right for you.

4. Change the channel. Through the act of meditation, and employing techniques you may learn in therapy, you can change the image you have in your mind. When a trigger causes you to spiral backward in your mind, take control of a virtual remote control and change the picture you've drawn for yourself.

Children play games like Simon Says, Hide and Seek, Duck Duck Goose and Red Light Green Light as a way to learn self-control and impulse-control. You can play your own impulse control games. When you're triggered, play a game with yourself as if you were a child. To now, you have simply acted on your desires, acting and reacting impulsively – but now, in recovery, you're training yourself to see things through, considering the ramifications of your actions and learning to think about the broader picture before acting or reacting.

5. Be patient with yourself. This is the most important tool you could employ. It takes time to overcome impulse control issues; it won't happen overnight. Consistency is key, and as they say, slow and steady wins the race.

"It's easy to get down on yourself, or worse, go back to how things were before," says Alyson. "It's tempting to go back to what you know and what feels better, but it's important to remember that what 'feels better' actually feels a hell of a lot worse.

"I've found I'm not always successful, but I celebrate when I am, and I don't hurt myself when I'm not," she continues. "I accept that this is something I have to live with and it won't be without conflict or difficulty. Being patient with myself is a form of self-love and it really does help me get through the day."

Dark Side of Human Consciousness Concept

"Dark Psychology is both a human consciousness construct and study of the human condition as it relates to the psychological nature of people to prey upon others motivated by psychopathic, deviant or psychopathological criminal drives that lack purpose and general assumptions of instinctual drives, evolutionary biology and social sciences theory. All of humanity has the potentiality to victimize humans and other living creatures. While many restrain or sublimate this tendency, some act upon these impulses. Dark Psychology explores criminal, deviant and cybercriminal minds." Michael Nuccitelli,

Dark Psychology is the study of the human condition as it relates to the psychological nature of people to prey upon others. All of humanity has this potential to victimize other humans & living creatures. While many restrain or sublimate this tendency, some act upon these impulses. Dark Psychology seeks to understand those thoughts, feelings and perceptions that lead to human predatory behavior. Dark Psychology assumes that this production is purposive and has some rational, goal-oriented motivation 99.99% of the time. The remaining .01%, under Dark Psychology, is the brutal victimization of others without purposive intent or reasonably defined by evolutionary science or religious dogma.

Within the next century, iPredators and their acts of theft, violence and abuse will become a global phenomenon and societal epidemic if not squashed. Segments of iPredators include cyber stalkers, cyberbullies, cyber terrorist, cyber criminals, online sexual predators and political/religious fanatics engaged in cyber warfare. Just as Dark Psychology views all criminal/deviant behavior on a continuum of severity and purposive intent, the theory of iPredator follows the same framework, but involves abuse, assault and online victimization using Information and Communications Technology. The definition of iPredator is as follows:

iPredator

iPredator: A person, group or nation who, directly or indirectly, engages in exploitation, victimization, coercion, stalking, theft or disparagement of others using Information and Communications Technology [ICT]. iPredators are driven by deviant fantasies, desires for power and control, retribution, religious fanaticism, political reprisal, psychiatric illness, perceptual distortions, peer acceptance or personal and financial gain. iPredators can be any age or gender and are not bound by economic status, race, religion or national heritage. iPredator is a global term used to distinguish anyone who engages in criminal, coercive, deviant or abusive behaviors using ICT. Central to the construct is the premise that Information Age criminals, deviants and the violently disturbed are psychopathological classifications new to humanity.

Whether the offender is a cyberstalker, cyber harasser, cybercriminal, online sexual predator, internet troll, cyber terrorist, cyberbully, online child pornography consumer/distributor or engaged in internet defamation or nefarious online deception, they fall within the scope of iPredator. The three criteria used to define an iPredator include:

A self-awareness of causing harm to others, directly or indirectly, using ICT.

The usage of ICT to obtain, exchange and deliver harmful information.

A general understanding of Cyberstealth used to engage in criminal or deviant activities or to profile, identify, locate, stalk and engage a target.

Unlike human predators prior to the Information Age, iPredators rely upon the multitude of benefits offered by Information and Communications Technology [ICT]. These assistances include exchange of information over long distances, rapidity of information exchanged and the seemingly infinite access to data available. Malevolent in intent, iPredators habitually deceive others using ICT in the abstract and artificial electronic universe known as cyberspace. Therefore, as the internet naturally offers all ICT users anonymity, if they decide, iPredators actively design online profiles and diversionary tactics to remain undetected and untraceable.

Cyberstealth, a sub-tenet of iPredator, is a covert method by which iPredators attempt to establish and sustain complete anonymity while they engage in ICT activities planning their next assault, investigating innovative surveillance technologies or researching the social profiles of their next target. Concurrent with the concept of Cyberstealth is iPredator Victim Intuition [IVI], an iPredator's IVI is their aptitude to sense a target's ODDOR [Offline Distress Dictates Online Response], online & offline vulnerabilities, psychological weaknesses, technological limitations, increasing their success of a cyber-attack with minimal ramifications.

Arsonist

The Arsonist is a person with an obsessive preoccupation with fire setting. These individuals often have developmental histories filled with sexual and physical abuse. Common among serial arsonists is the proclivity to be loners, have few peers, and absolutely fascinated by fire and fire setting. Serial arsonists are highly ritualistic and tend to exhibit patterned behaviors as to their methodologies for setting fires.

Preoccupied by fire setting, Arsonists often fantasize & fixate upon how to plan their fire setting episodes. Once their target is set ablaze, some arsonists experience sexual arousal and proceed with masturbation while watching. Despite their pathological and ritualistic patterns, the serial arsonist feels pride in his actions.

Necrophilia

Thanatophilia, Necrophilia and Necrologies all define the same type of disordered person. These are people, and they do exist, who have a sexual attraction to corpses. The Diagnostic and Statistical Manual of Mental Disorders, by the American Psychiatric Association, classifies necrophilia as a paraphilia. A paraphilia is a biomedical term used to describe a person's sexual arousal and preoccupation with objects, situations or individuals that are not part of normative stimulation and may cause distress or serious problems for the person. Hence, a Necrophile's paraphilia is sexual arousal by an object, a deceased person.

Experts who have compiled profiles of Necrophiles indicate they have tremendous difficulty experiencing a capacity for being intimate with others. For these people, sexual intimacy with the dead feels safe and secure rather than sexual intimacy with a living human. Necrophiles have divulged in interviews feeling a great sense of control when in the company of a corpse. A sense of connection becomes secondary to the primary need for perceived control.

Serial Killer

A serial killer is a true human predator typically defined as someone who murders three or more people over a period of 30 days or greater. Interviews with most serial killers have revealed they experience a cooling off period between each murder. The serial killer's cooling off period is a perceptual refractory period whereby they are temporarily satiated with their need to cause pain to others.

Criminal Psychology experts have hypothesized their motivation for killing is the pursuit for an experience of psychological gratification only achieved via brutality. After they murder, these individuals feel a sense of release combined with egotistical power. The experience for them brings such gratification that they become wanton of feeling the experience of release and gratification once again.

"The term 'serial killings' means a series of three or more killings, not less than one of which was committed within the United States, having common characteristics such as to suggest the reasonable possibility that the crimes were committed by the same actor or actors." FBI

Sexual assault, rape, humiliation and torture are often involved during the course of their murders. Experts at the Federal Bureau of Investigations have outlined other motivations in addition to anger, rage, attention seeking, thrill seeking and monetary gain. Often, serial killers exhibit similar patterns in their choice of victims, how they murder their targets, and methods for disposal of the body. Criminal experts trained in behavioral analysis concur serial killers have a history of significant emotional, behavioral and social pathology. Although not absolute, serial killers tend to be loners who have trouble engaging in functional relationships.

Provided above are four examples of offenders and offender groups who commit abusive and/or violent bizarre acts sharing the common bond of having deep psychological deficits with distorted worldviews. These serious psychiatric and/or personality constructs, which may metastasize throughout their being, defies reason. What is it about these human predators, how do they function and socialize in their day-to-day lives? These brief profiles speak volumes about the dark nature of the human condition. In addition to all sharing mild to severe psychopathology, they all are perceptual loners with deep-seated forces governing their decision-making capacities.

The serial arsonist may not assault other people or find gratification from being a human predator as does the serial killer, but he actually experiences joy and elation from his fire setting. In addition to joy, he feels a sense of accomplishment from the devastation he has caused. His episodes of fire setting are extremely dangerous given he can cause harm to others, but the goal of inflicting pain or bodily harm is not his modus operandi.

For the serial arsonist, the big payoff is his sense of pride and distorted perception of accomplishing a brilliant feat of genius. His perverted sense of achievement, at times, lead him to become sexually aroused and masturbation ensues. The arsonist's behavior is reprehensible, illegal and dangerous, but typically does not involve premeditated murder. They live within an abyss of infernal obsession.

Although the Necrophile is not causing pain to another person or victimizing others, his actions are extraordinarily bizarre and absent of any sense of logic. The Necrophile's need for perceived control is so insidious that he develops a sexual attraction to a corpse. Imagine what the experience must be for him. He is sexually aroused by a lifeless body that is expressionless and absent of warmth. Most people yearn for connection during sexual intimacy, but the Necrophile does not require this. He becomes aroused by the experience of a total and complete disconnect. Clearly, his mind has entered a very dark realm.

The serial killer is one of the most despotic characters that manifests from the dark side. In films, court cases and news coverage, the serial killer is frequently a subject of intrigue. The essence of this epitome of deviant evil echoes a part of the human psyche that only the serial killer himself can realistically experience. Just as an alcoholic craves his next drink or an opiate addict yearns for his next fix, the serial killer becomes addicted to murder.

The serial killer speaks of the gratification and elevated sense of release once his murder has come to fruition. Unlike the necrophile or serial arsonist, the serial killer's sole endeavor is to extinguish life. For many of these assailants, sexual arousal by torturing their victims is a common theme. Although a common theme, there are other equally disturbing drives causing them to torture their victims.

These four examples are illustrations of the extent to which humans will go for the experience of power, pleasure and/or goal attainment. All of the criminal profiles described, involve assailants feeling a sense of gratification from their abusive and/or heinous actions. The reality is that these examples are merely basic profiles of four segments of the population of men and women who participate in criminal, abusive or deviant acts. The extent to which humans will go for sexual gratification, perceived control or financial gain is quite extensive and elaborate.

Before the advent of scientific advancements and the capacity of society to explain deviant human behavior, monsters and demons were the cause of such chaos. Unable to understand how people could commit such atrocities, metaphysical beings were the only logical explanation. Instead of fearing their neighbors, early civilizations concocted legends and tales of demonic beings. Werewolves, Vampires and Ghouls prowled the night stalking their prey.

Although contemporary society deems itself as advanced in its ability to comprehend the potential for humans to commit violent and heinous acts, learning how to reduce and/or prevent bizarre and deadly actions perpetrated by humans remains elusive. Our species is the only group of living organisms that participate in actions antithetical to our survival.

Dark Psychology is both the study of criminal & deviant behavior and a conceptual framework for deciphering the potential for evil within all human beings. This writer does not claim to have the proverbial "holy grail" of defining deviant human behavior, but rather a framework for inquiry and further investigation.

Many years ago, when this writer first became interested in the study of forensic and criminal psychology, he posited that aberrant deviant behaviors were part of a psychiatric illness not yet determined. With the passing of time and research, intrigue followed from the vast array of theories and explanations for why humans maintain a capacity to prey upon other humans.

The idea of Dark Psychology entered this writer's theoretical exploration and he began to formalize a set of concepts he believed plausible. The sum of his attempts ended in narrow concepts aimed at trying to explain the psychopath and sexual predator. Four years ago, this writer experienced his first paradigm shift pertinent to his present theory.

"A psychopath, as described by psychologists, is emotionally flat, lacks empathy for the feelings of others and is free of remorse. Psychopaths behave as if the world is to be used for their benefit, and they employ deception and feigned emotion to manipulate others." Bill Steele, Chronicle

Online (2011)

The construct that follows is this writer's best attempt at defining why humans are predators with the potential to prey on others for reasons that seem to lack purpose and/or understanding. This writer presents to you, Dark Psychology.

Dark Psychology Defined

Dark Psychology is the study of the human condition as it relates to the psychological nature of people to prey upon other people motivated by criminal and/or deviant drives that lack purpose and general assumptions of instinctual drives and social science theory. All of humanity has this potential to victimize other humans and living creatures. While many restrain or sublimate this tendency, some act upon these impulses.

Dark Psychology seeks to understand those thoughts, feelings, perceptions and subjective processing systems that lead to predatory behavior that is antithetical to contemporary understandings of human behavior. Dark Psychology assumes that criminal, deviant and abusive behaviors are purposive and have some rational, goal- oriented motivation 99.99% of the time. It is the remaining .01%, Dark Psychology parts from Adlerian theory and the Teleology. Dark Psychology postulates there is a region within the human psyche that enables some people to commit atrocious acts without purpose. In this theory, it has been coined the Dark Singularity.

Dark Psychology posits that all humanity has a reservoir of malevolent intent towards others ranging from minimally obtrusive and fleeting thoughts to pure psychopathic deviant behaviors without any cohesive rationality. This is called the Dark Continuum. Mitigating factors acting as accelerants and/or attractants to approaching the Dark Singularity, and where a person's heinous actions fall on the Dark Continuum, is what Dark Psychology calls Dark Factor. Brief introductions to these concepts are illustrated below. Dark Psychology is a concept this writer has grappled with for fifteen years. It has only been recently that he has finally conceptualized the definition, philosophy and psychology of this aspect of the human condition.

"Dark Psychology is not just the dark side of our moon, but dark side of all moons combined."

Michael Nuccitelli, Psy.D.

Dark Psychology encompasses all that makes us who we are in relationship to our dark side. All cultures, all faiths and all humanity have this proverbial cancer. From the moment we are born to the time of death, there is a side lurking within us all that some have called evil and others have defined as criminal, deviant, and pathological. Dark Psychology introduces a third philosophical construct that views these behaviors different from religious dogmas and contemporary social science theories.

"It is the individual who is not interested in his fellow men who has the greatest difficulties in life and provides the greatest injury to others. It is from among such individuals that all human failures spring." Alfred Adler

Dark Psychology posits there are people who commit these same acts and do so not for power, money, sex, retribution or any other known purpose. They commit these horrid acts without a goal. Simplified, their ends do not justify their means. There are people who violate and injure others for the sake of doing so. Within in all of us is this potential. A potential to harm others without cause, explanation, or purpose is the area this writer explores. Dark Psychology assumes this dark potential is incredibly complex and even more difficult to define.

Dark Psychology assumes we all have the potential for predator behaviors and this potential has access to our thoughts, feelings and perceptions. As you will read throughout this manuscript, we all have this potential, but only a few of us acts upon them. All of us have had thoughts and feelings, at one time or another, of wanting to behave in a brutal manner. We all have had thoughts of wanting to hurt others severely without mercy. If you are honest with yourself, you will have to agree you have had thoughts and feeling of wanting to commit heinous acts.

Given the fact, we consider ourselves a benevolent species; one would like to believe we think these thoughts and feelings would be non-existent. Unfortunately, we all have these thoughts, and luckily, never act upon them. Dark Psychology poses there are people who have these same thoughts, feelings, and perceptions, but act upon them in either premeditated or impulsive ways. The obvious difference is they act upon them while others simply have fleeting thoughts and feelings of doing so.

Dark Psychology posits that this predator style is purposive and has some rational, goal-oriented motivation. Religion, philosophy, psychology, and other dogmas have attempted cogently to define Dark Psychology. It is true most human behavior, related to evil actions, is purposive and goal oriented, but Dark Psychology assumes there is an area where purposive behavior and goal-oriented motivation becomes nebulous. There is a continuum of Dark Psychology victimization ranging from thoughts to pure psychopathic deviance without any apparent rationality or purpose. This continuum, Dark Continuum, helps to conceptualize the philosophy of Dark Psychology.

Dark Psychology addresses that part of the human psyche or universal human condition that allows for and may even impel predatory behavior. Some characteristics of this behavioral tendency are, in many cases, its lack of obvious rational motivation, its universality and its lack of predictability. Dark Psychology assumes this universal human condition is different or an extension of evolution. Let us look at some very basic tenets of evolution. First, consider we evolved from other animals and we presently are the paragon of all animal life. Our frontal lobe has allowed us to become the apex creature. Now let us assume that being apex creatures does not make us completely removed from our animal instincts and predatory nature.

"The greater the feeling of inferiority that has been experienced, the more powerful is the urge to conquest and the more violent the emotional agitation." Alfred Adler

Assuming this is true if you subscribe to evolution, then you believe that all behavior relates to three primary instincts. Sex, aggression, and the instinctual drive to self-sustain are the three primary human drives. Evolution follows the tenets of survival of the fittest and replication of the species. We and all other life forms behave in a manner to procreate and survive. Aggression occurs for the purposes of marking our territory, protecting our territory and ultimately winning the right to procreate. It sounds rational, but it is no longer part of the human condition in the purest sense.

Our power of thought and perception has made us both the apex of species and the apex of practicing brutality. If you have ever watched a nature documentary, this writer is sure you cringe and feel sorrow for the antelope ripped to shreds by a pride of lions. Although brutal and unfortunate, the purpose for the violence fits the evolutionary model of self- preservation. The lions kill for food, which is required for survival. Male animals fight to the death, at times, for the rite of territory or the will to power. All these acts, violent and brutal, evolution explains.

"Defiant individuals will always persecute others yet will always consider themselves persecuted." Alfred Adler

When animals hunt, they often stalk and kill the youngest, weakest, or females of the group. Although this reality sounds psychopathic, the reason for their chosen prey is to reduce their own probability for injury or death.

All animal life acts and behaves in this manner. All their brutal, violent and bloody actions relate to the theory of evolution, natural selection and instinct for survival and reproduction. As you will learn after reading this manuscript, there are no Dark Psychology applications when it comes to the rest of life on our planet. We, humans are the ones to possess what Dark Psychology attempts to explore.

Theories of evolution, natural selection and animal instincts, and their theoretical tenets, seem to dissolve when we look at the human condition. We are the only creatures on the face of the earth that preys on each other without the reason of procreation for the survival of the species. Humans are the only creatures that prey upon others for inexplicable motivations. Dark Psychology addresses that part of the human psyche or universal human condition that allows for and may even impel predatory behavior. Dark Psychology assumes there is something intrapsychic that influences our actions and is anti-evolutionary. We are the only species that will murder one another for reasons other than survival, food, territory or procreation.

Philosophers and ecclesiastical writers over the centuries have attempted to explain this phenomenon. We will delve into some of these historical interpretations of malicious human behavior. Only we humans can harm others with a complete lack of obvious rational motivation. Dark Psychology assumes there is a part of us because we are human, which fuels dark and vicious behaviors.

As you will read, this place or realm within all our beings is universal. There is no group of people walking the face of the earth now, before, or in the future who do not possess this dark side. Dark Psychology believes this facet of the human condition lacks reason and logical rationality. It is part of all of us and there is no known explanation.

Dark Psychology assumes this dark side is also unpredictable. Unpredictable in the understanding of who acts upon these dangerous impulses, and even more unpredictable of the lengths some will go with their sense of mercy completely negated. There are people who rape, murder, torture, and violate without cause or purpose. Dark Psychology speaks to these actions of acting as a predator seeking out human prey without clearly defined purposes. As humans, we are incredibly dangerous to ourselves and every other living creature. The reasons are many and Dark Psychology attempts to explore those dangerous elements.

It is this writers aim to examine the nature of Dark Psychology and to understand the origin and development of psychological phenomena motivating human beings to exhibit predatory behavior in the absence of any apparent rational motivator. This writer realizes his endeavor to succeed at this is next to impossible, but he hopes Dark Psychology will foster an interest in further exploration.

As mentioned above, there have been a plethora of philosophers, great thinkers, religious figures, and scientists who have attempted to conceptualize in a cogent way Dark Psychology. For this writer, Dark Psychology encapsulates all previous theories and explanations for human brutality.

It is this writer's assertion that Dark Psychology exists universally throughout the human species and manifests itself as predatory behavior (inclinations) without apparent rational motivation. He suggests that examination of Dark Psychology and its evolutionary foundation is vital. He does not suggest Dark Psychology is part of our evolutionary heritage, but he does believe it is vital to investigate the evolutionary foundation of Dark Psychology.

To be exact, this writer means the basis or rudimentary constructs we all possess. Throughout this manuscript, you will read how redundant this writer is when it comes to reinforcing the basic tenets of Dark Psychology. He does this not only for the reader, but also for himself in order to remain focused on the core constructs. Remember, Dark Psychology is like a spider's web attempting to capture all previous theories of human victimization and communicate them to others inspiring awareness, and encouraging self-awareness.

The more readers can visualize Dark Psychology, the better prepared they become to reduce their chances of victimization by human predators. Before proceeding, it is important to have at least a minimal comprehension of Dark Psychology. As you proceed through future manuscripts expanding this construct, this writer will go into detail about the most important concepts. Following are six tenets necessary to fully grasp Dark Psychology as follows:

1. Dark Psychology is a universal part of the human condition. This construct has exerted influence throughout history. All cultures, societies and the people who reside in them maintain this facet of the human condition. The most benevolent people known have this realm of evil, but never act upon it and have lower rates of violent thoughts and feelings.

2. Dark Psychology is the study of the human condition as it relates to people's thoughts, feelings, and perceptions related to this innate potential to prey upon others devoid of clear definable reasons. Given that all behavior is purposive, goal oriented, and conceptualized via modus operandi, Dark Psychology puts forth the notion the nearer a person draws to the "black hole" of pristine evil, the less likely he/she has a purpose in motivations. Although this writer assumes pristine evil is never reached, since it is infinite, Dark Psychology assumes there are some who come close.

3. Because of its potential for misinterpretation as aberrant psychopathy, Dark Psychology may be overlooked in its latent form. History is replete with examples of this latent tendency to reveal itself as active, destructive behaviors. Modern psychiatry and psychology define the psychopath as a predator devoid of remorse for his actions. Dark Psychology posits there is a continuum of severity ranging from thoughts and feelings of violence to severe victimization and violence without a reasonable purpose or motivation.

4. On this continuum, the severity of the Dark Psychology is not deemed less or more heinous by the behavior of victimization but plots out a range of inhumanity. A simple illustration would be comparing Ted Bundy and Jeffrey Dahmer. Both were severe psychopaths and heinous in their actions. The difference is Dahmer committed his atrocious murders for his delusional need for companionship while Ted Bundy murdered, and sadistically inflicted pain out of sheer psychopathic evil. Both would be higher on the Dark Continuum, but one, Jeffrey Dahmer, can be better understood via his psychotic desperate need to be loved.

5. Dark Psychology assumes all people have a potential for violence. This potential is innate in all humans and various internal and external factors increase the probability for this potential to manifest into volatile behaviors. These behaviors are predatory in nature, and at times, can function without reason. Dark Psychology assumes the predator-prey dynamic becomes distorted by humans. Dark Psychology is solely a human phenomenon and shared by no other living creature. Violence and mayhem may exist in other living organisms, but humanity is the only species that has the potential to do so without purpose.

6. An understanding of the underlying causes and triggers of Dark Psychology would better enable society to recognize, diagnose and possibly reduce the dangers inherent in its influence. Learning the concepts of Dark Psychology serves a twofold beneficial function. First, by accepting we all

have this potential for evil allows those with this knowledge to reduce the probability of it erupting. Secondly, grasping the tenets of Dark Psychology fits our original evolutionary purpose for struggling to survive.

This writer's goal is to educate others by increasing their self-awareness, creating a paradigm shift of their reality for the better, and inspiring them to educate others to endeavor upon the path of learning to reduce the probability of falling victim to those possessed by the forces explored by Dark Psychology. If you have been a victim of the Dark Psychology guided predator, do not feel humiliated, because we all experience some form of victimization at one time or another in our lives.

We all have a dark side. It is part of the human condition but agreed not to be well understood. An unpleasant reality, Dark Psychology surrounds us waiting patiently to pounce. As this writer has previously mentioned, Dark Psychology encompasses all forms of cruel and violent behaviors. We need only look at the senseless cruelty to animals. Being a dedicated pet lover, animal abuse to this writer is both vicious and psychopathic. As recent studies have suggested, animal abuse correlates with a higher probability to commit violence against humanity.

On the milder side of the Dark Continuum is vandalism of others property or the increasing levels of violence in video games children and teens plead for during the holiday season. Vandalism and a child's need to play violent video games are mild compared to overt violence but are explicit examples of this universal human feature this writer's theory illustrates. Most of humanity denies and hides its presence, but still the elements of Dark Psychology quietly lurk beneath the surface in all of us.

It is universal and everywhere throughout society. Some religions define it as an actual entity they call Satan. Some cultures believe in the existence of demons as being the culprits causing malicious actions. The brightest of many cultures have defined Dark Psychology as a psychiatric condition or spawned by genetic traits passed down from generation to generation.

This writer attempts to examine Dark Psychology's origin and nature to understand how the average, well-socialized person can wind up in the news, having committed an atrocity no one could have predicted. At any point during the day and throughout the night, since the beginning of recorded history, atrocities inflicted by one human on another are infinitely occurring. Although macabre, it is amazing how apparently decent people could participate in or allow such horrors to occur.

Thousands of these atrocities are evident throughout history. The holocaust during World War II and ethnic cleansing presently occurring in neighboring countries are a few examples. History, with the remnants of what Dark Psychology has caused, abounds with examples. As described above, Dark Psychology is alive and well and requires a serious inspection. As you continue to explore the tenets and foundation of Dark Psychology, a cognitive framework of understanding will slowly develop.

Dark Continuum

The Dark Continuum is an essential element to comprehend in your passage through the dark side of humanity. The Dark Continuum is an imaginary conceptual line or concentric circles that all criminal, violent, deviant and sadistic behaviors fall. The Dark Continuum includes thoughts, feelings, perceptions, and actions experienced and/or committed by humans. The continuum ranges from mild to severe and from purposive to purposeless.

Obviously, physical manifestations of Dark Psychology fall to the right of the Dark Continuum and more severe. Psychological manifestations of Dark Psychology lie to the left of the continuum but can be equally as destructive as physical acts. The Dark Continuum is not a scale of severity, in terms of range from bad to worse, but defines typologies of victimization in the thoughts and actions involved. When this writer further expands his thesis of the Dark Continuum, you will have a conceptual illustrated line depicting all forms of Dark Psychology ranging from mild and purposive to severe and purposeless.

Dark Factor

The Dark Factor is defined as the realm, place and potential that exist in all of us and is part of the human condition. This concept is one of the more abstract terms of Dark Psychology, because it is so hard to illustrate via the written expression. According to an online dictionary, a factor is anything that contributes causally to a result i.e., a number of factors determined the outcome. This writer will attempt to extrapolate for you in a cogent manner how Dark Factor resembles an equation.

The Dark Factor is not a mathematical equation, but a theoretical one. The Dark Factor is a set of events that a person experiences, which increases their probability for engaging in predatory behavior. Although research has suggested that children who grow up in abusive households become abusers themselves, this does not mean all abused children grow to become violent offenders. This is merely only one facet of a multitude of experiences and circumstances that contribute to the Dark Factor.

The number of elements that are involved in the Dark Factor equation is large. It is not the quantity of elements causing Dark Factor to become extreme, but the impact those experiences have on a person's subjective processing that makes the Dark Factor dangerous. Some of these facets include genetics, family dynamics, emotional intelligence, peer acceptance, subjective processing and developmental milestones and experiences.

Dark Singularity

The Dark Singularity is a theoretical concept similar to the definition of singularity at the center of a black hole. When this writer attempts to illustrate the concept of the Dark Singularity, he uses astronomy and cosmology as a metaphor to describe this concept. In astrophysics, the singularity is the absolute center of a black hole that is incredibly small, but dense in mass beyond mathematical comprehension. The theory suggests that the singularity is so dense and powerful, modern laws of physics and their mathematical equations become entangled.

A black hole is the huge expanse of space surrounding the singularity and so dense light cannot escape its grasp. At the center of all galaxies as well as ours, the Milky Way, is an all-powerful black hole with an infinitely small singularity at its center chock full of awesome energy. The Dark Singularity, as it applies to Dark Psychology, is the absolute center of the Dark Psychology universe. Simply put, the Dark Singularity is made of pristine evil & unadulterated pure malevolence. Farthest to the right of the Dark Continuum is the Dark Singularity. Also, part of the human condition is the Dark Singularity that no one ever reaches. The person who comes closest to the Dark Singularity is the advanced & severe psychopath who victimizes others with minimal motivation or purpose for his actions.

Because all behavior is purposive, the Dark Singularity is a theoretical destination never reached. The Dark Singularity is approached, but without arrival. The center of Dark Singularity is best explained as "Predators Who Prey Without Purpose." The closer a person approaches the Dark Singularity, the more heinous and malevolent their behavior becomes. At the same time, their modus operandi becomes less purposeful. As stated, this is an abstract concept that this writer will outline in his later writings.

A psychological and philosophical tenet to comprehend when venturing to visualize cognitively, the Dark Singularity, is that all behavior is purposive. This writer was blessed to have completed his doctoral degree in the mid 1990's at the Adler University in Chicago, Illinois. What he learned in those four years of academic studies was the theories and philosophies of Alfred Adler. Alfred Adler was a turn of the century medical doctor and psychologist who was a contemporary of Sigmund Freud, Carl Jung and an incredible philosopher as well.

Through this writer's studies, he grasped hold of many of Adler's theories. To this day, this writer interprets his world as defined by Alfred Adler, this great medical doctor and psychologist. Adler had many theories of human behavior and this writer integrated many of them during his construction of Dark Psychology. The three most valuable concepts from Adler for developing the theory of are as follows.

Adler believed that all behavior was purposive. From the moment we are born to the day we die, everything we think, feel, and do has a purpose. Nothing we initiate during our life span occurs haphazardly. Although his philosophy may initially sound simplistic, it actually is quite complex. With this premise in mind, the reason why people are benevolent is that it serves that person to be so because they reap the rewards of acceptance by their peers, loved ones and community.

Children taught to be kind, caring, and contributory have greater levels of feeling accepted and being part of a group. For Adler, feeling part of or a strong need for acceptance by others was the purpose for healthy functional behavior. Taking his theory of all behavior being purposive to the opposite end of the spectrum, malevolent behaviors serve a purpose as well.

Adler posited that people who behave in hostile or non-accepting ways were responding to a deep sense of inferiority. When people perceive they are not part of or not accepted by a social group, they move into negative directions. As they move further away from their innate purpose to be part of a social construct, the further away they move from treating others with kindness, respect and dignity. Under this tenet, Dark Psychology assumes that 99.99% of all behavior is purposive. Like Freud and Jung, Adler subscribed to the philosophy of Teleology.

Furthermore, as humans increasingly become discouraged, isolated and his social environment becomes increasingly fragmented, the more they lash out towards others in volatile ways. A prime example and quick illustration would be the narcissistic psychopath. The narcissistic psychopath is incredibly selfish, finds delight in victimizing others and purposely takes advantage of others without remorse. The concept of purposive behavior is paramount to the understanding of Dark Psychology.

As mentioned above, this writer strongly believes all human behavior is 99.99% purposive. The left over .01% is where he differs from Adler. This .01% is the Dark Singularity. Of all Adler's theories, the assumption of all behavior as purposive is vital to understanding Dark Psychology but varies slightly in the severest form of malevolent human behavior(s).

The second theoretical tenet Adler defined central to Dark Psychology is the concept of subjective processing. We all have thoughts, feelings and actions, in which cognitions and affective states influence behavior. Conversely, a person's behavior influences his cognitions and emotions. Defined as a system or what Adler called a constellation, the triad or trinity of human experience is comprised as an orbiting system of thoughts, feeling and behaviors. Adler added subjective processing to this system of human experience.

He believed that childhood experiences, birth order positioning, family dynamics, quality of social acceptance and the dynamics of inferiority vs. superiority worked in a manner to create a person's perceptual experience and trajectory of interacting with his world.

The easiest way to understand subjective processing and the perceptual framework is by visualizing a pair of sunglasses. These shaded glasses filter light and protect your eyes from the sun's harmful rays. Your eyes represent true reality and the sunglasses represent your filtering mechanism distorting the reality of the harsh sun light. Hence, your "perceptual sunglasses "?filter, distort and alter how you interpret information and respond accordingly.

This is how our subjective processing works but applied to the human condition. Reality exists and occurs every moment all around us. Subjective processing filters our reality to both protect and shield us from what we feel may be counter indicated to our purposive goals. If the human develops in an environment where he perceives being part of, belonging to, and accepted, his subjective processing filtering mechanism allows input that is much more accurate. A person socialized in what he perceives as a discouraging environment, their subjective processing becomes distorted and convoluted with selfishness and narcissism.

Regarding Dark Psychology, the goal is to assume that all people filter their world using subjective processing. Those people who are aggressive, violent or abusive are wearing a pair of proverbial sunglasses that are myopic and blurry. These people perceive others are out to harm them and move to assault or manipulate them first. Their subjective processing distorts their common decency, charitable acts and selflessness. Acts of kindness become foreign experiences or used to manipulate their social environment guided by a selfish modus operandi.

The third tenet valuable to understanding Dark Psychology is Adler's theory of Social Interest. Social Interest, postulated by Adler, is the compilation of perceptions, thoughts, and feelings translated into benevolent behaviors. Simply stated, the greater a person feels accepted by others, the more they feel part of, and the higher sense of belonging directly links to a person's Social Interest. People with high Social Interest are inherently kind, selfless, giving and receptive. All of these qualities of Social Interest further solidify their subjective processing to be positive and compassionate. High Social Interest equals low Dark Psychology impact.

Given that, we all have a Dark Factor within us; the person with high Social Interest keeps his Dark Factor subdued. The lower the Social Interest, the higher the probability the Dark Factor manifests. When a person feels discouraged, does not feel part of, does not experience a sense of acceptance and perceives his world as isolating, he is at a higher risk for exhibiting dysfunctional hostile reactions. Related to Alfred Adler & purposive behavior, subjective processing and Social Interest are central to understanding Dark Psychology.

Dark Psychology is a theoretical construct made up of a compilation of the philosophical tenets of Alfred Adler, Carl Jung, this writer's clinical experience as a psychologist, his academic and professional experiences as a forensic/criminal psychologist, and the many discussions with loved ones and colleagues over the years regarding deviant behavior.

As mentioned earlier in this manuscript, this writer's goal is to take fifteen years of thoughts and observations and translate them for others to investigate. The second goal, and most important, is this writer's hope that others will read his work, investigate his postulations and use them to defeat those that walk-through life looking to harm, victimize and brutalize.

Others postulate an entirely different tenet that is not psychiatric but defined as a depletion of conscience. This writer does not spend much time going into clinical studies or academic explanations, given the massive quantities of work compiled by those studying deviant behavior. The approach is to cast a wide net to cover relevant theories that this writer feels are highly valuable to understanding Dark Psychology.

A portion of the information relevant to understanding Dark Psychology is an overview exploring child development, family dynamics and other factors that work to formalize Dark Psychology. Although there is no way to exactly define why and how some people turn to the dark side, there are areas for exploration that help to explain how the "laws of probability" exist in the development of the antisocial personality construct. Other areas discussed include psychiatric illness, personality disorders and alcohol/ drug addiction as catalysts to deviant behavior. Psychiatric and alcohol/ substance abuse do not explain violent behavior, but this writer concurs these disturbances contribute to the understanding of Dark Psychology.

Contemporary social sciences investigate the areas of psychopathy, narcissism and personality disorders. These profiles are very intriguing and fuel much of the interest in the field of forensic and criminal psychology. Based on this writer's investigation, there seems to be an intricate combination of these three-character disordered constructs that that create truly despotic people. Once this writer has presented Dark Psychology thoroughly, provided will be alternative explanations for violent behavior. Another element of Dark Psychology discussed will include rapists, pedophiles and sadistic sexual offenders.

In the concluding manuscripts to follow, this writer will move into the most important themes defining Dark Psychology. It is within these arenas this writer offers advice on how to insulate oneself from becoming a future target for the human predator. Once you have a grasp of Dark Psychology, you will then have the ability to assess other people's actions as being potentially dangerous.

Employed in mental health for the last 25 years, working as a psychologist and forensic examiner for 10 years treating patients, evaluating court entangled defendants, and learning as much as he can as a forensic psychologist has given this writer the opportunity to offer those not involved in the pursuit of Dark Psychology, a set of tools for protection.

Remember, Dark Psychology includes all criminal and deviant behaviors committed upon other people. Although many people are intrigued by the discussion of the serial killer and psychopath, the vast majority of predators hunting human prey are not engaged in murder or sexual deviance. If this writer were to make an estimate, he would put the percentage of human predators at roughly 70% of the total pool of people who are out to victimize others, but who are not involved in murder or sexual deviance. 30% have been estimated to include criminal, deviant and violent offenders where physical contact is planned.

At the beginning of this introduction, this writer presented what he believes is a sound theory of the human predator. Dark Psychology assumes what lives within all of us is a potential reservoir of violent malicious energy. All humanity lies somewhere on the Dark Continuum with most being in the category of subtle, mild and with fleeting thoughts and minor shortfalls. The reality though is Dark Psychology is a universal phenomenon, and there is no dispute all of us, at times in our lives, have had at least thoughts of sheer violence and predatory fantasies.

The difference is most of humanity has never acted upon those thoughts. The reason is that we have a low Dark Factor equation compared to the predators. For them, their Dark Factor is elevated; influencing them to move in a direction towards what many define as evil and this writer defines as a trajectory accelerating towards the Dark Singularity.

Carl Jung and Alfred Adler's theories were a powerful influence in this writer's creation of Dark Psychology. He strongly adheres to Adler's philosophy that behavior is purposive. The only slight philosophical divergence from Adler is this writer's belief that all behavior is 99.99% purposive. He holds the remaining .01% as being within the realm of the black hole of the Dark Singularity. The black hole of the singularity is the area of evil that the predator comes close to, but never reaches.

The Dark Singularity is the potential in all of us to behave as a predator, hunting human prey completely and utterly devoid of purpose. This writer also strongly subscribes to Adler's theory of subjective processing. Dark Psychology and the human predator have a highly distorted perceptual filtering mechanism. For them, it is no longer about being compassionate and kind. Their subjective processing colors all of their thoughts, emotions and perceptions with blackness and venom.

At some point in the development of the human predator, he/she actuates his thoughts and feelings and starts down the long road of what contemporary criminologist call psychopathy. Within time, their subjective processing filter becomes divorced from experiencing remorse. They come to perceive that the victimization of others is deserved by those who are too naive to protect themselves.

Given that, a large portion of human development surrounds social acceptance, the predator somehow moves into the arena where his Dark Factor becomes an active force fueling an urge for the destruction of others. Once touched by the realm of psychopathy, he has entered the point of no return. Just as light cannot escape a black hole, the human predator cannot escape the path towards the Dark Singularity. Interviews conducted by forensic profilers and research scientists with convicted notorious psychopaths have proven the theory of accelerated movement towards the Dark Singularity.

Not only have psychopaths divulged a perception of experiencing a sense that their evil acts accelerate in frequency, but also their experience of acting as predator takes on an addictive quality. Using cosmology once again as a metaphor for Dark Psychology, the closer matter approaches a black hole, the faster mass accelerates and can never swing away from the black hole's awesome gravity. Interviews with psychopaths almost exactly mimic this universal law of astrophysics.

As society moves further into what is defined as the Information Age filled with digital technology and cyberspace, Dark Psychology and its impact on humanity will be tested at greater rates. Given the veil of anonymity cyberspace offers all humanity, the question remains is if the nefarious aspects living within all of us will recognize there is a realm of free reign called the digital universe.

"Dark Psychology is the study of the chasm within us all, which only few enter, and even fewer ever exit. Without a natural predator to cause humans to rally, we prey upon one another." Michael Nuccitelli Psy.D.

A reserch on self -control

It is also important to exercise caution when interpreting these findings, for a number of reasons. One of these reasons is that the majority of studies on self-control training have used passive control groups; in other words, they compared the effect of practicing self-control to the effect of doing nothing (see Table 1). This is not an ideal design for testing the effects of an 6 intervention, as any improvements in the trained group are potentially attributable to factors other than training itself. For example, participants may improve because they are treated differently from the control group, because they have different expectations about their improvement, or because they believe that the experimenter has different expectations about their improvement. In other words, any improvements in self-control in the trained group may be attributable to Hawthorne effects, placebo effects, or demand characteristics (see Shipstead, Redick, & Engle, 2012, for similar criticisms of studies training executive function). This problem is compounded when self-control performance is assessed using subjective measures that are especially susceptible to such influences (Greenwald, Spangenberg, Pratkanis, & Eskenazi, 1991; Shipstead et al., 2012), and when adherence to the training task is not assessed, which makes it difficult to confirm that completion of the training task is responsible for any observed improvements in the trained group. Although most previous studies asked participants to keep records of task performance, the methods used may not have reliably assessed adherence (e.g., paper diaries submitted after training; see Table 1), and rates of adherence generally were not reported, presumably because these records were designed more to motivate adherence than to measure it. The upshot of these methodological decisions is that the effect of training on self-control performance may have been over-estimated in previous studies. It is also possible that the data in published studies represents only a subset of the total data on the effect of self-control training. Evidence from various sources suggests that statistically significant findings are more likely to be published, both within studies (e.g., selective reporting of variables with positive effects; Franco, Malhotra, & Simonovits, 2016), or across studies (e.g., studies with null effects are less likely to be published; Franco, Malhotra, & Simonovits, 2014). Both factors would mean that the published literature overestimates the true 7 effect of self-control training. A recent meta-analysis by Inzlicht and Berkman (2015) attempted to quantify the influence of publication bias on the self-control training literature by providing a 'p-curved' estimate of the training effect, employing an analysis which uses the distribution of p values in a set of studies to estimate the true size of the underlying effect. Findings suggested that after correcting for possible publication bias, the true effect of training could be as small as d+ = 0.17. This analysis suggests that the effect of training may not be as robust as previously thought. However, as corrections for publication bias can only estimate the impact of missing data on the observed effect, the only way to establish the true effect is through adequatelypowered empirical research (Inzlicht & Berkman, 2015). In sum, variability in previously reported training effects, methodological confounds in previous studies, and the possibility of publication bias all converge to indicate the need for research that establishes the reliability of training effects using rigorous methodology. Does Training Generalize Beyond Ego Depletion Effects? Aside from questions about the true size of the training effect, another limitation of previous research on self-control training is that studies have typically employed lab-based measures as outcomes, such as persistence in solving anagrams (Bertrams & Schmeichel, 2014; Gailliot et al., 2007) or performing a visual tracking task under distraction (Oaten & Cheng, 2006a,

2006b, 2007). With the exception of Oaten and Cheng's (2006a, 2006b, 2007) questionnaire measures of self-control behavior and Muraven's (2010b) study of the effects of self-control training on smoking cessation, all of the evidence to date concerning the effects of self-control training has been based on participants' performance in laboratory settings. Whether performance gains on such tasks translate into improvements in self-control outside the laboratory is largely an open question. Self-control training has the potential to help people to 8 overcome their everyday self-regulatory challenges, but this potential can only be realized if improvements in self-control transfer from the trained task to the struggles that people experience in their everyday lives, and not simply to other experimental tasks. Evidence from studies of executive function training suggests that we should not automatically expect such transfer. Executive function training studies investigate whether or not it is possible to train cognitive abilities such as working memory and inhibition through practice. This type of training is conceptually similar to self-control training, because executive functions are thought to subserve self-regulation (Hofmann, Schmeichel, & Baddeley, 2012). However, it is distinct in that researchers in these two areas are typically interested in different outcomes (improvements in cognitive abilities vs. improvements in performance on unrelated tasks that require self-control). Researchers studying the effects of training executive functions have highlighted the importance of ensuring that training-related improvements do not merely reflect task-specific learning, but indicate genuine improvement in the underlying ability being trained – which should then generalize to unrelated tasks that draw upon this ability. Enriquez-Geppert, Huster, and Herrmann (2013) distinguished between different levels of generalization: modality transfer (improvements on the same task used in training, but using new stimuli), near transfer (improvements in other tasks targeting the same domain as the training task), far transfer (improvements in tasks targeting another domain), and meta-cognitive transfer (improvements in "everyday behavior, health, or overall quality of life," p. 4). While there is some controversy about the extent to which executive function training generalizes, highly-powered studies comparing the effects of training working memory with active control conditions have observed little generalization beyond near transfer (e.g., Redick et al., 2013), and a recent meta-analysis concluded that there was "no convincing evidence" for generalization beyond near transfer 9 (Melby-Lervåg & Hulme, 2013, p. 270). In other words, trained participants demonstrate improvement in the trained ability and on closely related tasks, but do not seem to reliably improve on other tasks that are supposedly related to the trained ability. Given the theoretical and conceptual overlap between executive function training and self-control training, it is puzzling that studies training self-control and studies training executive functioning have observed such different effects. Typically, self-control training studies have found that effects generalize to both similar and dissimilar tasks (e.g., avoiding sweets for two weeks appears to improve both participants' ability to avoid cigarettes and their performance on a computer-based cognitive task; Muraven, 2010a, 2010b). If training executive functioning is conceptually similar to training self-control, why would one type of training generalize widely while the other does not? One possibility is that the disparity is due to differences in the methods used to investigate the effects of training, rather than to differences in the underlying effects of training. Specifically, studies investigating the effects of training executive functions, which typically find that effects do not generalize, tend to have active control conditions and stringent measures of adherence and training performance (e.g., Harrison et al., 2013; Redick et al., 2013). In contrast, studies investigating the effects of training self-control, which typically find that effects do generalize, tend to have passive control conditions and fail to measure adherence or training performance. Thus, it is possible that the wide-ranging benefits observed after selfcontrol training could be attributable to confounds such as Hawthorne effects, placebo effects, and demand characteristics. Clearly, there is a need for research that assesses the extent to which training self-control leads to generalized improvements in self-control using methodologically rigorous designs. 10 The Present Research As we have seen, the evidence supporting the effectiveness of self-control training may be less robust than it initially appears. In particular, the use of passive control conditions, reliance on laboratory-based measures of self-control, variability in observed effects, and possible publication bias each offer grounds for caution in concluding that self-control can be improved through practice. The primary goals of the present research were, therefore, to (a) investigate the effects of self-control training using a rigorous methodology that rules out alternative explanations for any observed effects, and (b) examine the presence and reliability of the effects of training across various measures of self-control. We conducted this assessment using appropriate control conditions, randomization checks, and measures of adherence; and examined the effects of training on a wide range of outcome measures in both laboratory and field settings. A secondary goal was to gain a deeper understanding of the nature of self-control training effects. There are many unanswered questions about exactly how, why, and when practicing selfcontrol leads to improvements in self-control. For example, a distinction has been drawn between practicing behaviors that require self-control, such as avoiding colloquialisms, and engaging in tasks that train an underlying cognitive ability thought to subserve self-control, such as training inhibition via the Stroop task (Berkman, Graham, & Fisher, 2012). Previous studies have generally assumed that these training tasks will have equivalent effects on self-control outcomes (either using them interchangeably, or combining them; e.g., Hui et al., 2009), but this assumption has yet to be tested. Similarly, the literature to date is largely silent about the mechanisms underlying the effects of training, and about whether training is more effective for some people than for others. The broader literature on self-control suggests some plausible 11 candidates as mediators and moderators: For example, trait levels of self-control, beliefs about self-control, and executive functions have each been shown to predict self-control outcomes in everyday life (e.g., Tangney, Baumeister, & Boone, 2004; Job, Walton, Bernecker, & Dweck, 2015; Hofmann, Schmeichel, et al., 2012). Thus, assessing these variables at baseline and tracking whether and how they change over the course of training may help us to identify both the mechanisms underlying self-control improvement, and the particular groups that might experience greater improvements. Thus, to investigate the processes underlying self-control training, we included pre- and post-training measures of these potential mediators and moderators, and trained self-control using both cognitive and behavioral tasks. Method Participants Participants were undergraduate and postgraduate students at a UK university, recruited via email. Figure 1 shows the flow of participants through the study. Of the 185 participants who began the study, 174 participants (59% female) completed their assigned training program and attended their follow-up assessment (i.e., there was a 6% dropout rate). Eighty-nine participants were randomized to the two training groups (cognitive training, n = 45; behavior training, n = 44), and 85 were randomized to the two control groups (active control, n = 45; no-contact control, n = 40). Power Analyses For each dependent measure, our key aim was to assess the effect of self-control training (i.e., the effect of practicing self-control vs. not practicing self-control on the outcome of interest). As such, the critical comparison was between the participants in the training groups (who exerted self-control), and participants in the control groups (who did not exert self-control). 12 Therefore, power calculations were based on the ability to detect differences in performance between these two groups. Power analyses based on the effect size estimate of d+ = 1.07 from Hagger et al.'s (2010) meta-analysis of training effects on ego depletion indicated that 40 participants would be required, split between the training and control conditions, to achieve 90% power (two-tailed). However, because this estimate relates to only one of our dependent measures (the ego depletion effect), and because concerns have been raised over whether this figure overestimates the true effect size (e.g., Inzlicht & Berkman, 2015), we based our power calculations on 90% power to detect a medium-sized effect (d+ = 0.50) between participants who received versus did not receive training (two-tailed). This power analysis indicated that 172 participants were required in total (86 training and 86 control). This sample size also affords 80% power to detect the average effect size observed across social psychological phenomena (r = .21, equivalent to d+ = 0.43; Richard et al., 2003), and is nearly 3 times larger than the average sample size in previous studies of the effects of self-control training (see Table 1).1 Training Paradigm We assessed the effectiveness of both a behavioral training task and a cognitive training task in two separate conditions, following recommendations that researchers should employ 'single-domain' training (Berkman et al., 2012). The behavioral training condition involved the task used most commonly in previous research, namely, using one's non-dominant hand for all daily activities (see Table 1). The cognitive training condition required participants to perform the Stroop task and the stop-signal task; both tasks involve inhibition (Miyake et al., 2000), the component of executive function that is most closely related to the prototypical definition of selfcontrol (i.e., overriding unwanted impulses; Hoffmann, Schmeichel, et al., 2012). 13 We included two control conditions that allowed us to control for, and assess the impact of, confounding variables (e.g., the amount of contact that participants had with the experimenter, effort invested in the study, and expectations about improvement). Participants in the active control condition undertook sets of math and linguistic problems each day (difficult tasks that involve effort and persistence, but – unlike the tasks designed to train self-control – do not require participants to inhibit responses), whereas participants in the no-contact control condition completed an online questionnaire each week about cognitive failures. All participants worked on their assigned training program for six weeks (longer than the typical duration of training; Table 1). Participants with daily training tasks (i.e., all participants except those in the no-contact control condition) completed their tasks five days per week, from Monday to Friday. Participants either completed their tasks online (cognitive training, active control) or completed a daily online measure of task adherence (behavioral training), using a link provided to them by email, which enabled us to assess adherence for all conditions. At the end of each online session, participants completed items assessing their perceptions of the training task (the extent to which it required self-control, effort, and motivation). Participants completed these items again post-training, and also rated their perceived improvement in self-control (among rating their perceived improvement in various other skills and abilities, which served as distractor items). Further details about the training protocol for each condition are provided in the Supplemental Materials. Dependent Variables We examined the effects of training on a broad range of outcomes relevant to selfcontrol. Inspired by Enriquez-Geppert et al. (2013), we classified our self-control measures as representing 'near transfer' to similar tasks (e.g., performance in a laboratory-based ego 14 depletion paradigm), 'far transfer' to other conceptually-related tasks (e.g., intentional control of behavior), and 'meta-cognitive transfer' to important real-life outcomes (e.g., wellbeing). Figure 2 shows the dependent variables in each category. An overview of our measures is provided below, and further details about all dependent variables are provided in the Supplemental Materials. Near transfer: Performance under ego depletion. As in previous research, we assessed the effect of training on the ego depletion effect (i.e., the extent to which performance on a selfcontrol task was influenced by previous exertion of self-control). To provide a strict test of performance under depletion, we employed the 'severe depletion' paradigm (Vohs, Baumeister, & Schmeichel, 2012), in which participants completed a series of four consecutive tasks that each required self-control. Our key measure of ego depletion was persistence on a hand-grip task, measured before and after this set of depleting tasks. Far transfer: Self-control behavior in the lab. Studies to date have tended to assess the effects of training on self-control via performance or persistence on demanding or tedious tasks. Another way to assess self-control in a laboratory setting is by simulating a real-life self-control dilemma (cf. Denson et al., 2011). As such, the present research measured participants' performance of two behaviors that have been shown to depend upon self-control resources, but have not yet been tested as training outcomes; eating chocolate and displaying prejudice. Chocolate consumption was measured during a task presented to participants as a measure of consumer decision making, and prejudice was measured using an unobtrusive test developed and validated by Webb (2011), in which participants could take advice from Asian or White targets.2 We tested for main effects of training on these behaviors, but also considered the hypothesis that training might improve self-control only among participants with a predisposition 15 to engage in that behavior (cf. Govorun & Payne, 2006, Friese, Hofmann, & Wänke, 2008). We measured these predispositions by assessing implicit attitudes towards both targets (chocolate, Asian people) using Implicit Association Tests (IATs; Greenwald, McGhee, & Schwartz, 1998) and used these measures to assess whether training effects were moderated by implicit attitudes. We also assessed several other individual differences that might influence performance of these behaviors: namely, explicit attitudes, motivation to respond without prejudice, and dietary restraint (see Supplemental Materials for details). Far transfer: Intentional versus habitual control of behavior. Research indicates that there is a substantial gap between people's stated intentions to act and their subsequent actions (Sheeran, 2002). This gap is especially large when people want to modify habitual behaviors (Ouellette & Wood, 1998; Webb & Sheeran, 2006), which are particularly difficult to inhibit. As self-control influences the extent to which individuals can overcome habits and enact intentions (De Ridder et al., 2012; Neal, Wood, & Drolet, 2013), it is possible that self-control training could reduce habitual control, and increase intentional control, over behaviors. We assessed this hypothesis by asking participants to complete measures of habit strength, intentions, and behavior for a wide variety of behaviors before and after training, including both behaviors that would usually be considered good habits (e.g., studying, tidying, eating fruit and vegetables) and bad habits (e.g., gossiping, drinking alcohol, skipping lectures). If self-control training helps people to translate good intentions into action, we might expect to observe not only main effects of training on the incidence of positive and negative behaviors and future intentions to engage in those behaviors, but also stronger prediction of behavior by intentions and weaker prediction by habits among trained participants. 16 Meta-cognitive transfer: Self-control behaviors in everyday life. To assess whether the effects of training transferred to real-life self-control efforts, we assessed the performance of everyday behaviors involving self-control by asking participants to complete daily reports on their performance of seven behaviors, and to provide specific details about either the frequency (e.g., number of alcoholic drinks) or duration (e.g., time spent watching TV or playing video games) of each behavior (for a retrospective measure of similar behaviors, see Oaten & Cheng, 2006a, 2006b). We also measured variables that have been shown to relate to behavioral enactment in studies using experience sampling (Hofmann, Baumeister, Förster, & Vohs, 2012; Hofmann, Vohs, & Baumeister, 2012), such as the strength of desire to perform each behavior. Finally, in keeping with the idea that successful self-control involves not only the effortful inhibition of unwanted behaviors but also the enactment of desired behaviors (cf. Fujita, 2011), we asked participants to report the amount of time that they spent engaging in behaviors such as exercising and studying daily, and to report their perceived success in achieving health, academic, and relationship goals each day. Meta-cognitive transfer: Well-being. Greater self-control is associated with improved well-being (e.g., De Ridder et al., 2012) and training self-control might therefore be expected to enhance well-being. The present research operationalized well-being in terms of changes from pre- to post-training in positive and negative emotions and well-being, and included a measure of life satisfaction after training. Participants also completed measures concerning their use of emotion regulation strategies before and after training, as strategy use could mediate any effects of training on well-being. In particular, we hypothesized that self-control training may increase the resources available to employ strategies such as reappraisal (cf. Urry & Gross, 2010), a highly effective means of managing emotions (Webb, Miles, & Sheeran, 2012). 17 Potential mediators and moderators of training effects. To discover more about how training works and for whom it works best, the present research measured three individual difference variables: trait self-control, implicit theories about willpower and temptation (i.e., the extent to which participants believe that willpower is a limited resource that can be depleted by resisting temptations), and executive function (assessed using three tasks measuring the components of inhibition, shifting, and updating; Miyake et al., 2000). All of these variables were measured both before and after training, as they constitute both potential moderators (pre-existing differences between participants could influence the effectiveness of training) and potential mediators (changes in these variables over time could help us to understand the mechanisms underlying training effects on self-control). Additional individual differences (impulsivity, regulatory focus, and conscientiousness) were also measured at baseline in order to confirm the success of our randomization procedure.3 Procedure The study was presented to all participants as an investigation of whether "brain training" could enhance cognitive function. The rationale for the measures and training tasks did not mention self-control (e.g., the stated purpose of the behavioral training task was "to strengthen visuo-motor co-ordination, an ability that is often inhibited in people who have a cognitive impairment"). Participants could receive up to £65 (approximately $100) for participating in the study, depending on their performance, and could also earn entries into prize draws. After random assignment to conditions, participants completed baseline assessments online. All participants then began their assigned training task on the same date in order to minimize variability due to time-of-semester effects. After completing six weeks of training, participants completed online assessments, a 7-day self-control diary, and attended the laboratory 18 in person to complete follow-up assessments (detailed information about the timing of each assessment in relation to the training period can be found in the Supplemental Materials). Figure 3 shows the structure of the study. Results Randomization Checks To establish whether participants in the training and control conditions were equivalent at baseline, we tested for group differences on all baseline measures relevant to self-control (see Supplemental Materials for descriptive statistics for all variables). Trained participants had higher levels of trait self-control at baseline, $t(172) = 2.24$, $p = .03$, $d+ = 0.34$, and marginally higher levels of conscientiousness, $t(172) = 1.95$, $p = .05$, $d+ = 0.30$, all other $ps > .08$. We therefore conducted all analyses of the effects of training on outcomes both with and without these variables as covariates; unless otherwise stated, the inclusion of these covariates did not alter our observed effects. Manipulation Checks To ensure that participants completed the training program to which they had been assigned, we assessed the number of sessions that participants in each condition completed. Participants in the cognitive training condition completed an average of 28 training tasks out of 30 ($M = 28.44$, $SD = 1.84$, range 23-30), participants in the behavioral training condition completed an average of 29 out of 30 reports concerning use of their non-dominant hand ($M = 29.18$, $SD = 1.65$, range 23-30), and participants in the active control condition completed an average of 29 tasks out of 30 ($M = 28.53$, $SD = 1.77$, range $= 22-30$). There were no differences between these conditions, $F(2, 131)$

= 0.43, p = .65. Participants in the no-contact control condition completed an average of 4.70 out of 6 questionnaires (SD = 1.91, range = 0-6). 19 For the behavioral and cognitive training conditions, we also analyzed data from the training tasks, which allowed us to determine whether participants performed the training tasks correctly and whether performance improved over time. Findings from these analyses are reported in the Supplemental Materials and supported the idea that participants adhered to the training procedures (we did not exclude any participants on the basis of these analyses). Perceptions of Training and Beliefs About Its Likely Effects We first analyzed whether participants in the training and control conditions perceived the tasks as requiring equal amounts of effort and self-control and were equally motivated to undertake training. We analyzed both the overall judgments provided at the end of the study, and daily ratings provided at the end of each training task (by all participants except no-contact controls). Training participants perceived that their tasks required more self-control than control participants, as rated both at the end of training, t(171) = 3.31, p = .001, d+ = 0.50, and on a daily basis, t(132) = 3.09, p = .002, d+ = 0.56. Training participants also reported that their tasks required more effort, but only when rated retrospectively, t(171) = 3.70, p < .001, d+ = 0.56, and not when rated immediately after each task, t(132) = 0.00, p = 1.00, d+ = 0.00. Follow-up analyses suggested that these effects were driven by participants in the behavioral training group providing higher ratings of effort and self-control than participants in each of the other groups, ts > 2.83, ps < .006, d+ > 0.60. Participants in the training and control conditions did not differ in their reported motivation to complete the tasks, either assessed retrospectively or daily, ts < 1.61, ps > .11, d+ < 0.30. Participants in the training and control conditions differed in the extent to which they felt that training had improved their self-control, t(171) = 3.58, p < .001, d+ = 0.54. Follow-up comparisons showed that participants who received behavioral training believed that their self- 20 control had improved to a greater extent than did participants in the other three conditions, ts > 2.51, ps < .02, d+ > 0.54, which did not differ from one another, ts < 1.67, ps > .10, d+ < 0.36. Near Transfer Our primary test of the effect of self-control training on ego depletion was change in persistence on the handgrip task from pre- to post-depletion (see Table 2). A repeated-measures ANOVA with time (pre- vs. post-test) as a within-participants IV, condition (training vs. control) as a between-participants IV, and handgrip performance as the dependent variable, revealed a significant effect of time, F(1, 171) = 7.66, p = .01, partial $\eta2$ = .04, but no significant effect of condition, F(1, 171) = 3.37, p =.07, partial $\eta2$ = .02, and no interaction between condition and time, F(1, 171) = 0.03, p = .86, partial $\eta2$ < .001. Participants held the handgrip for longer after completing the four self-control tasks (M = 56.96, SD = 49.65) than before doing so (M = 48.14, SD = 45.09), d+ = -0.30, but this change in performance over time did not differ between training and control participants. In other words, we neither observed the standard effect of ego depletion, nor did we find any influence of self-control training on the ego depletion effect. While the main purpose of asking participants to complete a series of self-control tasks was to increase the likelihood that self-control performance would be subsequently impaired (as Vohs et al., 2012, observed), ego depletion studies typically find that self-control performance suffers after completing only a single self-control task, and previous training studies have found that training attenuates this effect. Thus, we might expect to observe performance differences between trained and control groups not only after the depleting tasks, but also within the series of depleting tasks, and these differences might become more pronounced as participants complete more self-control tasks. We therefore computed standardized performance scores for each of the four tasks, and assessed whether condition influenced performance across the series of tasks. A 21 repeated-measures ANOVA with task (first, second, third, fourth) as a within-participants IV, condition (training vs. control) as a between-participants IV, and performance as the dependent variable showed no effect of condition, F(1, 171) = 0.22, p =.64, partial $\eta2$ = .001, and no interaction between condition and task, F(3, 513) = 0.27, p =.85, partial $\eta2$ = .002. Thus, consistent with the findings of the effect of training on handgrip performance, these analyses suggest that training did not affect self-control performance. MANOVA also showed no effect of condition on participants' judgments of the amount of effort or self-control required by each of the depleting tasks or how motivated they were to perform the tasks F(3, 167) = 1.14, Wilk's Λ = 0.98, p = .34, partial $\eta2$ = .02. Far Transfer To determine whether training influenced the performance of behaviors requiring selfcontrol, we examined our measures of chocolate consumption and prejudice.4 Participants in the training and control conditions did not eat different amounts of chocolate, t(167) = 0.47, p = .64, d+ = .07, nor were they more biased toward Asian targets in the advice taking task, t(156) = 0.01, p = .99, d+ = .002 (see Table 2). We also conducted hierarchical regression analyses to examine whether the association between implicit attitudes and behavior was moderated by training. Implicit attitudes toward Asian people (standardized scores) and a dummy-coded variable for training condition (0 = control groups, 1 = training groups) were entered in the first step of an analysis to predict prejudiced behavior; however, neither variable significantly predicted prejudice (ps > .79). At the second step, the interaction term was entered, which was also nonsignificant, β = -0.05, t(154) = -0.45, p = .65. The same analysis with the amount of chocolate eaten as the dependent variable also revealed that neither implicit attitudes nor condition 22 significantly predicted chocolate consumption (ps > .65).5 At the second step, the interaction term for these two predictors was also non-significant, β = -0.06, t(165) = -0.48, p = .63. To assess whether training increased participants' intentions to engage in positive behaviors (e.g., studying, tidying, eating fruit and vegetables) and decreased participants' intentions to engage in negative behaviors (e.g., gossiping, drinking alcohol, skipping lectures), we performed a repeated-measures MANOVA on intentions to engage in the 27 measured behaviors. For this analysis, all measures were coded so that higher scores indicated 'good' intentions (e.g., intentions to binge drink were coded such that higher scores represented weaker intentions to engage in the behavior, whereas for studying higher scores indicated stronger intentions). The within-participants IV was time (pre- vs. post-training) and the betweenparticipants IV was condition (training vs. control). There was no effect of condition, F(27, 145) = 1.19, Wilk's Λ = 0.82, p = .26, partial $\eta2$ = .18, indicating that participants in the training and control conditions had similar intentions. There was, however, a significant effect of time, F(27, 145) = 3.88, Wilk's Λ = 0.58, p < .001, partial $\eta2$ =.42, indicating that participants generally reported stronger intentions to engage in good behaviors and avoid bad behaviors at the end, as compared to at the start, of the study. The interaction between condition and time was nonsignificant, F(27, 145) = 1.24, Wilk's Λ = 0.81, p = .21, partial $\eta2$ =.19, indicating that this positive change in intentions from pre- to post-training was similar in both conditions. In order to assess whether training changed participants' behavior, we carried out a MANOVA with performance of each the 27 behaviors at post-test as dependent variables and condition (training vs. control) as the between-participants IV. All measures were coded so that positive scores reflected greater performance of the behavior in question.

As there were some extreme outliers, all values ±3 SD from the mean for each behavior were replaced with the next 23 most extreme value (resulting in the replacement of 50 values, or 1.1% of the total). There was no effect of condition on behavior, $F(27, 141) = 0.99$, Wilk's $\Lambda = 0.84$, $p = .48$, partial $\eta2 = .16$, indicating no overall difference in behavior between participants in the training and control conditions.6 We then investigated whether habit strength and intentions were differentially predictive of behavior between conditions. Following Danner, Aarts, and de Vries (2008), a measure of the extent to which each behavior was habitual was created by converting the rating for context stability to a -4 to +4 scale, and multiplying this by frequency of past behavior. For each participant, we then computed the correlation between the strength of habits and post-training behavior across the 27 behaviors, as well as the correlation between intentions at baseline and post-training behavior. As correlations are not normally distributed, we tested for differences in the magnitude of these correlations between conditions using Mann-Whitney U tests. These tests showed that there was no significant difference between the training and control conditions in how well behavior was predicted by habits, $U = 3346.50$, $p = 0.28$, or how well behavior was predicted by baseline intentions, $U = 3296.00$, $p = 0.18$. Habits positively predicted behavior among both participants who received self-control training (median correlation; $r = .21$) and participants in the control conditions (median $r = .32$). Likewise, intentions positively predicted behavior among both participants who received self-control training (median $r = .31$) and participants in the control conditions (median $r = .36$). However, the magnitude of the correlations did not differ significantly between participants who received versus did not receive training. Meta-Cognitive Transfer 24 The information that participants provided in the diary was used to compute the amount of money spent on non-essential items over the 7 days, the number of unhealthy snacks and meals eaten, the total number of minutes that participants spent engaging in negative behaviors related to self-control (namely, internet use, social networking, socializing, and watching TV), and the total number of minutes that participants spent engaging in positive behaviors related to self-control (namely, exercising, studying and doing household chores). Across all behaviors, a total of three outliers (> 3 SD above the mean) were replaced with the next most extreme value. Data for each of the behaviors was positively skewed, such that most participants performed the behaviors relatively infrequently. A square root transformation was therefore performed on each variable to improve normality. A MANOVA on these four variables found no effect of condition on behavior, $F(4, 168) = 0.53$, Wilk's $\Lambda = 0.99$, $p = .71$, partial $\eta2 = .01$. The amount of alcohol that participants reported consuming was extremely skewed (participants reported consuming no alcohol on 78% of days within our sample, and 38% of participants did not drink alcohol on any day during the week). Therefore, chi-square was used to assess whether training condition influenced the likelihood that participants drank on more than one day during the diary period (43% of participants drank on more than one day). There was no significant effect of condition, $\chi^2(1, N = 174) = 2.22$, $p = .14$. Similarly, condition did not influence perceived success at achieving health goals, relationship goals, or academic goals, $F(3, 169) = 1.32$, Wilk's $\Lambda = 0.98$, $p = .27$, partial $\eta2 = .02$. As no group differences in behavior were observed, we did not conduct mediation analyses to investigate whether participants' ratings of their desire to perform each of the different behaviors, whether they wanted to control the desire, experienced conflict between the desire and other goals, the extent to which they attempted to resist the desire, and the extent to 25 which they took action to reduce the desire mediated the effect of training. Indeed, consistent with the lack of effects of training on behavior, a MANOVA with condition (training, control) as a between-participants IV and scores for each of these five questions as the dependent variables confirmed that there was no overall effect of condition on these ratings, $F(5, 167) = 0.30$, Wilk's $\Lambda = 0.99$, $p = .91$, partial $\eta2 = .01$. To examine the effect of training on well-being, a MANOVA with time (pre- vs. posttraining) as a within-participants IV, condition (training vs. control) as a between-participants IV, and positive emotion, negative emotion, and overall well-being as the dependent variables revealed a multivariate effect of time, $F(3, 169) = 30.66$, Wilk's $\Lambda = 0.65$, $p < .001$, partial $\eta2 = .35$. Follow-up univariate tests revealed that participants reported similar levels of overall wellbeing ($p = .98$) but fewer negative and fewer positive emotions ($ps < .001$) at the end of the study as compared to the beginning. There was also a significant effect of condition, $F(3, 169) = 2.81$, Wilk's $\Lambda = 0.95$, $p = .04$, partial $\eta2 = .05$, but no interaction between condition and time, $F(3, 169) = 1.14$, Wilk's $\Lambda = 0.98$, $p = .33$, partial $\eta2 = .02$, indicating that participants in the training conditions had higher overall well-being than participants in the control conditions ($p = .004$), but that this effect was not driven by an increase in well-being from pre- to post-training. The effect of condition was no longer present when covarying for baseline differences in trait self-control and conscientiousness, $F(3, 167) = 1.83$, Wilk's $\Lambda = 0.97$, $p = .14$, partial $\eta2 = .03$, however. Life satisfaction was measured at follow-up only: Participants in the training conditions reported being more satisfied with their lives than participants in the control conditions, $F(1, 171) = 5.49$, $p = .02$, partial $\eta2 = .03$, but again, this effect was no longer present when covarying for baseline differences in trait self-control and conscientiousness, $F(1, 169) = 3.44$, $p = .07$, partial $\eta2 = .02$. Multivariate analyses also indicated no effect of condition on daily 26 reports of positive and negative emotional experiences, $F(2, 170) = 1.17$, Wilk's $\Lambda = 0.99$, $p = .31$, partial $\eta2 = .01$. Overall, these findings suggest pre-existing differences in well-being between participants in the training and control conditions, but provide no evidence for changes in well-being as a function of training.7 Effects of Training on Potential Mediator Variables Levels of trait self-control, implicit theories about willpower, implicit theories about resisting temptation, and scores on each of the measures of executive function were entered into a repeated-measures MANOVA with time (pre-training vs. post-training) as a within-participants IV and condition (training vs. control) as a between-participants IV. 8 There was an overall effect of time, $F(6, 159) = 21.04$, Wilk's $\Lambda = 0.56$, $p < .001$, partial $\eta2 = .44$, but no significant effect of condition, $F(6, 159) = 1.71$, Wilk's $\Lambda = 0.94$, $p = .12$, partial $\eta2 = .06$, and no interaction between condition and time, $F(6, 159) = 0.48$, Wilk's $\Lambda = 0.98$, $p = .83$, partial $\eta2 = .02$. These findings indicate that participants tended to improve on these measures over time but that the improvements were similar in the training and control groups.9 Did Training Work For Some Participants But Not Others? To investigate the hypothesis that training might only be effective among some participants (e.g., people lower in relevant abilities might benefit more from it), we conducted a series of hierarchical regression analyses to examine the interaction between the relevant baseline variables (measures of trait self-control, implicit theories about willpower, and executive function) and training (control = 0, training = 1) in predicting each fo the key dependent variables in Table 2. Due to the large number of tests undertaken, we controlled the family-wise error rate using the Holm-Bonferroni correction (Holm, 1979). Using this correction, none of the variables significantly moderated the effect of condition on outcomes (without this 27 correction, 7% of these analyses reached significance, similar to chance level; we report the raw analyses in the Supplemental Materials). We conclude that the hypothesis that training particularly benefited specific groups of people is rejected. How Confident Can We Be in Our Null Findings? The analyses reported thus far suggest that repeated practice of tasks involving selfcontrol did not improve self-control. Compared to participants who did not receive self-control training, trained participants did not show reduced ego depletion effects, and were no better at intentionally controlling their behavior or exerting self-control in everyday life. To assess whether our findings provide conclusive evidence for a null effect of self-control training, we undertook Bayesian analyses. A non-significant effect in traditional null hypothesis testing could indicate either the absence of a true effect or that the data are not sensitive enough to detect a true effect. Bayesian analyses allow conclusions to be drawn about whether non-significant results provide conclusive support for the null hypothesis, relative to a pre-existing theory (Dienes, 2011). The outcome in our study that maps most closely onto previous research, and for which we have a prior estimate of the expected effect size, is the impact of training on ego depletion. We therefore used the estimate of the effect of training on ego depletion reported by Hagger et al. (namely, d+ = 1.07) as the basis of our experimental hypothesis. This estimate was transformed to Fisher's Z to ensure a normal distribution (using the formulas described in Lipsey & Wilson, 2001) and represented the experimental hypothesis using a half-normal distribution with a mean of zero and this estimate as the standard deviation (see guidelines in Dienes, 2011). The Bayes factor indicates the relative strength of the evidence for the null hypothesis versus this experimental hypothesis, given the data. Bayes factors below 0.3 indicate substantial evidence 28 for the null hypothesis, Bayes factors above 3 indicate substantial evidence for the experimental hypothesis, and a Bayes factor between 0.3 and 3 indicates that the data are unable to differentiate the two hypotheses (Jeffreys, 1939/1961). As the present research included multiple measures of self-control performance under depletion, our analysis compared participants in the training conditions with participants in the control conditions on a combined score representing performance across the second, third and fourth self-control tasks and change in handgrip performance from pre- to post-depletion (i.e., performance on all tasks after the initial exertion of self-control). The Bayes factor was 0.23, which indicates that our data are more consistent with a null effect of training on ego depletion than with the experimental hypothesis. Bayes factors for individual tasks ranged from 0.11 (performance on the second self-control task) to 0.33 (performance on the fourth self-control task), indicating relatively consistent evidence for the null hypothesis across the series of tasks. We can therefore conclude that our data are more consistent with the null hypothesis than with Hagger et al.'s effect size estimate and that our data are sufficiently sensitive to distinguish between these hypotheses. If the effect size estimate from Hagger et al.'s (2010) meta-analysis was influenced by confounding factors as well as training effects, or if publication bias resulted in the omission of studies with null effects from their overall estimate, then the effect size used as the basis of our Bayesian analysis could overestimate the strength of prior evidence for training effects. Indeed, as discussed earlier, a recent paper estimated that the actual effect of training might be small (d+ = 0.17, Inzlicht & Berkman, 2015). Given uncertainty about what can be concluded from past data, we also performed a Bayesian analysis to test whether our data supported this smaller estimate of the effect of training, using the same method described above. The Bayes factor for 29 this revised analysis was 0.93, which indicates that our data are consistent with both a true effect of d+ = 0.17 and with the null hypothesis (i.e., d+ = 0.00), and cannot differentiate these two possibilities (indeed, demonstrating a between-groups effect size of d+ = 0.17 with 80% power would require 429 participants per group, one-tailed). Thus, our data cannot confirm whether self-control training truly has a null effect, or whether its effects are merely so small that hundreds more participants would be required to reliably demonstrate them.10 Discussion The present research involved a rigorous and comprehensive test of the effects of two types of self-control training on a wide variety of outcomes relevant to self-control. There was good evidence that participants engaged with the training tasks and that performance on the tasks improved during the 6-week training period. However, we found no evidence that training led to any improvements in self-control. We could not replicate the substantial effect of self-control training on ego depletion observed in a previous meta-analysis (Hagger et al., 2010). In fact, Bayesian analyses suggested that our findings provided substantial support for the null hypothesis relative to this prior estimate of the training effect size. Furthermore, we did not obtain any evidence that training generalized to performance of behaviors involving self-control in either the laboratory or the field, to intentional versus habitual control of behavior, or to wellbeing. Overall, the present findings suggest that practicing self-control does not improve participants' performance on non-trained self-control tasks. Integrating the Present Findings with Previous Research Differences from previous work on self-control training. Our results stand in contrast to previous studies that have observed effects of training on performance under ego depletion (as reviewed in Hagger et al., 2010) and generalization of training effects to everyday behaviors 30 involving self-control (Oaten & Cheng, 2006a, 2006b). Given that the present research assessed training effects using both a much larger sample and improved methodology as compared to previous studies, we have reason to believe that our null findings more accurately reflect the true effect of training on self-control. We note here that, while participants in our behavioral training condition did not differ from participants in the other groups on objective measures of selfcontrol, they nevertheless reported believing that their self-control had improved, suggesting that participants may sometimes believe that training has improved their self-control even when it has not. This observation may shed light on the processes underlying the positive effects observed in previous studies; namely, that they may be a function of participants' expectations of the likely effects of training. Motivational accounts of self-control failure (e.g., Inzlicht & Schmeichel, 2012) may also help to explain why participants might show group differences in performance in the absence of true increases in the trained ability. Most previous research on self-control training lacks the design features necessary to disentangle the effects of beliefs, expectations, and motivation from the actual effects of practice. The present research also moved beyond the outcomes assessed in previous studies to examine the effects of self-control training across a much broader range of dependent measures, all of which had established associations with self-control and thus should have benefitted from training, according to the strength model (Muraven & Baumeister, 2000). Our consistent finding that training did not influence these outcomes suggests that previous studies may have overestimated both the effectiveness of self-control training and the extent to which effects generalize beyond the lab. Similarities with previous work on other types of training. The null effects of training observed in the present study are consistent with research in other areas and, in particular, with 31 work on executive function training. Although some studies have observed that training executive functions can influence conceptually-related cognitive outcomes such as fluid intelligence (e.g., Jaeggi, Buschkuehl, Jonides, & Perrig, 2008), these studies often share similar limitations to those examining the effects of self-control training (e.g., a lack of active control conditions; Shipstead, Redick, & Engle, 2010). Studies comparing executive function training with active control conditions have tended to find that training leads to improvements only on tasks that are very similar to the trained task, with no evidence for generalization beyond those tasks to other cognitive abilities (e.g., Dougherty, Hamovitz, & Tidwell, 2015; Harrison et al., 2013; Redick et al., 2013). In the few studies that have assessed the effects of executive function training on self-control outcomes, there is also a lack of consistent evidence for transfer. Working memory training has been found to reduce alcohol consumption (Houben, Wiers, & Jansen, 2011), but does not appear to decrease rumination (Onraedt & Koster, 2014; Wanmaker, Geraerts, & Franken, 2015). There is evidence that performing a single inhibition task can temporarily influence behaviors such as snacking, alcohol consumption, and gambling, but no evidence that training inhibition over time has long term effects on these behaviors (e.g., Verbruggen et al., 2013; Allom, Mullan, & Hagger, in press). This failure to observe transfer from an intervention to conceptually related outcomes is also common in other domains. For example, researchers have often observed that interventions targeting clinical problems, such as cognitive bias modification for anxiety or self-management for ADHD, do not generalize across symptoms, responses, or settings (e.g., Barry & Haraway, 2005; Beard, 2011; Corrigan & Basit, 1997; Evans, Axelrod & Sapia, 2000). Similarly, in educational contexts, it is widely recognized that students may not transfer learning from one situation to another, leading McKeough, Lupart, and Marini (2013) to comment that "researchers 32 have been more successful in showing how people fail to transfer learning than they have been in producing it" (p. vi). In short, the overall pattern of findings observed across these different literatures is consistent with the findings obtained in the present research – namely, that selfcontrol training did not generalize to untrained outcomes. Implications for the ego depletion effect. The present findings also have implications for the other key prediction of the strength model – that exerting self-control temporarily reduces self-control performance. In contrast to previous studies that have used hand-grip persistence as a measure of self-control and found that performance suffers under depletion (as reviewed in Hagger et al., 2010), we found that performance on the handgrip task improved following the exertion of self-control (i.e., a negative effect of depletion, d+ = -0.30). This finding is consistent with observations that self-control performance can improve when individuals are required to exert self-control for sustained periods of time (Converse & DeShon, 2009; Dang, Dewitte, Mao, Xiao, & Shi, 2013) and lends support to recent empirical and meta-analytic work which has concluded that the published record is likely to have overestimated the magnitude of the ego depletion effect – perhaps due to publication bias – with the true effect of ego depletion likely to be either small or nonexistent (Carter et al., 2015; Hagger et al., in press). Taken together, it is becoming clear that people do not inevitably falter under high self-regulatory demands, but that whether performance suffers or benefits may depend upon factors such as motivation and beliefs about self-control (e.g., Hopstaken, van der Linden, Bakker, & Kompier, 2014; Bernecker & Job, 2015). Is Training Inhibition the Right Way to Improve Self-Control? Although the central idea of programs designed to train self-control involves improving peoples' ability to inhibit a dominant response, self-control involves more than just the effortful 33 inhibition of impulses (Fujita, 2011) and, as such, there may be multiple ways to improve this skill (Inzlicht, Legault, & Teper, 2014). Indeed, there is emerging evidence that people with higher levels of self-control may not actually be better at inhibiting impulses or spend more time doing so, which implies that the ability to inhibit responses is not in fact responsible for the higher levels of success and well-being experienced by people with good self-control. Indeed, Hofmann, Baumeister, et al. (2012) found that people with high trait self-control reported resisting fewer temptations, and Imhoff, Schmidt, and Gerstenberg (2014) found a negative correlation between trait self-control and the frequency with which participants actively engaged in self-control. Taken together with recent findings which suggest that trait self-control might be associated with reduced experience of temptation, rather than increased control of temptation (Hofmann, Baumeister, et al., 2012), and related evidence that people who are good at selfcontrol may actively avoid temptation (Ent, Baumeister, & Tice, 2015), these findings call into question the idea that inhibition training should necessarily result in improved self-control outcomes. If the goal of self-control training is to train the abilities and skills that are possessed by people with high levels of self-control, then this goal may be better accomplished by training people to proactively avoid temptation rather than to reactively inhibit temptation. Inzlicht et al. (2014) also offer a number of other promising suggestions for improving self-control that go beyond the conception of effortful inhibition, such as changing goal appraisals and responding to self-control failures with acceptance. Limitations and Future Directions Our study differed from previous work in that participants trained for six weeks as compared to a modal training period of just two weeks in previous research. One potential limitation, therefore, is that this longer-than-average training period could have resulted in 34 selection bias – perhaps only participants who are already relatively high in self-control were willing to sign up for a lengthy study, and these participants were least likely to benefit from training. We do not believe, however, that this bias characterizes our study, or that selection bias could be responsible for our null effect, for two principal reasons. First, our participants scored no higher on measures of trait self-control than participants in previous studies. Two previous studies of self-control training assessed participants' trait levels of self-control at baseline using the Brief Self-Control Scale (BSCS; Bray et al., 2015; Sultan, Joireman, & Sprott, 2012). Our participants' scores on the BSCS were not significantly different from those observed in either of these studies (ts < 1.45, ps > .15) and did not differ from the original norms reported by Tangney et al. (2004), t(778) = 0.57, p = 0.57. Second, levels of trait self-control did not moderate the impact of training on any of the outcome measures in the present research, suggesting that preexisting differences in trait self-control did not influence the effectiveness of training. These observations suggest that it is unlikely (i) that selection bias is a serious problem in the present research, or (ii) that selection bias could account for the difference in findings between our study and previous research. We do, however, acknowledge that research in this area has almost exclusively involved educated, student participants (see Table 1), and tests with more representative samples are overdue. It is also possible that the effects of practicing self-control are nonlinear, which might mean that increasing the length of training does not increase its effectiveness. The time course of training effects, and whether or not they increase as a function of the length of the intervention, are as yet unknown (Berkman, in press). The possibility of non-linear effects is not explicitly considered by the strength model, which appears to assume that more practice should equal more strength. However, an alternative is that participants experience an initial boost from engaging in 35 a new activity (e.g., using their non-dominant hand) which fades over time, perhaps as the activity becomes more automatized, more habitual, and demands less effort. While no study has yet compared the effects of different durations of training on outcomes or studied how the effects of training change over time, one recent study has found that the effects of self-control training wear off relatively quickly once training is complete: Bertrams and Schmeichel (2014) found that practicing logical reasoning for one week influenced ego depletion effects when tested immediately afterwards, but not one week later. Our data do not allow us to test the possibility that training effects were present near the beginning of the training program. However, we would note that self-control training has limited practical value if its effects are so short-lived. Conclusion Determining the effectiveness of psychological interventions such as self-control training is important both to further our understanding of the nature of self-control and to answer applied questions about how best to help people to change their behavior. Whereas previous studies have reported improvements in self-control after practice, the present research rectified several methodological problems with previous studies and observed that self-control training did not improve self-control. Given mounting evidence that self-control performance may depend upon more than self-control resources, and that the exertion of self-control does not necessarily impair performance in the short term nor improve it in the long term (Carter et al., 2015; Inzlicht & Berkman, 2015), we suggest that future research could benefit from taking a broader perspective on self-control. Our suggestion is that programs that do more than train people to effortfully inhibit impulses may achieve greater real-world impact.

Is There A Downside To Good Self-control?

The evolutionary beginnings of selfhood may have been part of the attempt to exert control over the external environment, but selves soon began to develop the capacity to exert control over themselves too, in the sense that the self came to alter its own inner processes, inner states, and behavioral responses. The terms self-control and self-regulation have been used to refer to the capacity of the self to alter itself. The need to be able to alter behavior to accord with standards has figured prominently in human social life because of the proliferation of standards: laws, distant goals, social norms, religious ideals, moral and ethical principles, traditions and customs, and more. Civilized life in human cultural societies would be unthinkable without self-regulation, and inadequate self-control would be central to the inability of most nonhuman animals to live and function in the human social world. Viewed in that way, self-regulation is a highly desirable and adaptive trait. And in fact an assortment of field studies and applied research has confirmed that exercising effective self-control is highly beneficial, both to individuals and to society. Yet an accumulating body of laboratory studies has depicted the immediate effects of exercising self-control to be mainly detrimental and negative. In this manuscript, we shall review both sets of findings, consider their contradictory nature, and seek to offer a resolution.

Self-regulation refers to the efforts by the self to alter its own responses. Dictionaries define regulation as change designed to bring something into agreement with a standard. Applied to the self, then, regulation involves changing the self or aspects of it to bring it into line with any sort of standard, such as a social norm, a cultural ideal, or a personal goal. Self-regulation can be used to change the person's thoughts, emotions or moods, motivated behaviors (aka impulse control), or task performance. We use the terms self-control and self-regulation interchangeably, though we recognize that some scholars make a distinction. The distinction typically treats self-control as a large subset of self-regulation. In this view, self-control is seen as the conscious, effortful form of self-regulation, but there are also nonconscious processes and forms of self-regulation that would not be encompassed as self-control. Our focus is on the conscious, effortful variety, and so in our writing the terms self-regulation and self-control refer to the same phenomenon. State and trait aspects of self-control can be distinguished. The state is the current act. The trait would be the broad, dispositional tendency to exert self-control. Measures of trait self-control have begun to appear in recent years (e.g., Tangney, Baumeister, & Boone, 2004). These have some relationship to several more traditional trait concepts. One is impulsivity, but as the term impulsivity implies, it focuses on strength of impulses as much as on the restraints. Another relevant trait is Conscientiousness, which is one of the so-called Big Five dimensions of personality. According to Roberts, Walton, and Hogg (2005), Conscientiousness in the Big Five is a blend of self-control, traditionalism, industriousness, responsibility, and orderliness. Trait self-control is thus a narrower, more specific concept than both. There is also a question of how to define benefits and beneficial effects. Although these clearly refer to positive, desirable outcomes, one may ask who desires and benefits from them. In Freudian theory, for example, there was an overt tradeoff between personal and societal benefits. The superego was the Freudian analog to self-control, and Freud (1930) was explicit in depicting the superego as costly to the self even while beneficial to the larger social group. In fact, he proposed that the superego was created by having the socializing agents turn the child's aggression inward against the self, so that the young person learned to deprive himself or herself of desired pleasures in order to live by society's rules. A second tradeoff involved gaining safety in exchange for sacrificing one's own chances for untrammeled indulgence: I agree not to rob or harm you, and you agree not to rob or harm me. But, Freud went on to say, the tradeoff is not quite equal, because the mechanism by which it is accomplished (the superego) had a side cost of inducing guilt, and the rise in guilt was an extra added cost, constituting the "discontent" in civilized life. Thus, in that view, self-control was net costly to the individual, whereas the gains were primarily found in the harmonious and smooth functioning of society. Even the concept of good can be debated. We shall argue that self-regulation is a tool, and that it is a good tool, which means that by using it people can improve their chances of getting what they want. But they may use it for ends that others would condemn. Most likely a mass murderer with good self-regulation would succeed in killing more people than a sloppy, careless, undisciplined one. Hence our use of the term "good" refers to pragmatic benefit within the basis of chosen goals, and it does not extend to passing moral judgment on those goals.

Why should self-control be beneficial? A context for answering this question begins with the basic principle that all organisms need to achieve some sort of harmony with their environment so that they can live in reasonable security and peace and can satisfy their needs. Changing the environment to suit the self is one way of achieving such harmony, but changing the self to fit the environment is also a viable strategy (Rothbaum, Weisz, & Snyder, 1982). In many cases, the environment cannot be changed to suit the wishes of the individual, and so changing the self may be the most promising option for achieving harmony. This fact may be especially true about social environments, because whenever people disagree or want incompatible things, one or more of these people must be disappointed. Hence social life places demands on the individuals to accommodate themselves to external circumstances. Increased flexibility of behavior is a second important benefit of self-regulation. We have said that self-regulation can be conceptualized as the self overriding its current, incipient, prepotent response. Instead of acting on first impulse, the selfcontrolling individual can stifle that response, which makes it possible to act differently. The resulting freedom of action has tempted some writers to connect self-regulation with the folk notion of free will (e.g., Baumeister, 2008; Dennett, 2003). The advanced requirements and opportunities in human social life are again relevant, because they involve complex decisions, and the behavioral flexibility stemming from self-regulation enables the person to capitalize on them. Needless to say, these benefits of self-control can be recognized for both individuals and social systems. Self-control enables individuals to fit in to societies and to navigate their way through the myriad constraints and opportunities society presents. The self-control of individuals also enables social systems to operate smoothly and serve their functions, because self-controlling individuals obey the society's rules and perform their roles within it. Ample research has confirmed the benefits of self-control. Some of the most impressive evidence that self-control benefits individuals was provided by Mischel, Shoda, and Peake (1988) and Shoda, Mischel, and Peake (1990). They followed up children who had participated in laboratory studies of delay of gratification when they were four years old. In these procedures, which have become widely known under the rubric of "the marshmallow test," children had to choose between an immediate but small reward (e.g., one marshmallow) and a larger but delayed reward (e.g., three marshmallows after 20 minutes). Self-control is required to resist the temptation to take an immediate pleasure in order to procure a better outcome in the long run. ("Better" in this case involves the assumption, dubious to adults but presumably embraced by children, that three marshmallows are preferable to one.) The participants who had shown the best self-control at age 4 became more successful than others as adults, both socially and academically. The diversity of benefits of self-control was suggested in a pair of studies by Tangney, Baumeister, and Boone (2004). A trait measure of self-control significantly predicted a host of positive outcomes, including interpersonal success, school achievement, and adjustment. That is, people scoring high on self-control were more likely than others to report good grades in school and college. They were more likely to report secure and satisfying relationships and less likely to report angry aggression. They were less prone to report an assortment of pathologies, including depression, anxiety, eating disorders, drinking problems, and psychoticism. Their emotional stability was better. These effects remained significant after controlling for social desirability, which suggests they are not some mere expression of selfreport bias. What about bad effects? A noteworthy feature of the Tangney et al. (2004) investigation was that it contained a determined search for curvilinear effects, which would reveal negative effects of very high self-control. Such analyses were done on the presumption that some self-control is superior to little or none but that "over control" was possible and would be reflected in a downturn in positive outcomes among the people scoring highest on the scale. No hint of such effects was found. On that trait scale, at least, the higher the scores, the better. Although the results in the Tangney et al. (2004) study were exclusively based on self-report, other studies have confirmed the benefits with objective measures. Smith and Baumeister (2006) used the same scale to predict actual grade point average, obtained from registrar's records, and the findings confirmed that students scoring high in self-control really did get better grades than others, even after correcting for academic ability as measured by the SAT Reasoning Test. Wolfe and Johnson (1995) tested 32 trait predictors of actual grade point average in a large sample and found self-control was the only one to have a significant impact after controlling for high school Grade Point Average and SAT scores. Perhaps most dramatically, Duckworth and Seligman (2005) showed that self-control predicted academic performance better than IQ. (This is dramatic because predicting academic performance was the central purpose of IQ scores and they have been quite consistently successful at doing so.) High self-control predicted higher grade point average, higher scores on tests of academic achievement, and better admission to selective high schools, as compared to low self-control. Students with high self-control had fewer school absences, spent more time on homework, and started their homework earlier than other students. Another approach to providing objective confirmation is to have other people rate the target individual. Cox (2000) found that supervisors who scored high on selfcontrol were rated more favorably by their peers and subordinates. The fact that having good self-control makes someone a better boss brings up the second category of benefits, which is benefits to society. The supervisors themselves may have benefited from their good work and from the appreciation of subordinates, but this is inferred, whereas it seems safe to assume that the appreciative subordinates have benefited most directly. Another domain where the benefits of self-control for individuals and society overlap is the maintenance of long-term relationships. Individuals in satisfying longterm relations experience fewer mental and physical health problems (Bloom, White, & Asher, 1979; DeLongis, Folkman, & Lazarus, 1988), are less likely to have fatal heart attacks (Lynch, 1979), and are more likely to survive cancer (Goodwin, Hunt, Key, & Samet, 1987). Happily married individuals are also less likely to commit suicide (Rothberg & Jones, 1987) and less likely to commit crimes (Sampson & Laub, 1993). Self-control is related to one important facet of relationship maintenance: accommodation. Accommodation involves an individual's tendency to avoid responding destructively to the negative behaviors of his or her partner (Rusbult, Verette, Whitney, Slovik, & Lipkus, 1991). A series of four studies showed that individuals' self-reported trait self-control was consistently correlated with three of the four aspects of accommodation (Finkel & Campbell, 2001). Individuals with higher self-control were more likely to respond to a partner's negative behavior by trying to talk through the problem and were less likely to respond by avoiding the partner or ending the relationship than individuals with lower self-control.

To be sure, in general the benefits of self-control to society are somewhat more difficult to document than the benefits to individuals, but they may be quite important. An influential work by Gottfredson and Hirschi (1990) concluded that poor self-control is the single most important cause of criminality. (We assume crime is detrimental and costly to society.) Subsequent research has confirmed strong links between poor self-control and criminal, violent, and antisocial behavior patterns (see Pratt & Cullen, 2000, for a review). Thus, good self-control is vital for sustaining socially desirable, law-abiding behavior and thus for the smooth and effective functioning of civilization. Benefits of self-control to both the individual and society are evident in recent studies with a population notorious for low self-control, namely prison inmates. Among a sample of incarcerated offenders, low self-control was associated with more drug use, higher unemployment, and less education (preceding incarceration), as compared to people high in self-control (Mathews, Youman, Stuewig, & Tangney, 2007). More importantly, trait self-control was significantly correlated with recidivism. Even after controlling for IQ and social desirability, inmates with low self-control were more likely to be arrested again or report committing undetected crimes than those with high self control. Insofar as being arrested again for a new crime signifies a bad outcome for both the individual and society, good self-control appears to be a broadly beneficial trait. Costs of Self-control When assessing the costs and benefits of self-control, it is important to note that selfcontrol is ultimately just a tool, and it can be used for bad purposes just as easily as for good, praiseworthy ones. Given that most individuals' goals seem to align with general social norms, self-control is most often used for positive ends for the self and society. However, some applications of effective self-control can produce destructive or antisocial results. A criminal or torturer with good self-control will be all the more effective at his or her heinous occupation, and the harmful results would thus be intensified. Still, this is a complaint that can be leveled against any tool, from physical ones (effective hammers can destroy more items than poorly designed ones) to psychological ones (intelligent evildoers will accomplish more harm than incompetent ones). For society, the cost of self-control is the negative effects of those individuals who use self-control for antisocial goals. Whether they have socially acceptable goals or not, individuals bear costs from exerting self-control. These come in two quite different forms, sacrifice and process. Self-control and Sacrifice The very nature of self-control entails overriding some impulses and desires, and so forfeiting those satisfactions is a very real and substantial cost. The exertion of selfcontrol in everyday life means that people do not eat or drink what they want, do not purchase items they desire, do not have sex with partners they fancy, do not strike or shoot people they despise, and in many other ways forfeit the satisfaction of their desires. To be sure, self-control brings benefits to individuals too, as already noted, and the sacrifices are in many ways directly tied to those benefits. Tradeoffs (the theme of this special issue) are thus at the heart and essence of self-regulation. The self-regulated citizen respects the property of others, and in return lives in a social world in which his or her property is equally respected by others. The sacrifice of not helping oneself to others' possessions is compensated by the secure enjoyment of one's own possessions. The direct link between these costs and benefits of self-regulation is especially obvious in delay of gratification. In the laboratory, participants face choices between an immediate gain and a delayed but greater gain, and foregoing the immediate satisfaction is essential to the enjoyment of the delayed benefits (e.g., Mischel, 1974, 1996). Delay of gratification is thus a paradigmatic example of enlightened self-interest, because it increases the benefits to the self in the long run, even though it may involve short-term costs. Outside the laboratory, a great many patterns in human cultural life depend on the same sort of enlightened tradeoff. Agriculture, for example, would be impossible without delay of gratification, because it requires taking what is often edible food and burying it in the dirt instead of eating it now. That short-term sacrifice is exacerbated by risks of drought, blight, and theft, but throughout most of human history, the sacrifice has generally paid off well in terms of greatly increased yield of food when the crop ripened at the end of summer. Today, most citizens in the developed world are no longer farmers, but delay of gratification is still central to many forms of success in cultural life. Young people may forego taking a job that would pay enough to enable them to afford an apartment, nice clothes and food, and a car, and instead they attend a university where they live amid the chaos and squalor of dormitory life and eat the institutional food served in dining halls. The short-term sacrifices are thus palpable, but they are compensated. In the long run the university degree increases their lifetime earnings by approximately a million dollars. Costs of Self-regulatory Process The second cost of self-control is the cost of the internal mechanism and processes that override responses and make self-regulation possible. In that respect, it resembles Freud's (1930) analysis of the superego and guilt, though psychology's understanding of the processes and its costly side effects has come some way since Freud was writing. These costs of self-regulation have been a central focus of the research program with which we are affiliated, and so we furnish here a brief overview. The idea that self-control requires the expenditure of energy has roots in folk wisdom and the colloquial concept of willpower. Whether folk psychology understood willpower as a limited resource that was subject to depletion is unclear, but there was at least the sense that some form of inner energy or strength was needed to resist temptation and remain on the path of virtue. To be sure, folk theories have had very mixed success in the psychology laboratory, and alternative theories of self-regulation (such as based on skill or computational models) were certainly plausible. These were noted by Baumeister, Heatherton, and Tice (1994) in an early literature review. Those authors concluded that the energy or strength model seemed to fit a smattering of observations better than the alternative theories. Direct tests of the limited resource theory of self-regulation were first reported by Baumeister, Bratslavsky, Muraven, and Tice (1998) and Muraven, Tice, and Baumeister (1998). They showed that exerting self-control in one sphere led to impaired capacity to regulate one's behavior in another, ostensibly unrelated, sphere. For example, regulating one's emotions while watching an upsetting video clip 120 R. F. Baumeister & J. L. Alquist caused a significant drop in a test of physical stamina (handgrip). The implication is that a common, limited resource is used for many different exertions of self-control. When the resource was expended by the person in a first act of self-control, less of it remained to enable the person to regulate effectively on the second task. There are many different situations in which individuals require self-regulatory resources to overcome impulses, habits, and temptations in order to respond in more beneficial and appropriate ways. Because of this, it is not surprising that performance is impaired on a variety of tasks when self-regulatory resources have been depleted. When individuals have their self-regulatory resources lowered by a previous act of regulation, they are more likely to spend impulsively (Vohs & Faber, 2007), to fail at upholding their diets (Kahan, Polivy, & Herman, 2003; Vohs & Heatherton, 2000), and to indulge inappropriate sexual impulses (Gailliot & Baumeister, 2007a), as compared to participants whose resources were not depleted by prior acts of self-regulation. Interpersonally, those with lowered self-regulatory resources are more likely than their non-depleted peers to respond aggressively to provocation (DeWall, Baumeister, Stillman, & Gailliot, 2007; Stucke & Baumeister, 2006), to present themselves in ways that fail to make the desired or optimal impression (Vohs, Baumeister, & Ciarocco, 2005), and to be persuaded by weak arguments (Wheeler, Brin~ol, and Hermann (2007). Thus, each individual act of regulation temporarily depletes self-regulatory resources, leading to decreased performance in a variety of domains. These impairments in performance reflect one important category of costs of self-regulation: In the aftermath of self-regulation, people's ability to perform effectively in many important spheres, including reasoning, acting appropriately, and dealing effectively with others, is compromised. How the Cost is Paid Just what is it that gets depleted? The folk concept of willpower was admittedly merely a metaphor, and the very idea that the self depended on a genuine energy source was considered fairly implausible if not downright absurd when these findings first came out. In fact, Baumeister et al. (1998) used the term "ego depletion" in homage to Freud, because Freud had been one of the last theorists to suggest that the human self depended on energy processes. In the intervening half century, writings about the self had depicted it almost exclusively as a cognitive structure (e.g., Greenwald & Banaji, 1989; Kihlstrom & Cantor, 1984). In the 1990s, however, the influx of biological thinking into psychological theory made energy models seem more plausible than they had been. Biological processes do involve energy, and indeed life itself can be understood as a matter of energy transformations. Human life depends on frequent ingestion of food, from which the body derives the energy needed for all its activities. Recent work has begun to suggest that the energy from food is linked to willpower. The mediating processes involve glucose, a chemical typically found in the bloodstream, which serves as the proximal source of energy for much of the body's work. In particular, neurotransmitters in the brain are made from glucose, and insofar as psychological processes are based on the firings of brain cells, one could argue that all psychological activities depend on fuel from glucose. Of particular importance is the fact that some psychological and brain activities consume considerably more glucose than others. Self-regulation might well be one of these biologically expensive forms of psychological activity.

Suggestive links between blood glucose and self-regulation can be found scattered through multiple research literatures, as compiled in a recent review by Gailliot and Baumeister (2007b). For example, performance on the Stroop task, which is a classic test of attention control, has been linked to glucose availability and consumption (Benton, Owens, & Parker, 1994; Fairclough & Houston, 2004), and other tests of attention control, such as dichotic listening and vigilance tasks, show similar covariation with glucose. Having more glucose seems to improve people's abilities to regulate their moods and tolerate frustration (e.g., Benton, Brett, & Brain, 1987; Benton & Owens, 1993). In many studies impulsive crimes and violence have been linked to low glucose and poor glucose tolerance. Alcohol, which is associated with deficits in self-control on almost any behavioral sphere one studies, reduces glucose (e.g., Altura, Altura, Zhang, & Zakhari, 1996; Wang et al., 2000). Direct laboratory tests of the possible link between glucose depletion and self-regulatory impairments were reported by Gailliot et al. (2007). They found that blood-glucose levels dropped significantly from before to after performing tasks that involved self-regulation, whereas comparable tasks that did not require self-regulation had no such effect on glucose. Furthermore, low levels of blood glucose were associated with subsequent deficits in behavioral self-control, consistent with the view that ego depletion reflects a state of diminished availability of glucose in the bloodstream. Last, the patterns of ego depletion were counteracted by giving participants a dose of glucose. Recent electroencephalogram (EEG) research suggests that the neurological costs of self-regulation may be incurred in individuals' abilities to nonconsciously monitor for errors in their behaviors (Inzlicht & Gutsell, 2007). Participants were asked to watch an emotional movie and either suppress their emotions or react normally. After the movie, participants completed the Stroop task while their neural activity was recorded. Neurological research has shown that there is a sharp negative voltage following behavior that is thought to reflect preconscious error monitoring (Nieuwenhuis, Ridderinkhof, Blom, Band, & Kok, 2001). This spike is referred to as error related negativity (ERN; Falkenstein, Hohnsbein, Hoorman, & Blanke, 1990; Gehring, Goss, Coles, Meyer, & Donchin, 1993). Participants who had suppressed their emotions showed diminished ERN during the Stroop task compared to participants in the control group. Even more impressive is that the relationship between emotion suppression and Stroop performance was mediated by ERN. This suggests that the preconscious monitoring of errors plays an important role in self-regulation and previous acts of self-control weaken this error monitoring system. In plain terms, one cost of having exerted self-control is that afterward the person will be more prone than usual to make mistakes. Does ego depletion indicate a state of reduced capability or reduced willingness to exert further self-control? Evidence suggests both (and they may be related). Muraven and Slessareva (2003) showed that providing a motivational incentive to self-regulate despite ego depletion seemed to counteract the impact of depletion—but it left the person that much more depleted. Thus, the incentive did not truly replenish the depleted state. Rather, it appears to have motivated the person to continue spending the diminished resource, resulting in even more severe depletion. Thus, the present state of evidence indicates that acts of self-control have an immediate and direct cost to the self-regulating person. Some limited resource, apparently involving the blood glucose that serves as fuel for brain and bodily activities, is depleted by effortful self-control.

As a result, the person's capability and willingness to exert self-control are temporarily impaired. 122 R. F. Baumeister & J. L. Alquist Indeed, the costs may go beyond self-control. Recent studies have found that the same resource needed for acts of self-control is also used for decision making (Vohs et al., 2008). After exerting self-control, people become reluctant to make decisions, preferring to avoid or postpone them (Pocheptsaya, Amire, Dhar, & Baumeister, in press). If they do make choices when their resources have been depleted by recent acts of self-control, these decisions tend to follow relatively simple and more errorprone pathways, such as choosing a simple extreme rather than a compromise option and succumbing to irrational heuristic biases (Pocheptsova et al., in press). Glucose likewise appears to be involved in these choices, as shown by the finding that a dose of glucose after self-control can reduce the tendency to follow an irrational short-cut to an easy decision (Masicampo & Baumeister, 2008). Several studies have also suggested that the same resource used for self-control is used for initiative, which is to say for responding actively rather than passively. The avoidance of decision making noted above (Pocheptsaya et al., in press) is one sign of this. More direct evidence of passivity was provided by Vohs et al. (2008), who assigned participants to perform a visual task and then left the room, after which the equipment obviously malfunctioned. Depleted participants waited longer before taking action to find the experimenter and report the problem. A similar finding was reported by Baumeister et al. (1998), who found that depleted participants were more likely to follow the default option rather than one that required an active response. Coping with the Costs Self-regulation is vitally important for effective human functioning and contributes to social, academic, and occupational success. Given that exerting self-control depletes a multiply useful resource and temporarily impairs the person's ability to function, how do people cope with this fact so as to maintain their capacity despite ongoing demands? The challenge is one of managing the limited resource so as to get the best results from it. One approach to managing limited self-control resources is to reduce the amount of resources a desirable behavior requires by automatizing it. One basic tenant of the limited resource model is that controlled behaviors consume resources whereas automatic behaviors do not. Waking up early to go to the gym may initially leave one depleted but constant repetition will making going to the gym the dominant response. In a daily diary study, participants who were assigned to engage in depleting tasks performed fewer non-habitual behaviors than participants who were not assigned to do depleting tasks. However, there were no differences between conditions on habitual behaviors (Neal & Wood, 2006, as cited in Neal, Wood, & Quinn, 2006). Whether they were desirable or undesirable behaviors, these habits endured in the face of depletion because they no longer required resources. Another standard response to limited resources is to conserve them (e.g., Hobfoll, 2002). Indeed, one way of looking at all the ego depletion effects is that they represent efforts to conserve a resource that has been only partly depleted, instead of viewing them as signs that the resource has been so thoroughly depleted that nothing can be done until it is replenished. The strength model of self-control compares it to a muscle, and muscular fatigue conforms to the pattern of conservation (e.g., Baumeister, Vohs, & Tice, 2007; Muraven & Baumeister, 2000). That is, athletes or physical workers begin to conserve their remaining strength as soon as they start to become tired, rather than exerting full effort until they reach exhaustion.

Direct evidence for conservation was reported by Muraven, Shmueli, and Burkley (2006). They adapted what had become the standard two-task procedure into a three-task one: a first task depletes the resource (or not, in the control condition), and a second task measures self-control performance, while a third task is anticipated to place further demands on self-regulatory resources. Crucially, participants were told about the third task before they performed the second. Muraven et al. (2006) found that anticipating a third self-control task led to poorer performance on the second, mainly among participants whose resources had been depleted by the first task. Thus, when one's resources have been depleted, one reduces current exertions so as to conserve the resources for upcoming demands. The conservation occurred only when the later task was expected to place demands on self-control, and not when the third task was possibly arduous but not a matter of regulating the self. Is conservation effective? Muraven et al. (2006) included measures of performance on the third task. Sure enough, the demands and exertions of self-control in the first and second tasks led to poorer performance on the third—but these decrements were mitigated among participants who conserved. That is, by exerting less effort on the middle task, some participants were able to conserve their diminished resources, and these enabled them to perform relatively well on the third task. Participants who exerted more self-control on the second task despite being depleted suffered poorer performance on the third task. These findings strongly support the limited resource model and suggest that people know to conserve their resources—and that conserving them is effective at improving subsequent selfcontrol. Conservation is clearly a short-term strategy with regard to self-regulatory resources. A long-term strategy would be to increase the resource. The muscle analogy (Baumeister et al., 2007) would suggest frequent acts of self-control may increase the person's strength, just as a muscle becomes stronger as the result of regular exercise. There is, in fact, some evidence that self-regulatory power can be increased by regular exercises (see Baumeister, Gailliot, DeWall, & Oaten, 2006, for a review). Multiple exercises have been used and proven effective, including correcting one's posture, using one's nondominant hand for minor routine tasks, cleaning up one's speech, modifying one's habits of money use and spending, and taking up an exercise program. These have been shown to reduce susceptibility to depletion on laboratory tasks. In some studies, they also led to improvements in other areas of self-regulation. For example, it is perhaps not surprising that several weeks' worth of regulating one's money usage can result in improvements in saving—but participants who completed the money course also reported that they began to study more regularly and effectively, became more scrupulous about completing household scores, smoked fewer cigarettes, and seemed to have better self-control in other spheres (Oaten & Cheng, 2007). They even reported improvements in healthy eating, which is noteworthy because healthy food tends to be more expensive than junk food, and given that they were concentrating on saving money, one might have expected them to shift toward cheaper (and less healthy) food. To be sure, the results from research studies aimed at improving self-regulation have not been uniformly effective. In our laboratory, about half the studies have been successful. The basis for the mixed results remains unclear. It appears that self-control can be improved significantly via exercise, and these benefits have been replicated, but they are not yet thoroughly reliable. Further work is needed to establish what factors moderate their effectiveness and how the gains can be maximized. Are There Other Costs? As reviewed earlier, individuals with high trait self-control attain better grades, have more satisfying relationships, and report fewer symptoms of psychopathology than those with low trait self-control. However, is there a cost to being able to resist temptation? Reduced emotional sensitivity may be considered a cost, though in principle one might also regard it as a benefit. In a recent study by Zabelina, Robinson, and Anicha (2007), individuals were asked to answer the question, "What are you thinking?"

on a daily basis for seven days, when they were prompted. In response to this prompt, participants with high self-control were less likely to write about either positive or negative affective states than participants with low-self control. This finding suggests that high self-control dampens affective responding (which could be regarded as either a cost or a benefit!). The same study also showed that individuals high in self-control were perceived as less spontaneous and extraverted than individuals low in self-control. Other research has shown that individuals describe the most self-controlled person they know as significantly less open to experiences than the least self-controlled person that they know (Stillman & Alquist, 2007). Insofar as people like spontaneity, extraversion, and openness to experience high self-control may have some interpersonal costs. Some possible interpersonal costs of self-control have formed the basis of a research program by Kashdan and his colleagues (e.g., Kashdan, Elhai, & Breen, 2007). Some people (i.e., a subgroup of socially anxious individuals) believe that in their social environment, hedonic and risky indulgence promotes popularity, whereas restraint would reduce it. These people conclude that abandoning self-control is necessary in order for them to make and keep friends, and so they engage in binge drinking, heavy drug use, sexual promiscuity, and possibly other risky behaviors—all apparently in a deliberate and strategic manner. At a more physiological level, another possible cost has been identified by Segerstrom and Nes (2007). Their findings suggest that exerting self-control increases variability in heart rate. One way of understanding these findings is that the body has several homeostatic mechanisms that help maintain the internal environment, such as by stabilizing heart rate, and that these regulatory processes use some of the same resources needed for effortful self-regulation of behavior. Hence when the resource is depleted, the body's homeostatic maintenance is compromised. Further work might explore whether these effects extend to matters such as immune system functioning. If so, that could explain why some people seem to become more vulnerable to illness when under stress or otherwise facing demands on their limited self-regulatory resources. Integration of Costs and Benefits To sum up what we have reviewed thus far, it seems necessary to distinguish trait self-control (as a capacity) from the state associated with current exertions. The costs and benefits are somewhat different when sorted in that way. To be sure, the distinction is imperfect, and trait self-control undoubtedly contributes to the ability to exercise self-control (as a state) on particular occasions

Trait self-control seems an unmixed blessing. It benefits both individuals and society. People high in trait self-control end up better off in a multitude of ways, as compared to people with low or poor self-control. Society benefits because such people perform fewer antisocial acts (including violent and criminal ones) and because their superior performance contributes more goods, services, and social capital to society. The closest things to downsides of good self-control that we found were mainly from one study (by Zabelina et al., 2007) and were that the reduced emotional lability of people with high self-control entailed lesser reporting of positive emotional reactions (though this was balanced against lesser negative emotional reactions as well), and that other people tended to perceive them as relatively less spontaneous and less extraverted. Even so, it seems dubious to extol spontaneity as a definite advantage of low self-control, because its benefits are likely linked to drawbacks. Spontaneity means responding in unplanned, unpredictable, spur-of-the-moment ways, and self-control presumably evolved in order to enable people to behave in planned, predictable, and consistent ways, which in the long run are advantageous to the individual and socially appealing. In contrast, current exertions of self-control carry a cost in depleted resources, even as these exertions contribute to pursuing benefits and achieving goals. The depleted resources undermine the person's ability to exert effective self-control subsequently, and may also hamper decision making. Physiological costs of having recently exerted self-control have begun to be identified, including temporarily diminished stocks of glucose (which is the basic energy source for the body's mental and physical activity), variable heart rate, and some compromise of the brain's capacity to monitor for errors. These costs seem best understood by invoking a limited resource model. The capacity for self-control is based on a single, common resource that is used for a great many different and beneficial acts, and these acts may extend even beyond self-control to encompass decision making, initiative, and possibly other controlled processes. As with any limited resource (e.g., money), spending it on one thing means having less for something else. The conservation studies by Muraven and Slessareva (2003) highlight the dilemma of the limited resource. When the resource has already been somewhat depleted by exertions of self-control on an initial task, people often seek to conserve what is left for possible future demands and opportunities. Spending more of it on a second task entails having that much less left over for a third task. Some people conserve more than others, but this reflects the tradeoff of spending the limited resource on the second versus the third task. The limitations of the resource present a particular challenge themselves. To negotiate human social life effectively, it may be necessary to make the right choices about where best to expend those limited resources. For example, should one expend one's limited resources to resist fattening food at lunch or conserve them for making important decisions in the afternoon? The obvious irony is that judicious management of the resource likely places further demands on that same resource. That is, the self likely depletes its resources to some extent in deciding where and when to allocate those resources. To be sure, this conclusion remains speculative at present, but it is hard to see why or how this could not be true. Almost certainly, however, these demands must normally be relatively minor, or else the cost of deciding when to exert self-control would undercut the capacity to exert self-control at all and hence wipe out many of its potential benefits. 126 R. F. Baumeister & J. L. Alquist Concluding Remarks We have suggested that self-control is largely, even crucially, beneficial and adaptive. In considering its costs, we distinguished between trait and state. The trait capacity for self-control appears to be largely an unmixed blessing. In contrast, the momentary exertion of self-control, even though it is typically used to pursue outcomes that are positively valued by both the person and society, may produce significant costs. These are found in the diminished capacity for further self-control and for performing other psychological acts that depend on the same underlying resource, such as logical reasoning, wise decision making, and initiative. If the costs of self-control stem from the limited nature of the resource it consumes, why has not evolution endowed human beings with a more abundant resource pool? One can easily speculate that human life would be better and happier if everyone's capacity for self-control were much greater than it is. But such wistful fantasies of limitless strength and virtue do not mesh well with the reality that psychologically beneficial acts are costly in physiological and psychological terms. Although cross-species comparisons of advanced psychological processes are hazardous, it does appear that the human capacity for self-control is already quite a bit more advanced than that of humans' evolutionary forebears. The glass of self-control is thus very much both half full and half empty. Moreover, crucially, evolution will only favor devoting more of the body's precious energy to advanced psychological processes such as self-control insofar as they contribute to improved survival and reproduction in a competitive environment. The environment in which humans evolved was certainly competitive, but it did not likely contain the vast range of challenges and opportunities for which the modern individual finds self-control useful. Should natural selection continue to function amid modern cultural life so as some day to create a superior version of the human being, it seems likely that one central trait of this superior person would be an (even) greater capacity for self-regulation. Among other benefits, that would solve most of the problems we have found associated with self-regulation, so that even the momentary exertions of self-control could become purely beneficial without apparent downsides. Seen from the present, however, such a Utopian outcome seems extremely remote, and in the very long mean time, people will continue to have to cope with the fact that their capacity for self-regulation remains limited. Still, by managing the limited resource carefully, they can still enjoy the extraordinary benefits that human self-control has afforded to individuals, both in terms of direct benefits to them and indirectly via the facilitation of culture.

www.ingramcontent.com/pod-product-compliance
Lightning Source LLC
Chambersburg PA
CBHW031301160726
47993CB00001B/246